The Lost Slipper of Soul

Stefan G. Meyer

The Lost Slipper of Soul

An Adventure in Contemporary Spirituality

Stefan G. Meyer

The quotes attributed to Andreas Leo are adapted from the following works by Paul Twitchell: *The Tiger's Fang,* copyright by Paul Twitchell, 1967. *The Kandjur: The Words and Wisdom of Paul Twitchell* and *The Key to ECKANKAR,* copyright by Illuminated Way Press, 1968. *The Shariyat-Ki-Sugmad, Book One* and *Stranger by the River,* copyright by ECKANKAR, 1970. *The Shariyat-Ki-Sugmad, Book Two,* copyright by ECKANKAR, 1971. Brad Steiger's *In My Soul I Am Free,* copyright 1968, transferred 1982. *ECKANKAR: Illuminated Way Letters 1966-1971,* copyright by Gail Twitchell Gross, 1975.

The quote from Bob Dylan's "A Hard Rain's A-Gonna Fall" on page v is copyright 1963, renewed 1991, by Special Rider Music.

The quote from Hermann Hesse's *The Journey to the East,* originally entitled *Die Morgenlandfahrt,* on page 7 is taken from the translation by Hilda Rosner, copyright 1956 by Hermann Hesse, and published by Farrar, Straus and Giroux, pp. 10-11.

The passage on pages 13-14 is adapted from *ECKANKAR: The Key to Secret Worlds,* by Paul Twitchell, copyright by ECKANKAR, 1969, 1987, p. 17.

The A. E. Housman poem on page 33 is taken from *The Collected Poems of A. E. Housman,* copyright 1965 by Holt, Rinehart and Winston, published by Henry Holt and Company, p. 165.

The poem on pages 34-5 is Laurence Housman's "Failure," quoted by T. E. Lawrence in *Minorities,* copyright 1972 by Doubleday.

The passages on page 195 are adapted from *The Temple of ECK,* by Harold Klemp, copyright by ECKANKAR, 1991, p. 26, and *The Dream Weaver Chronicles,* by James Paul Davis, copyright by James Paul Davis, 1993, published by ECKANKAR, p. 27.

The quote from Arnold Brown's *Are You Looking at Me, Jimmy?* on pages 201-2 is copyright 1994 by Arnold Brown, published by Methuen, pp. 25, 27.

The passage on page 206 is adapted from *The Mystic World,* a confidential publication for members of ECKANKAR, December 2002, p. 5.

The paraphrase from Elsa Joy Bailey's *The Uncommon Book of Prayer* on page 240 is copyright 1987 by Elsa Joy Bailey, published by Lord and Bilder.

The quote from Anatole France's *Thaïs,* first published in 1909, on page 251, is from the translation by Robert B. Douglas, published by Wildside Press, pp. 21, 25.

The quote from Robert Camp's *Exploring The Little Book of the Seven Thunders* on pages 270 is copyright by Robert Lee Camp, Seven Thunders Publishing, 2001, p. 169-170.

The retelling of the Arabian Nights tale by Jorge Luis Borges on page 284 is adapted from *Seven Nights,* translated by Eliot Weinberger, copyright 1984 by Eliot Weinberger, published by New Directions, pp. 53-4.

Cover sculpture by Louise McCagg. Cover design by Graphinity, Inc. Publicity photo by José Pereyra.

"But I'll know my song well before I start singin'."

—Bob Dylan

This book is dedicated to the memory of Paul Twitchell, whose writings, by whatever means crafted, have been a source of inspiration to me for most of my adult life.

Contents

Introduction

From the Viewpoint of Soul

"Entering the unknown is the most fearful step to the mind."
—Andreas Leo, *The Face of the Eternal, Book Two*, 21

THE IDEA OF writing a chronicle of my experiences in the League first occurred to me in a daydream when I was a young novitiate. I was driving down the freeway on a clear, bright day, pondering the idea of detachment. At the time, detachment meant to me a kind of stoicism in the face of the succession of trials, frustrations, embarrassments, and miseries that constituted my life. Ever since I had been introduced to this concept as a member of the League, I had relied on it to explain, rationalize, ward off, and cope with my unhappiness.

Now, as I drove along, I could visualize the book clearly in my mind. I could see myself picking it up from a display, being congratulated on it, and basking in the warm glow of accomplishment and recognition. At another point in the daydream, I backtracked. The book had not yet been written. The current President and Living Master of the League approached me in the company of another initiate, and introduced us to one another. "This young man will write a book on the subject of detachment," the Master declared to the student, gesturing toward me. "There is no one better qualified to write such a book than he."

"Why is that?" the initiate inquired.

"Because he has so much to learn!" he replied, glancing at me with a mischievous smile.

Spurred on by youthful enthusiasm, I spent an entire summer working on the book. Finally, I took the manuscript to a high initiate of the League to critique. She was a kind, soft-spoken woman, but very direct in her manner. "Your writing is too forced," she said. "Try to write from the viewpoint of Soul."

"The viewpoint of Soul! What could that be?" I wondered. I realized that, despite having devoted myself to the League teachings on this subject, I had no idea what it was like to see from this viewpoint. I felt as if I was looking up, hoping to see the night sky brilliantly illuminated by stars, only to stare at a plaster ceiling.

That evening, I had a dream that I managed to copy down verbatim. I remember writing the words down as if taking dictation, their style seemingly borrowed from a child's fairy tale:

> For many years, I lived near the Shadowlump of Grayling. My abode was a little hut that stood, all alone, under the massive cliff. The hut served as an inn to passing strangers. In those days, the only ones who passed by were robbers, or mutants, or both—miscreants fleeing the Righters of Wrongs, but I gave them a bed and let them go on their way, asking no questions, for I did not wish to share in their ill fortunes.
>
> One day, however, a little girl appeared in this forsaken place. I found her walking about under the great walls of the cliff face, seemingly unconcerned for her own welfare. Now, I had not seen a child for many years, and when I saw this one, I became filled with foreboding. I felt she must surely be some angelic spirit come to test me, for many ages past I had been found wanting in the Way of Love.
>
> I did not ask her name, but humbly walked at her side, answered her questions, and strove to see her safely through the forest of jagged rocks and canyons. It was not long before we came to the Master Cliff, and—behold! It stood open, as it had never been in all the years of my memory. I was

sorely afraid and urged the little child not to enter, but she would not heed me, and ventured within.

There, in the dimly lit cavern, stood an entablature, and upon that smooth stone was the Lost Slipper of Soul, a slipper of yellow filigree. I saw that it had fallen from its pedestal and now lay on its side. The little girl stretched out her hand as if to right it, but at this point, I called out, "Do not touch the slipper!" and she stopped as if frozen in mid-air. I explained that if she put her hand to it, she could not fail to be drawn into the evil kingdom of Röo-kel, where there were far too many dangers for a little creature such as she. For proof, I brought her close to the far end of the cave. Here the ground sloped down and the passage narrowed slightly. Beyond this portal, we could see another world, swimming as if in a dream.

"What is that?" she cried. A wicked guardian was approaching, eyeing the portal, as if aware that someone watched him. He wore a vest of red silk with gold brocade, and pantaloons of green. In his hand, he carried a scimitar, sharp as a razor. He came closer, examining the entrance ever more suspiciously, truly terrifying with his shaved head, monstrous moustache, and gleaming teeth.

"Young miss," I addressed her, "take heed that you never come here again. Do not enter the cave, nor walk up to the entablature. Do not touch the royal slipper, not even to right it, for you will then inevitably find yourself within the evil kingdom, where the guardian is only the first of many dangers that will confront you." So saying, I escorted her from the cave, bade her well, and made my way back to the inn.

As soon as I returned, I found a note lying upon the table. It was addressed "To the Innkeeper" in a childish hand. I tore open the letter and the only word written upon the

> sheet inside was "Röo-kel." I knew then that she was already in the shadows of that dark land, and that it was my task to follow and save her.

I had only the vaguest idea of the meaning of the dream. "The Lost Slipper of Soul" was a suggestive phrase, for according to the teachings of the League, Soul referred to man's identity as a spark of God. As a follower of these teachings, I interpreted the royal slipper to be a symbol of this birthright, a token left behind in this world to remind us of our spiritual identity.

Andreas Leo, who first made these teachings available to the public, was quoted in Brett Singer's *In My Heart I Am Free*, as follows:

> Man is a monarch clothed in rags, a master of the universe begging for a crust of bread. He is a king bowing before his own servants, a prisoner held in chains by his own ignorance. If he could only walk out of his self-constructed prison, where none holds him but himself, he would be free. (140)

In this passage, I could hear an echo of my dream. If each one of us was a king whose true home lay in the spiritual worlds, the lost slipper must be a symbol of our spiritual inheritance. Why, however, had I perceived the kingdom that was home to the slipper to be an evil one? What was the identity of the guardian that I had seen at the portal of that world?

Not long afterwards, I had occasion to visit a photographer's studio. The photographer was an elderly man with curly, dyed blond hair, and a South American accent. "I need an eight by ten, black and white, glossy photo," I said. "But I don't want a nice, smiley kind of photograph. I'm interested in a shot that brings out my character, not one that just looks good. I've got an idea of what I want—something cropped close, no shoulders. I want it to zero right in on my face, my expression a little aggressive, eyes squinting a little, chin jutting out, head cocked to one side."

"There are two ways of looking in a picture in which you don't smile," the photographer commented. "You can look sad or you can look mad."

"I don't want to look either, but I want to look like I've got attitude," I said melodramatically.

"Well, you're doing a good job of that," he quipped. He ushered me into the studio, had me sit on a sofa, and tried various camera angles. I made various expressions for him—one smiling, another scowling deeply, and yet another in the midst of speaking. He seemed to be enjoying my performance. "Did you ever notice how people, in their interaction with you, comment on your appearance?" he asked. "If you're in an argument with them, they'll say 'You look angry.' It's a way of gauging you, and at the same time influencing you."

"I think I know what you mean," I said. "People are always asking me what I mean by the face I'm making, yet I'm not aware that I'm making any kind of face at all."

"Exactly," the photographer said. "It's because we pay too much attention to ourselves. Our faces acquire a set, rigid expression. When we forget ourselves, however, our faces come alive, as if they are freed from their prison routine."

After the session, the photographer brought out four prints and set them on the counter. I was shocked at the wide divergence of expressions. One was too happy, another too glum, and a third simply aggressive. "I think the first one is really the best. Unless maybe this one," I said, pointing to the third. "What do you think?"

"I like that one," he said, indicating the latter. "The first one is too wishy-washy. You look like you're going along with something—not because you want to, but because you have to. The other one is stronger. You look like you're saying 'I'm not going to take any crap from anyone.'"

"You're right. Let's go with the third one," I agreed. I paid for the session, and made arrangements to pick up the finished prints the next day. In return, he gave me the initial prints of the four pictures I had rejected. I took them home, sat down, and started scrutinizing the four initial prints. First, I looked at the "happy" one, which I had disliked when I first saw it. As I stared at it, it seemed to come to life.

I had experienced this phenomenon many times before. The

technique involved staring at a person's picture in a slightly oblique manner. It helped to focus not on the eyes, but on another feature, such as the tip of the nose. Eventually, the picture would begin to change. First, there would be merely changes of expression. If one persisted in staring, however, the face would transform into other faces. Eventually, there would be a cascade of faces quite distinct from one another—not the face of the original personality, but of other individuals entirely. It didn't always happen in equal measure with all pictures. Some people's pictures proved to be amazingly powerful, providing a dazzling cascade of images. Others produced little effect at all. I wondered what it meant. Perhaps I was seeing images that represented the past lives of the individual. Maybe these "past lives" were not merely in the past, but were continually present as aspects of the individual's personality. Eventually, I concluded that each of us was not one, but many. We were clearly not ourselves, or at least not what we thought ourselves to be.

After staring at all the photographs, I decided that the effect was stronger with the cheerful picture than with the others. The next day, I returned to the photographer's studio. "I think we chose the wrong one to enlarge," I said. "The one of me smiling is the best."

"Why do you say that?" he inquired. "I think we made a good choice."

"I guess I just realized that I came in with an attitude," I admitted. "I didn't want a picture in which I looked happy. That says something about my state of mind."

The photographer laughed. "I work with a bunch of narcissists all the time," he said. "Actors and actresses—they account for a large portion of my business. They come in for publicity shots. They have the biggest egos in the world. If you put them in water, they would float! What I mean is, they don't know themselves. They have to borrow from the characters they play. They have no personality of their own, so they're difficult to photograph. A few great actors, however, know this about themselves, and that's what makes them great. They're easy to photograph."

"What does that have to do with me?" I asked.

"You were easy to photograph. You have the qualities of a great actor, even if you're not aware of it. Your personality started to come through as soon as I started to shoot you. We play roles in life in the same way that actors do. Sometimes we get locked into our role, and take life too seriously. But if we have the ability to slip out of our roles now and then, we're OK."

I took out a notepad and started jotting down his words. As I did so, I realized that photographer and I had switched roles. The day before, it was he who had been the observer, trying to bring out my personality in a photograph. Now I was capturing his personality, not in an image, but through his words. For a moment, I had stepped outside of myself. I was able to see myself the way the photographer had seen me, as an array of personalities, not simply one single image that I was intent on preserving in a photograph.

To write about the League, however, was not so easy. What was the League? To a casual observer, faced with a proliferation of spiritual groups as bewildering as that of supplements in a health food store, it had all the earmarks of a religion. That, however, was only its outer form. In *The Journey to the East*, which first introduced the League to the reading public, Hermann Hesse had written of a similar plethora of spiritual groups in his own day:

> There were Bacchanalian dance societies and Anabaptist groups...There was...a widespread leaning towards Indian, ancient Persian and other Eastern mysteries and religions, and all this gave most people the impression that our ancient League was one of the many newly blossomed cults.

Was the League merely one of these newly blossomed cults? Was it the true path, the highest path, or just one path among many? In the course of writing this manuscript, I discovered that describing the League was like looking at my own photograph. At first, I saw what I was used to seeing, or what I wanted to see. Then I saw what I didn't want to see, and was overcome with disappointment and disillusion. Finally came a cascade of images—the viewpoint of Soul—and I realized that the lesson of detachment applied not only to my view of my self, but to my view of the League, as well.

This book is largely concerned with the difference between religion and spirituality. A religion provides us with a guide for living, moral and ethical rules or standards, and ritual that satisfies our need for meaning. A spiritual path, on the other hand, is a return journey into the heart of life. A religion is like looking at one's own picture, and seeing what one wants to see. A spiritual path is like seeing the infinite possibilities and potentialities in that image. Whether the League was a religion or a spiritual path depended on what one wanted to see, and what one was prepared to see.

I once went to a Chinese restaurant and got a fortune that said "He who falls in love with himself shall have no rivals." This paradoxical statement, I realized, could equally refer to vanity or enlightenment. The vain man had no rivals in the sense that no one else could love him. The enlightened man had no rivals because he had no peers. The same was true of the League. It was possible to fall in love with it, as long as one set aside one's ideas, opinions, theories, and beliefs. The human tendency, however, was to make an edifice out of the League, in which case one worshipped only a reflection of one's own ego. The whole thrust of one's experience as a League initiate was to either bind one ever closer to a single image, or to find the truth, which was in that multiplicity of images.

Spirituality is first and foremost concerned with unraveling the mystery of one's self and then going on to become an agent in a higher cause. If a person makes himself an agent in that cause, day in and day out, he is living the spiritual life. To become such an agent, however, it is necessary to participate in life unconditionally, without any reservations. To this end, we must drop the fixed ideas, attitudes, and opinions that separate us from life, and become more accepting of the world as it is, other people as they are, and ourselves as we are. This is the true meaning of detachment. We have to go beyond our comfort zone, our habitual patterns of thought, and our congratulatory assumptions about our belief systems, religious affiliations, or cultural identities. We need to crack the hard shell we have built around us.

There comes a time for each of us when we realize that the slipper of Soul has slipped from our grasp, and then it is necessary to embark on a mission to retrieve it. This is our moment of crisis, our call to action. We each have to face the challenge of entering the secret portal in our own way. We have to trust the child within ourselves to take the initiative and lead us there, despite our reluctance to face the unknown. Our greatest obstacle is fear. Fear tends to immobilize us, to render us incapable of action. No matter how great our insight or how pure our intentions, if we don't translate our thoughts and feelings into action, we risk failing to achieve our spiritual goal in this lifetime.

If we belong to a particular religion or spiritual group, we have to work to keep it a source of continual spiritual renewal. Remaining within the fold can't be allowed to become merely a matter of brand loyalty, and adhering to its disciplines can't be simply a matter of habit. In that case, we will find ourselves in danger of closing ourselves off to life all around us. The approach to our faith and spiritual practice has to be the same as our approach to life—to greet each day and each moment with new eyes, a young heart, and an open mind.

Thus begins the story of my journey…

PART ONE

THE INVISIBLE THREAD

"The Force is the invisible thread that binds together all universes throughout time into eternity. When the first glimmer of intelligent consciousness dawned on humanity, this thread was there. Man predates religion, but the Force is older than all life on Earth. It was with us in the beginning of Creation, and sustains us today."

—Andreas Leo, *The Face of the Eternal, Book One*, 17

CHAPTER 1

THE DARK SIDE OF THE MOON

"Spirituality germinates in man's heart by the grace of the God. By attending the League study group meetings, the individual becomes purified in the company of others, and makes progress in becoming an instrument of God. He moves spiritually closer to the Living Master, allowing them to secretly communicate with one another."
—Andreas Leo, *The Face of the Eternal, Book One,* 189

I FIRST ENCOUNTERED the League while still a university student at a now-defunct metaphysical bookstore in Belle Harbor. Above the counter, I had noticed a crude little poster, with a hand-drawn illustration that was copied from a book with which I was familiar, called *The Secret of the Golden Flower.* This was a Taoist text originally translated into German, with an introduction by Carl Jung. The picture was of a monk in contemplation, with his spirit form rising above his head. At the top of the poster were the words: **The Order of the League—Practicing the Ancient Science of the Soul.** Below this, it read:

> A class is now forming for anyone interested in studying the Ancient Science of the Soul as a means of liberation. It will follow the techniques as set down by Andreas Leo, President and Living Master, following in the unbroken line of Masters of the Order of the League. The creed of the League is

> that all life flows from the Creator into the lower worlds, and nothing can exist without this universal force, which can be experienced as sound and light. Therefore, it is necessary for man to always be aware of the light and sound emanating from the body of the Creator in order to dwell in the spiritual realms. (Not for the seeking of phenomena, but as an individual and arduous path to the higher states of consciousness.)

I immediately received a number of positive impressions from this poster. First, I had been looking for a system of meditation that I could easily learn to practice. I had already been led to certain books that discussed out-of-body experiences. The poster, with its reference to the Science of the Soul and its use of the illustration from the Taoist text, implied that the two practices could be combined within a single set of techniques. Secondly, I understood from the poster that a spiritual Master—in fact, an entire line of Masters—was associated with these teachings. I could see that a methodology was involved—a set of practices aimed at achieving specific goals. Moreover, those goals were lofty, involving the attainment of higher states of consciousness and, ultimately, spiritual liberation. Finally, the Science of the Soul was presented as an arduous path. That appealed to my romantic instincts. I felt that a true spiritual path shouldn't be easy, but should be only for the bold and adventurous.

The poster included the name of a contact and a phone number. I called the number, and, in response, received a visit from a mysterious young man with shoulder-length hair and a goatee, who lent me several books. He mentioned a conference that was to take place that weekend in a neighboring state. Andreas Leo, President of the League and Living Master, would be there. When he invited me to come along, I hesitated, then declined. Instead, I went upstate with some friends. We all got jobs in town and lived communally in an isolated cabin in the woods. During the next three months, I spent most of my free time taking long walks in those woods and reading the volumes the young man had lent me, all written by the mysterious Andreas Leo.

Hermann Hesse's *The Journey to the East*, the first book to speak openly about the League and its then young President and Living Master, was the story of a man who had failed a spiritual test. The League at that time was a secret organization. Hesse's narrator was a former initiate of the League who had lost his way, convinced that its great mission, cloaked under the guise of the fabled Journey to the East, had disbanded. Succumbing to vanity, he imagined himself as the lone survivor of this mission, and its sole potential chronicler. He set out to write a history of the Journey to the East, but his memory failed him. Eventually, he discovered that the League still thrived in the very city where he lived. He was forced to confront his own spiritual shortcomings, to acknowledge anew the authority of the President of the League, and to subordinate the rest of his life and work to serving his spiritual Master.

Forty years after the publication of Hesse's work, Andreas Leo had brought the teachings of the League into the open. He presented it not as an offshoot or sect of any other religion, but as an invisible thread of spiritual teachings that extended back through world history and beyond into the mists of time, which had at times remained secret, and at times been taught openly. The Masters of these teachings were part of an unbroken line of spiritual authority, charged with the task of gathering those souls who were spiritually ready and leading them back to God. Hermann Hesse had named Zoroaster, Lao-Tse, and Pythagoras as co-founders and brothers of the League. The writings of Andreas Leo extended the League's lineage to include Socrates, Paul of Tarsus, Rumi, Milarepa, and many other sages of history.

The teachings of the League centered on the technique of uniting the individual with the Audible Life Stream, or Sound Current, considered to be the creative and sustaining force of the universe. According to its doctrine, the ultimate goal of Soul's journey was to return to its true home in the spiritual worlds. Soul was kept here by the cycle of death and rebirth, perpetuated through the mechanism of karma and reincarnation. Liberation from this cycle could be achieved only through the intervention of a spiritual Master appointed specifically to lead Soul back to its true home. Without such a Master or guide, the individual was like a ship without a rudder, doomed to be tossed up and down by the tides of life, without a clear purpose or direction.

Andreas Leo—simply Leo to his followers—didn't claim that his teachings were unique. In fact, he emphasized their ancient nature. Nevertheless, his writings possessed an authoritative quality that was more than the sum of the sources from which he had borrowed. As soon as I began to read these books, my attention was completely absorbed by them. They were complex, sophisticated, and highly paradoxical. What impressed me more than anything else was the feeling that I would need a lifetime to get to the bottom of them.

Leo was the ultimate Renaissance man, who seemed to have the pulse of the universe at his fingertips. He had an unbelievable degree of familiarity with spiritual history, and an uncanny ability to break that history down to its essentials. He was also a real writer, with the facility of projecting his personality onto the page. Even when he borrowed directly from other people's work, he somehow made it his own. In addition, he projected an image of spiritual daring and adventure. He didn't just sit in his armchair and write about spirituality, but rather went out and lived it. He presented himself as risk taker who lived outside the rules of common humanity, without allowing himself to be forced into the position of a rebel.

Even Leo's writing style was risky and unconventional. Each of his books was different, as if tuned to a particular level of interest or spiritual receptivity. Some merely outlined his philosophy, while others were poetic. He wrote novels, and even science fiction. On each genre, he put the mark of his own personal style. Even those books that did not seem to have been written with great care were impressive. Their very imperfections seemed calculated with precision, as if they sought to persuade by their very genuineness, spontaneity, and candor.

Still, it took quite some time before the fire of devotion was lit within me. I remember the moment this occurred. I was sitting in the woods one day, reading a book entitled *The Mirror of God*, the last of the volumes by Andreas Leo that I had borrowed in Belle Harbor. I came to a chapter called "The Way to Success in God Consciousness," and read the following passage:

> The way to liberation is to resign your destiny to God. One must relinquish the feeling of need, and become genuinely detached toward all. This is release via self-renunciation, the act of dying to be reborn. To achieve it, a corner must be turned within; a latent hardness must dissolve and liquefy. This experience often occurs quickly and naturally, leaving the individual with the feeling of having been blessed by God, and causing him to turn from the viewpoint of the outer consciousness to that of the real self. It separates religious people from moralists, and the spiritual from the religious. Those who undergo it fully cannot doubt its reality, for in giving up their personal will, they have felt the Divine Power. (33-4)

As I read these words, I felt something break down within me, just as the text described. It was as if my heart had ruptured, spilling its fluid, and engulfing me in ecstatic liquidity. Sitting in the woods, with the dappled sunlight on my notebook, I responded by writing the following poem in the form of a prayer:

Lord, I open myself to thee. I make myself ready to receive thee.
I relax. My aches and pains melt as with a caress.
I feel your thought flow through me. Your love overwhelms me.
Soft as snow, thy eternal Gift.
There is no worry, no self for which to labor,
Yet, a thirst springs from me, as from a bottomless well, run dry,
A thirst to know myself,
To awaken from this dream that is poverty unto me,
And bathe in the pure Light that is wealth itself.

It took me weeks of pacing in the woods, as I read and absorbed the material in Andreas Leo's books, before it occurred to me to inquire about formally putting my feet upon this spiritual path. Finally, I sent away for the League discourses—monthly lessons written by Andreas Leo for study at home. I remember the day I received the first of these crudely printed mailings. The moment I opened it up, I felt that a presence had entered the room and permanently settled in with me. I returned to Belle Harbor to finish my university studies, and joined the League study group that had recently been formed there—the first in the state. At the initial meeting, I was told that Andreas Leo had passed away during the conference that I had declined to attend, and a new President and Living Master had taken his place.

The League study group became the focus of my life. Much of my effort, like that of the other students in the group, was concerned with cultivating experiences that would have appeared to most people to be so subtle, arcane, and elusive as to be of little value. In pursuit of these experiences, the League discourses offered various spiritual exercises for students to practice, many of which involved the use of certain charged words that were repeated inwardly as an aid to contemplation. A common practice involved carefully noting one's dreams, recording them in a notebook, and sharing these experiences with fellow members of the group. Still other exercises required the student to listen inwardly for various sounds, or look inwardly for a spontaneous flash of light. It was said that the Masters of the Order of the League hovered invisibly over these study sessions, revealing themselves only to those with the eyes to see.

According to the teachings of Andreas Leo, the initial purpose of cultivating such inner experiences as dreams, out-of-body travel, the inner perception of sound and light, or meeting with the Masters, was to prove for oneself the reality of survival after the death of the physical body. The ultimate goals of the spiritual path, however, were far more ambitious. They included self-realization, God-realization, and becoming a co-worker in the Divine cause. The League taught basic spiritual principles familiar from eastern religions, such as the laws of karma and reincarnation. Life was conceived as an endless cycle of death and rebirth, yet there was a means of liberation from this cycle via unswerving loyalty to the Living Master. Only the Living Master was said to be able to offer the spiritual student a way out of the perpetual cycle of action and reaction known as karma, and to assure him of never being obliged to return to earth again for yet another lifetime.

Gradually, I began to have the type of inner experiences that were the goal of these spiritual exercises. On a few occasions, I had the sensation of literally waking up within a dream and being able to control the dream experience by my own intention and will. Certain dreams were so vivid that I remembered them more clearly than my waking experiences. This convinced me that there was, in effect, little difference between dreams and waking life. If one could remember dreams just as well as waking experiences, and if one could write down what occurred in a dream just as one could record a physical experience, then how could one say that one type of experience was more "real" than the other?

I had a number of highly symbolic dreams during this early period of my membership in the League. A particularly notable example was one in which I found myself in my room, together with the new Living Master. Silently, the Master pointed to the floor, and I saw that it was made of earth. He then produced a shovel, with which he proceeded to dig a pit in the center of the room. When the pit was the size of the grave, he signaled me to lay down inside, and then covered me up until my eyes, ears, and every organ of sense was sealed in darkness. I woke up with the impression that this scene of ritual burial had represented my preliminary initiation into the Order of the League.

On another occasion, Andreas Leo himself appeared to me in a dream. Again, the scene unfolded in my room, this time on a beautiful spring day. The departed Master entered via a door that opened to a splendid garden. He left the door ajar. I was sitting in the opposite corner of the room. All around me were shelves filled with neat stacks of books—a library that any scholar would envy. As Leo entered, he carried a large bound volume, face open, in his hands. Instead of looking down at the pages, he stared directly at me, smiling broadly and enigmatically, without saying a word. Finally, I looked at the book he held, and saw that it was upside down. I awoke with the sense that the dream was telling me that book knowledge had no meaning for a true Master, that it had taken me as far as it could, and from this point on, I needed to gain experience in a non-intellectual manner.

In yet another dream, I found myself wading through a swamp, together with my sister. The swamp gradually changed to a beautiful, clear pond, in which I was able to swim freely. I looked back and saw that my sister was still struggling in the swamp, but felt that I couldn't help her. On the opposite shore of the pond, I glimpsed a light, and began swimming toward it. I was able to see that the source of the light was a temple built in the style of a Japanese pagoda. I reached the shore, and entered the temple. Inside, I was surrounded by a fragrance of unspeakable beauty, which I realized signified the presence of the Living Master. The dream was showing me that my consciousness was moving beyond that of the members of my family, and that I could not turn back and help them. They had to find their way to the path themselves, in their own time and according to their own pace, whether in this lifetime or a subsequent one.

While dreams were a relatively easy way to gain spiritual experience, contemplation was a more difficult matter. The mere discipline of sitting down for twenty minutes a day was a challenge for me. On a few occasions, a friend of mine who was not a member of the League took me to Zen meditation sessions at the local Quaker meeting house. I was amazed at the ability of the Zen students to sit solid as rocks for an hour at a time, while I fidgeted around in intense discomfort. One time I lost my balance entirely, landing with a profound thud on my back, and causing everyone in the room to look up with a sharp glance of condescension.

Even more difficult was learning to see, hear, and be aware of inner experiences during contemplation. According to the League teachings, one was supposed to hear sounds inwardly, but I wasn't aware of hearing anything. Frustrated, I remembered that there was a broadcasting lab in one of the university buildings that contained several soundproof rooms, which were unlocked and often vacant. I began to frequent these rooms in order to practice my contemplation. I immediately discovered that a soundproof room wasn't silent at all, for as soon as I sat down, I was aware of a loud buzzing sound in my head, like that of a high-tension electrical wire. I suppose I had always heard it, but had never given it a second thought. Still, I wasn't sure if this sound was that which one was supposed to hear in contemplation, so I continued my experimentation.

Eventually, I became aware of another way of hearing, which was to listen to inner music. The experience was like replaying a tune in my head, except that I didn't rely on memory or make up the music as I went along. Rather, the experience was like plugging into a symphonic stream that was ever flowing and ever available. The trick was simply to wait until the silence changed to sound. One could compare it to surfing, to catching and riding an auditory wave. The music was indescribably complex and ever changing. It was like replaying an eternal concert in my mind, except that I did nothing to initiate or maintain the flow of sound.

I experienced the same mental hang-up with respect to seeing in contemplation as I did with respect to hearing the inner sounds, in that I could never "see" in the same way that I did with my physical eyes. I never felt transported to a world that was as tangible as the physical world. In this matter, however, I was aided by my participation in the study group. One day, the group leader had us try a spiritual exercise together. We sat in contemplation and were then instructed to write down what occurred. I wrote in my notebook for a long time. Finally, the group leader asked the members to share their experiences.

I began with an elaborate apology. "I'm not very visually oriented," I told the group. "I don't really 'see' anything in my contemplation. It's more like a feeling." Then I began to describe what I had experienced. I went on and on, adding detail upon detail. Eventually, I noticed the smiles on the faces of the other students in the class.

They were on the brink of laughing out loud at me. There was such a comic disparity between my attitude toward my contemplation and what was actually occurring that I finally "got it." I had been having experiences all along, but I just hadn't understood that they were experiences until I was asked to write them down and talk about them. The fact that I had written and described them in such detail was proof of their reality that even I could not deny.

I also found that I was able to use my dreams to help me in other aspects of my spiritual discipline. One of the League discourses, for instance, involved choosing three words to use in combination during contemplation. I already knew which words I wished to use in the first and last places of the combination, but was stuck on what word to use in the middle. One night, after wrestling with this problem, I fell asleep. In the morning, I awoke with the memory of a vivid dream in which I had stood before three statues like those of ancient Greek goddesses. The statues to the right and left sides were darkened, but the one in the middle was illuminated. I looked more closely at the base of the middle statue, and saw a word lit up in golden letters. I remembered the word, and was able to use it in my contemplation.

During this period, I also attended my first League conference and met the new President and Living Master. At the time, I felt so unworthy that I was unable to meet his gaze. At that same conference, the Master made the unprecedented gesture of singing to the assembly. The audience was rapt, overwhelmed by his charismatic presence. Afterwards, as we exited the hall, I heard someone comment that the atmosphere was "just like Christmas." When I got back from the conference, I put a picture of the new Living Master on my bedpost so it would be the first thing I would see in the morning and the last when I went to bed at night.

I even had my brush with meeting the mysterious masters of the Order of the League in the flesh. The first time I gave a public talk on the Science of the Soul was at a public library in Belle Harbor. A large number of people showed up. I had an entire yellow pad full of notes for my presentation, and was very nervous. I gave a very detailed, intellectual treatment of my subject, complete with diagrams that I drew on a chalkboard. About two-thirds of the way through my talk, I felt a tremendous urge to speed up, almost as if an outside force was pushing me to do so. I broke into a sweat, scanned the rest of my notes, and managed somehow to wind up my lecture in a few more sentences.

About a week later, I attended a gathering of League members. At one point during the meeting, a woman named Dorothy got up with an intense and authoritative expression on her face. "I just can't keep silent about this," she burst out, passionately. "I just have to tell you. I had my first out-of-body experience at that talk last week! I met one of the Masters! I talked to him!"

She proceeded to relate how she had come to the library and suddenly found herself out of the body just in time to see one of the Masters entering the room, disguising himself as an ordinary member of the audience. "He was sitting there the whole time," she went on, breathlessly. "The young-looking man in the dark beard. Didn't anybody else see him?"

Then Dorothy turned to me. "The Master gave me a special message for you," she said.

"A message for me?" I stammered.

"Yes. He told me to tell you not to forget to welcome the people in the audience at the beginning of your talk. You neglected that. It wasn't polite!"

I was completely taken aback by this. A master of the invisible hierarchy of the League had attended my talk and given me a special message via this individual, just to tell me that I hadn't been polite? It was a lot for my ego to handle. I didn't know whether to be flattered to be singled out for such attention, or to be ashamed to be so publicly criticized. I might have dismissed Dorothy as a madwoman if not for my memory of the force that had manhandled me at the podium, causing me to abruptly conclude my talk. There was no explanation for it, other than that an unseen and powerful presence had taken charge of my presentation.

On another occasion, I went to a diner for breakfast early one Sunday morning. It was a seedy place just around the corner from my apartment that I used to call "The Sleaze Café." The place was completely empty so I chose a booth and took my seat. A waitress came. I ordered some eggs, and she left. As I sat waiting for her to return with my order, an old bum shuffled into the place. He stood in the middle of the dining area, looking at all the empty booths around him. Then he trained his eyes on me, sitting there all alone. He honed right in on the fact that I resented company, and approached me without any hesitation.

"Mind if I sit down?" he asked.

What could I do—say no? I allowed him to take a seat, and we started talking. It was clear right away that this was no ordinary bum. He talked intelligently on every subject. I can no longer remember all that we talked about, but the topics ranged from the career of a young politician who was prominent at that time, to speculation about what was on the dark side of the moon. The bum was not only intelligent, but also perceptive. He was immediately able to pick up on all my weak spots and sensitivities. After a while, I started to suspect that I was talking to a Master of the Order of the League in disguise, but I could do nothing to confirm this. He was in total control of the situation. If he was acting a part, he was doing so in such a virtuoso manner that it would have been useless for me to ask him who or what he really was.

"What's your ethnic background?" he eventually asked me.

Now, at the time, I was rebelling against my ancestry. When people asked me about it, I tended to avoid a direct answer. On this occasion, however, I went a step further and lied outright. "I'm Irish," I told him. It was a ridiculous reply, since there was nothing remotely Irish about my appearance. As soon as I said it, I felt that something in the bum's manner had pushed me into giving the most ludicrous possible answer.

"Oh yeah, you're Irish all right," he nodded with a wink.

I felt unbelievably stupid, and was completely on the defensive after that. The feeling that I was sitting across from a Master became overpowering. I kept thinking, "It's not supposed to be like this." I had absorbed some kind of romantic notion that if a person met with a Master in disguise but became aware of his identity, the Master would be forced to reciprocate by acknowledging his identity. Nothing of the kind was happening, however. If the bum was truly a Master, he must have been aware of what I was thinking, and yet he continued the pretense. I felt like I was the butt of some kind of cosmic joke.

Moreover, I felt resentful. By what power or even right could this individual—whoever or whatever he was—walk around in disguise and pretend to be something he was not? What was Mastership, anyway? Did it confer on an individual the freedom to put on whatever act he or she wanted? Was that what separated a true Master from a fake, charlatan, or dilettante? Was Mastership simply a matter of good acting versus bad acting? Did life boil down to knowing who one was merely so that one could pretend to be someone else?

Finally, the bum either fell asleep in a drunken stupor or did a good imitation of it as a sign that he was through with me. I got up and went home to ponder the experience. With each step out the door of the café, I felt that I was possibly walking away from a true spiritual Master. I wanted to turn around, walk back, and question him about all the secrets of the universe. I knew it was useless, though. He would just continue the pretense.

Shortly after this, I had a dream in which I returned to my old high school. It had been built in a modern style, with several buildings laid out separately like a junior college campus. All the buildings were made of poured concrete, studded with crystalline stones. There was a separate gym building, administration building, main classroom building, and agriculture building. The walkways between the buildings had canopies over them to protect transiting students from the rain and snow. The main classroom building was rectangular, with a single central hall and the classrooms all laid out on the perimeter.

The sun was so bright that I had to squint my eyes to see, and yet the light was not only dazzling, but also soothing and comforting.

The arrangement of the classroom building had changed. The classrooms were still on the perimeter, with a large hall in the center, but now all the entrances to the classrooms were on the exterior of the building. The rooms faced outward to the sun, their doors were thrown open, and sunlight filled the classrooms. The students were happy, energetic, engaged in their studies, and appreciative of their teachers. The bell rang, and as the classrooms started to empty out, I recognized one of the teachers. He recognized me, too. I went up to him, and he greeted me.

"Hello, O'Connor," he said.

I greeted him in return. "My name isn't O'Connor, though," I corrected him.

I told him my real name, pronouncing it very carefully and distinctly. After that, we reminisced a while. I had a number of mixed feelings during this conversation. Although I felt soothed and comforted by the light, I had the nagging feeling that I was wasting my life. By contrast, this teacher had devoted himself to service. He was close to retirement, and as the sun shone down on him, I sensed that he could look back on his life with satisfaction, knowing that he had helped so many young people along on their way in life. There was an undertone of anxiety to my feelings, for I could think of nothing comparable that I had achieved. Nevertheless, I was comforted by the soothing quality of the light that shone on everything.

I awoke with this dual awareness of anxiety about my lack of accomplishment in life, on the one hand, and the soothing, uplifting quality of the light that had flooded the dream, on the other. I couldn't reconcile these two feelings that the dream had produced in me. I called up a fellow member of the League named George Blackstone, and told him the whole dream.

"There's one detail that strikes me," he said. "The teacher called you O'Connor. What associations does the name bring up for you?"

"None that I can think of," I replied.

"You don't know anyone named O'Connor?" he asked.

"No. It's an Irish name, that's all," I said.

"OK," he persisted. "What associations does an Irish name bring up for you?"

I was about to say none, but then I checked myself, remembering my experience with the bum at the café. I had told him I was Irish. The potential significance of the dream dawned on me. "I told the teacher my real name," I replied. "I said it slowly, clearly, and distinctly. I think the dream is telling me that some fundamental insecurity I have been suffering from is gone." As I expressed this idea to George, I felt that the worry about my lack of achievement was of no consequence compared to that beautiful sunlight. I remembered the last line of the poem I had written when I first joined the League—about bathing in a pure light that was wealth itself. This was that light. It represented something that had no connection with outer forms of achievement. It had only to do with my true relationship to my self.

I thought back to my conversation with the bum (if that's what he had been), and particularly to our talk about the dark side of the moon. The image of the moon struck me as a metaphor for the human state of consciousness. What, after all, did we know about our own state of consciousness? Our moments of illumination were fleeting, to be captured in an instant—in a moment of déjà vu, a chance encounter, or the remembrance of a dream. If we had the good fortune to experience that light however briefly, we could know only that a hidden portion of ourselves had been revealed, and a small portion of God's grace had been bestowed upon us.

Chapter 2

The Cardinal's Red Hat

"Life is like a river, always flowing to the ocean. Only serene detachment can release us from that flow, and allow us to stand upon the river's banks and gaze upon its course. Thus, it is wise to be neither for nor against, remaining self-contained, and living only for God."

—Andreas Leo, *Sermon by the River*, 63

ONE NIGHT, I had a dream that appeared to be symbolic of a past life. I found myself in fourteenth century Italy, living the life of a monk. The dream progressed, and I saw myself at a later stage of life in a position of authority, wearing a strange hat. When I awoke, my clearest memory was of the hat. It had been bright red and oddly unbalanced in shape, with a close-fitting crown like that of a skullcap and a wide, floppy brim, as big as that of a sombrero. With its garish color and utter lack of proportion, the hat struck me as completely silly and improbable. Nevertheless, as a member of the League, I took dreams seriously, and cast around for a source of reference. My father was a walking encyclopedia, and the handiest authority. A typical intellectual, he had no use for the League teachings, so I didn't mention the dream to him. I merely described the hat—bright red, close-fitting crown, and wide brim—and asked if he knew what it might be.

"Show me," my father demanded, handing me a paper and pencil. I drew a sketch of the hat. "That's simple," he said, without hesitation. "It's the hat of a cardinal. There's no doubt about it. You can look it up!"

I dug out an encyclopedia and found a colored illustration of priests, monks, and other church officials down through history. Sure enough, there was a picture of a cardinal from the late Middle Ages or early Renaissance period, wearing the exact same outlandish hat that I had worn in the dream. The fact that I had never seen an illustration of such a hat before confirmed my conviction that the dream was a recall of a past life. Moreover, it seemed more than a coincidence that I had consulted my father on this topic. I wondered whether my connection to him was not possibly traceable to this same past life that had been reflected in the dream.

To get a picture of my father, whose name was Alfred, you must imagine a sharp-featured individual with a highly intelligent, kind, and witty expression. He had an enormous nose and aquiline brow—the features of a quintessential professor and scholar, and his habit of rapidly turning his head and cocking it to one side when considering a question gave him the appearance of a large, cerebral bird. Having divorced himself from his ancestral religion along with many other middle-class Jews in pre-war Germany, he was a confirmed atheist, with no apparent need for the solace offered by religion. Ironically, however, one of his greatest passions was choral music. He was a member of the local choir, and loved nothing more than listening to works such as Handel's Messiah, to which he would sing along full-throatedly, the libretto perfectly committed to memory. He also had a strange penchant for dressing up like a priest, particularly in front of his college students. His close-fitting black turtleneck jersey, augmented with a dark sport coat, made him look just like a cleric. He loved it when friends reacted to his appearance by addressing him as "Father Al."

At the same time, however, my father could be quite stridently anti-Christian. I once had a debate with him about which religion—Christianity or Judaism—was preferable. He expressed his preference for Judaism, while I voted for Christianity. My reasoning was that Judaism was the older, and hence more primitive of the two faiths. I regarded it as a tribal religion based on race and ethnicity, whose sense of exclusivity was elitist and patronizing. What I admired about Christianity was its ecumenical spirit, the fact that it made itself available to all, Jew and Gentile alike. My father, on the other hand, saw a danger in this very inclusiveness, which to his mind fostered the urge to proselytize, convert, and conquer. He pointed out the atrocities committed in the name of the Christian Church—the inquisitions, the pogroms, and the extermination of Native Americans, as evidence of this tendency.

In the course of this discussion, I made the mistake of bringing up my dream about the cardinal's red hat. When I suggested that we might have been Catholic clerics in a previous life together, his intellectual tolerance reached its limit. Something about my remark offended his sense of pride. Perhaps it was the suggestion that, in some realm of knowledge, I possessed greater authority than he did. Despite his permissiveness, my father possessed an Old World patriarchal streak. He was the father, and I was the son. Any blurring of that distinction offended his sense of pride.

After that, the League became a significant barrier between my father and me. I think he considered it my one true act of rebellion against him. To compensate, I looked for mentors within the League, and found one in the person of an elderly woman in her seventies, crippled with arthritis, named Kaye Tyson. Kaye and I came from completely different generations and backgrounds, and must have seemed like an odd pair indeed—yet appearances could be deceiving. A spiritual path often produces strange friendships and alliances. Individuals who share such bonds have something in common that goes beyond the conventions of ordinary life. It's the stuff of human mystery.

Kaye and I both took life seriously. It wasn't that we lacked a sense of humor, but when it came to the gut issues of life, neither of us was inclined to mess around. Kaye was a lifelong student of spirituality, and everything she experienced she sifted through this spiritual perspective. Because she couldn't be physically active, she was inclined to use her very passivity as a way to be of service. In a number of cases, she let other people take gross advantage of her. She was involved for years with a young man named Blair Davis. He was an unscrupulous character who borrowed Kaye's credit cards, ran up thousands of dollars in debts on them, and never paid her back a dime. His abuse culminated in a sexual act. Blair was a big man, and Kaye a tiny woman. There was a fifty-year age difference between them. That fact alone made the issue of whether or not she could have put up any resistance, even if she had wanted to, irrelevant.

Kaye confided this to me alone. Even knowing her as I did, I was shocked by the revelation. If she had told anyone else, they would probably have thought she was crazy. As it was, she was regarded as eccentric even within League circles. There was, however, a method to her madness. While she appeared to let people push her around and take advantage of her, she in fact accepted responsibility for everything she did. To allow Blair to run roughshod over her was her way of being a channel for the Force. According to her way of thinking, by maintaining strict neutrality, she was stepping aside, allowing Spirit to work its will and deliver its karmic lesson to Blair as he needed. If you tried to convince her that she would have been better off asserting her own will, she would give you sort of a weary look. Then, with her jaw firmly set, she'd let you know (if you didn't already) that your words were useless.

Kaye had a special affection for men, and was not shy of expressing feelings that would startle some people to hear them voiced by an elderly woman. She always felt that there was something of a man's experience in her, and that her affection for men came from the well of past life experience. A hint of this attitude might be seen in one of her few surviving poems:

> *Bold men are gentle yet ruthless when the occasion demands. Their touch is tender and hesitant. They are aware of the force within.*
>
> *They hold tight rein on their passions; control learned through eons of time and bodies left on bloody fields in many places.*

They seek permission, asking wordlessly with gleaming brightness in their eyes, and proceed slowly.

Their initial kiss is a soft brush on the cheek, and the touch of their lips is benevolent reverence from an unseen realm!

Kaye had a favorite poem that perfectly summed up the viewpoint that the two of us had most in common. It was by the early twentieth century British poet, A. E. Housman:

I to my perils of cheat and charmer,
Came clad in armour
By stars benign.
Hope lies to mortals and most believe her,
But man's deceiver
Was never mine.
The thoughts of others were light and fleeting,
Of lovers meeting
Or luck or fame.
Mine were of trouble, and mine were steady,
So I was ready
When trouble came.

The attitude of wariness, of skepticism, of being ready for trouble, that the poem expressed was one in which I was, curiously, as steeped as Kaye. I couldn't remember having inherited this attitude from my parents, nor was it the result of tragic life experience. It came from somewhere else. Other people tended to chuckle at the poem, commenting that a person's experience was in accordance with their expectations. Yet, beneath its fatalistic tone, I felt, was a bedrock of truth. Hadn't Andreas Leo written that the obstacles, trials, and tribulations of life must be considered as aids on the spiritual path? Hadn't he said that man must learn the extremes of life the difficult way? Hadn't he admonished that the renunciation of life was repulsive only to those who had no knowledge of the eternal?

This concept of the spiritual path as one of darkness, testing, and sacrifice was at the very heart of our relationship to the League, and Kaye and I reflected this attitude back to one another. She was good at coming up with aphorisms that often had the same fatalistic tone as the Housman poem. Sometimes I would match her aphorisms with my own. When she threw out the dictum, "The longer the road, the lonelier it gets," I responded with, "The greater one's strength, the less help is allowed." She likened the spiritual path to a roller coaster, and when things got heavy, her advice was to just hold on tight. Prompted by an experience I once had in Mexico, I wrote a prose poem that expressed this attitude in an extreme form.

Thus, IT works ITS will upon you, as it has always done, only that now you are fatally aware of ITS purpose.

Once, in a foreign land, I passed a slaughterhouse where pigs were being butchered, and I heard the squealing—the infernal squealing of those animal souls condemned to the knowledge of what was being perpetrated upon them, yet powerless to resist. Those squeals reminded me, all too vividly, of the slaughter of my own will at the hands of the Force.

Thus, IT works ITS will upon you, as IT has always done. Only now you can see the glint of the blade as it comes down on your neck, smell the sweat of your own fear, and hear the squealing of your mind, whose every instinct is to resist that which it can not comprehend.

Thus, IT works ITS will upon you, as it has always done, only that now you are fatally aware of ITS purpose.

One day, I stumbled on a poem by A. E. Housman's brother, Laurence, in T. E. Lawrence's collection of favorite poems, entitled *Minorities:*

When you are dead, when all you could not do leaves quiet the worn hands, the weary head, asking not any service more of you, requiting you with peace, when you are dead;

When, like a robe, you lay your body by, unloosed at last:

how worn, and soiled, and frayed: is it not pleasant just to let it lie unused, and be moth-eaten in the shade?

Folding earth's silence round you like a shroud, will you just know that what you have is best: thus to have slipped unfamous from the crowd; thus having failed and failed, to be at rest?

Or having not to know? Yet O my Dear, since to be quit of self is to be blest, to cheat the world, and leave no imprint here: is this not best?

I sent the poem to Kaye for her comment, and she gave her interpretation of it. "The first stanza of the poem," she wrote me, "talks about a respite from activity, which could be likened to a rest point in eternity. The second depicts the individual, or Soul, as still in control in the process of giving up the body. You release yourself from the physical limitations of the body, and it, being released, is left to return to its elements. In the third stanza, the words, 'Will you just know that what you have is best,' expresses the awareness that is Soul, and in the fourth stanza, the words, 'Since to be quit of self is to be blest,' is Soul speaking to Soul.

"On the last line, 'To cheat the world and leave no imprint here,'" she commented, "Any adulation is hollow glory from a spiritual point of view. Saints and Masters do not think of themselves as such. They know the magnitude of the whole and realize how small their contribution is to what is yet to be." Of the last words, "Is this not best?" she wrote that the writer "ends with a question. The day will come, when we will have no further questions."

These exchanges with Kaye on the subjects of detachment and death may have helped to prepare me to deal with my father's protracted illness, which began with a heart bypass operation that led to a stroke. I was living in an apartment of my own at the time, and teaching at a high school in Fairfield, which was about a forty-minute commute from Belle Harbor. When I wasn't teaching, I was preoccupied with my father's care. Although my mother was the primary caregiver, she was not consistently up to the task, and in many ways, I had taken responsibility for both of them. I taught early in the morning, usually returning to my own place after my classes were over, and often checking in with my parents later in the day.

One brisk winter morning, I took the Marine Road exit from the highway, and stopped at the traffic light. I decided to stop off and pick up something from a storage locker that I rented nearby. Two left turns got me onto the little-used service drive adjacent to the highway, which led to the storage facility. Melted snow lay in patches by the road, and I noticed a thick flock of crows circling overhead on the left-hand side. It didn't take me long to get what I wanted from the locker. Doubling back on the deserted road, I noticed the crows just up ahead on the near side of the road. I was in no hurry, so I stopped to investigate.

I got out of the car and saw a little rabbit sitting by the side of the road at the point where the grass left off and the shoulder began. It was sitting upright, its paws stretched out in front of it, awake and alert. I came closer, expecting it to bolt, but it remained immobile, staring straight ahead, hardly noticing me. Then I saw that its hind legs were splayed out in back, obviously broken. The crows were overhead, some hovering and a few hopping on their elastic legs only a few feet behind. In the middle of the rabbit's back was a gaping wound like a crater. Horrified, I watched as one of the crows jumped right up behind the rabbit and took a few vigorous pecks from its living flesh. The rabbit endured it, with only a few flinches passing over its face.

The crows were eating the rabbit alive. My first impulse was to pack it immediately into the trunk of my car and take it to a vet. Then I looked closer at the wound. The hole went right down to the spine. No vet could save an animal in that condition. The most that could be done would be to put it to sleep right away. It would be a messy scenario to put it in the trunk. I envisioned it thrashing around in a terrified state, resisting my attempt to grab it, and even biting. The way it was enduring its plight was extremely dignified. It seemed to be in a trance, its attitude of acceptance equal to that of the Buddha. What would be the point of despoiling this natural event? Convinced that there was none, I got back in my car and drove away.

By the time I got back to my apartment in town, I was having doubts. Did I do the right thing? At that moment, the crows were, undoubtedly, still pecking the rabbit to death. I was unable to get the image out of my mind. Several times, I had the urge to get back in my car, go back to the location, and try to rescue the animal, but I overruled myself.

A few days later, I took the exit ramp off the expressway at about the same time of day, with the urge to go back to where the gruesome incident had occurred. In my imagination, the rabbit was still by the side of the road, being eaten by those crows. Only seeing the remains of the corpse, or the roadside completely bare, would dispel that image. As I neared the stoplight at the end of the exit ramp, I got into the left lane. The light was red, the intersection deserted. I flicked on my turn signal, came to a complete stop, and waited for the light to change.

The next moment, I felt a tremendous impact behind me and saw a pickup truck careen off to my right and continue through the intersection. I got out of my car and looked at the rear. The bumper was completely smashed in. The pickup came to a halt at the shoulder of the exit ramp on the opposite side of the road. I got back in the car and drove it carefully into the median of the intersection, put on my emergency signal, and got out, expecting to have a word with the driver. Just then, however, I saw the pickup rev-up, spin around, and head off down the entrance ramp and back onto the highway. In a few seconds, it was gone.

As I cursed the driver, I had the feeling that this event had a meaning connected with the rabbit and crows. I had gotten into the left-hand lane, intending to revisit the site of that spectacle, and that was exactly the point at which I was rear-ended! Maybe the incident had something to do with second-guessing myself. The message was that I couldn't go back and relive the past. I had made the decision to leave the rabbit by the side of the road. There was no point in replaying the scenario over in my mind or looking back over my shoulder, like Lot's wife.

A year later, I left my father in my mother's care, moved to the East Coast, and settled in the town of Huntington Park to pursue a graduate degree. I became friendly with a young man named Zevon, who worked at a local newspaper. He inhabited a bedraggled apartment in the middle of the city, just behind the central bus station. His roommate, a statuesque young woman from the south of England named Kit, also worked at the newspaper. I used to visit them on Thursdays, which was their day off. I would arrive late in the evening, and we would sit and talk into the early morning hours. No matter how cold the apartment was, Kit was always barefoot, in jeans and a threadbare sweater. Zevon would drink beer, they both smoked, and I'd nibble on whatever they had lying around while the TV flickered in the corner of the room.

One evening, I told them the story about the rabbit and the crows. As I described the scene, I noticed Kit wincing. I felt encouraged to tell the story with a bit of flourish and dramatic effect, and I noted with satisfaction that both Zevon and Kit were leaning forward on the couch as I built up to the conclusion. The atmosphere in the dingy apartment was hushed as they waited for the punch line. When I gave them my interpretation, however, they were both disappointed.

"I thought the meaning of it had something to do with the rabbit's hind legs," Kit said. "You got rear-ended, and it was the rabbit's hind legs that were broken."

Kit's reaction made me reconsider my own interpretation of the incident. I began to wonder if I had overlooked something about it.

During Christmas vacation, I planned to take a brief vacation in Florida before returning to Belle Harbor. After that, it would be my mother's turn to vacation in Florida, while I took care of my father. Now, however, word came that my father might not have much time left to live. I called my mother to find out what she wanted me to do.

"I think it would be best for you to come here for a couple of days, just to assess the situation," she said. "If his condition stabilizes, then you can go on to Florida."

When I arrived, I was surprised to find my father seated upright in bed. He greeted me cheerily, gave me a firm handshake, and we sat and talked for hours. He was not in much different shape than when

I had last seen him. The next morning, the physical therapist came and gave him a good workout. In the middle of the day, I took my mother on an errand, leaving my father in the care of a hospice volunteer. When we returned, he was in his easy chair, apparently sound asleep, except that we couldn't rouse him. We looked at him, wondering if he was going into a coma. In the evening, the social worker came, and said if he stayed in that state, he would have to be moved to his bed. She suggested we try it ourselves. I got hold of him under one arm, and she under the other. We lifted him to his feet. He started putting one foot in front of the other, but he was fast asleep! After a few more hours, he simply woke up and was fine again.

That evening, I had to decide whether to go to Florida. I knew that I was taking a chance of not being around when my father died. My mother urged me to go anyway. "We've been in this situation so many times," she said. "Your father has been ill for a long time. There's a chance that he may not survive the next ten days, but there's an equal chance that he could still last a long time. There's no need to cancel your vacation. Go to Florida and relax for a while."

"If I go," I told her, "and he's still around when I get back, then you'll be in the same position that I'm in now. If you want to take a vacation in early January, you'll be taking the same chance. Will you go if it comes down to that?"

"Yes, I will," she replied.

I told her that I'd sleep on it, and went to bed that night with the mental resolution that I would have the answer in the morning. When I woke up the next day, it was clear to me if I didn't go to Florida I'd be asking my mother to do in January something that I wasn't willing to do now. When I realized this, I felt that I had come to the point where I had to utterly let go of the situation. At that moment, I remembered the rabbit and the crows, and a new interpretation of the incident occurred to me. It had been about my father the whole time! The rabbit symbolized my father, and the crows stood for the forces of nature, which decreed that his time on earth was nearing an end. My role was that of a spectator, and my lesson was to learn not to interfere in this process. My choice to leave the rabbit by the side of the road had been correct. By merely watching, I had contributed my presence to the situation. I had shown my respect for life in the face of the spectacle of death, and that was the most that I could do.

My father lived for a year after that. There was more letting go that I had to do, but I had already turned the corner and gone through the most important part of the process. I was with him during his last moments at the hospital, and remember the response of the muscles in his hand as I held it in mine. I remember, too, the mixture of stoicism, calm, and weakness that I felt in him, and the feeling of desolation I experienced as he acknowledged his impending death. When he told me that he was ready to go, I had no words to contradict him.

My father was a very gifted man, rich in intelligence, humor, knowledge, culture, and life experience. My mother, my sister, and I all lived in his shadow for most of our lives. He had many personal qualities that I didn't possess, and could count many achievements that I would never be able to emulate. He had a prodigious memory, and loved to entertain people with stories from his life or facts that came from a seemingly inexhaustible store of knowledge and experience. His abilities in this respect went far beyond making an impression on casual friends, colleagues, or acquaintances. I lived with him all my life, and yet up to his dying day, it still amazed me that he could tell me things within his sphere of knowledge and experience that I had never heard before.

Unfortunately, my mind was like a sieve, and all this information was lost almost as soon as it was told to me. That's what made his passing hardest for me. It represented not just the passing of an individual, but of a whole generation of cultural experience. One couldn't retrieve it by reading a book or watching a documentary. The only way to get it was by being in my father's presence, and listening to him speak.

My father was a gentle and moral man. He was a peacemaker by nature, disliked strife, and had no notion of enmity. He was not religious, yet he seemed to have all the ethical qualities of a religious man built into him. He was an unselfish man, with a natural inclination to serve others. There is a passage in Andreas Leo's *The Face of the Eternal*, which describes such a man of virtue and excellence:

> Our only purpose in life is to serve others. The wise see inaction in doing and action in not doing. Such men are always content because they have given up all interest in the consequences of their actions. They are in harmony with the Force and depend on none but the Living Master. Their minds are replete with wisdom and their deeds are truly noble, for their first impulse consists solely of sacrifice. (2:46)

My father had weaknesses, to be sure. He didn't know everything there was to know about life, the world, other people, or himself. He wasn't curious about some aspects of life, and he didn't inquire into certain facets of his own nature until it was too late. His heart disease may have been preventable, but such prevention requires awareness of the laws that govern health and life. The current Living Master once wrote that self-mastery simply means that a person has the ability to run his own life according to the laws of Spirit, but that this presumes that one knows the laws of Spirit. It could be said that our whole task in life is to learn the underlying spiritual laws behind all of life, and this task is a challenge even to the most learned and erudite among us.

An experience I had when I was already well into adulthood says a great deal about my father's hidden vulnerability and the difficulty of my relationship with him. I was alone in my parents' house one day, and sitting in my father's study. A black bookshelf stood against a wall in this study, laden with books. On the bookshelf, two photographs were displayed—one of a man, the other of a woman. They had sat atop this bookshelf ever since I could remember, and had probably been displayed in our house even before we moved to Belle Harbor. I had never inquired into the identities of the couple, and my father had never volunteered the information. Curiosity suddenly took hold of me, and I started staring at the picture of the man. His face made a deep impression on me. Whoever it was, he had been a very powerful person. In an instant, I realized that the two people in the photographs were my father's parents.

My father's parents perished in the Holocaust, and he suffered from the guilt of knowing that he failed to save them. For much of his life, he kept the pain of this experience buried. Only in later years he realized the error of this, and began to talk about his parents, his upbringing, and his experiences during the war. An emotional barrier had already been built up by that time, however, and this had a great deal to do with the cause of his later illness. His bypass operation brought about a big change in him. When he awoke from it, the room was filled with flowers from family members and friends. When he saw the flowers, his eyes brimmed with tears. I think that this was the most emotional moment of his entire life. The fact that he was loved and appreciated by others touched him in a way that only his illness opened him up to fully experiencing.

One of the last things my father said to me before his death came in the form of a question. I was alone with him in the hospital room, and he asked if I felt it was a privilege or an imposition to watch him die. He had a way of probing with questions of this sort that were more rhetorical in nature than anything else. I think that if the situation were reversed, he would have replied unhesitatingly that it was a privilege. Since his innate sense of reverence for life did not have the support of a philosophy, however, he expressed it in the form of questions, and tested others with their answers. I, of course, replied that I felt it was a privilege, but added that all experiences in life were a privilege for which we should be grateful.

In his last words, he muttered something about Prometheus being nailed to the cross. I received an impression of the death experience as one in which the dying person is literally strung between heaven and earth. I considered that just as our actions in life are sustained by sacrifice, at the time of death it must be that each of us becomes the sacrifice itself. In that case, for those who had dedicated their lives to serving others, there must truly be little distinction between life and death. As Andreas Leo wrote in *Sermon by the River:*

> If you know in your heart that death is an illusion, you have no reason to fear. When the physical body wears out, the temple of flesh and bone disintegrates, but God is an endless sea of love, and since man is a drop in this sea, he can never die. (125)

Kaye passed away a few months after my father. She was in a nursing home, and I had promised to visit her regularly. I kept putting off my visit, however, and when I finally came, it was just in time to see her lapse into a stroke. The last time I saw her, she was back home under her daughter's care, but had lost many of her faculties. When I came in, she looked at me fixedly for a few brief seconds, and in that moment of recognition, managed to say my name. Then she turned away, exhausted and ashamed of her condition, and did not look at me again. Her daughter took her out on the porch and started combing her hair. I watched them together for a while, and then I quietly left. The fatalism that I carried with me in the wake of the deaths of these two loved ones stuck with me for many years, and it was only much later that I began to call these assumptions about life and my spiritual path into question.

Chapter Three

The Divine Inheritance

"Every Soul is freed upon initiation by the Living Master, to whom the Supreme Deity has solely granted this power. The initiates of the Inner Circle of the League live out the rest of their lives on Earth, and move directly to the higher worlds when they die. They need not stand before the King of the Dead, from whom all uninitiated Souls must receive judgment."
—Andreas Leo, *The Face of the Eternal, Book One,* 57

The pinnacle of my experience in the League came with my high initiation, which occurred at a League conference in Boston. It was a cold and blustery day in February, and I had driven for half a day from Huntington Park. Along the edges of the highway, the wind created dune-like patterns in the dry patches of snow, and whipped the fringes of my coat as I got out of my car. The custom was to bring a gift of a flower or fruit to present to the initiator as a gift. I had about twenty minutes to do my shopping. I found a florist shop only a couple of blocks away, entered, looked around, and decided that I wanted to buy a live plant instead of cut flowers. I told the saleswoman what I was looking for, and she disinterestedly indicated various plants on display. I didn't see anything suitable, however.

"You can look outside," she said. "We have some things on sale." I stepped back out onto the street. There was a rickety wooden stand in front of the store window, containing little plastic pots of crocuses, some of them just coming into bloom. The diminutive blossoms were yellow and purple, with bright orange-colored stamens, their petals buffeted by the harsh wind. My attention focused on one in particular. A tingle crept up my spine. Its frail flowers mirrored something that I felt at the very core of my being. "I am that crocus!" I thought. I felt a strange anticipation, as if I was on the verge of a transformation.

I purchased the plant, carrying it out the door across a blustery intersection and into the hotel where my initiation was to take place. The deep carpets in the hallways silenced the sound of my steps. I knocked on the door. A tall, broad-shouldered man with sandy hair answered the door, greeting me in a broad Scottish accent. He admitted me to his suite, and gestured for me to take a seat in the corner. I asked to go to the bathroom first.

"Nervous?" he inquired when I returned. When I nodded my head, he tried to reassure me. "You're here. That's the main thing," he chuckled. "You could have turned around at any time, but you didn't. You've earned the right to be here, OK?"

I nodded my head again, still somewhat uncertainly, as I looked out the window at the city skyline.

"You're not going to jump, are you?" he asked sardonically. I smiled for the first time and assured him that I was not. I was still agitated, however, and asked to be excused to the bathroom one more time. When I returned, I finally made myself comfortable in the chair. The crocus was on the table between us. "This is a holy moment," he said in a matter-of-fact tone, accompanying his words with an enigmatic smile. I felt nothing that I associated with holiness, only a gradual decrease in my nervousness. Now that the moment had come, I was ready.

"I will now read from a portion of the sacred text," he said. "You may listen for a while, and then go into contemplation at any point." I sat staring at him with a sense of expectation.

> With this initiation, you find yourself in the true world of Spirit. You will find that your old balance will be swept away, and that a new and truer balance must be found. You

> will find yourself on trial, for you have left the path of the ordinary seekers of truth. It will be some time before you settle into the true ways of a member of the Brotherhood.

I closed my eyes, and let the words of the initiator flow over me like a wave. I felt a sense of trust, as well as a hint of confidence, and began to lose track of the words that the initiator was reading.

> If you fail the tests that must be confronted constantly during your daily life, you may slip back into the world of the Mind, where one chews upon all ideas and thoughts before releasing them. This is the transfiguration, when the Mind has finally come under control and become balanced with the rest of the personality. From this time on, you are the illuminated one. You will know and see the spiritual realities, and understand those around you from a new perspective. You will begin to use your faculties for a greater cause. You are ruled by Soul, and see from the viewpoint of Soul.

I listened distantly to the words, and began to take a series of long, protracted breaths. I felt as if I were floating, and gazed intently onto the screen of my mind. All was blackness. After a while, however, I noticed a prickly sensation on my skin. It increased in intensity until it seemed that a golden light had enveloped my body and was scouring my skin like thousands of tiny Brillo pads. The energy was intense. Then I felt as if an outside force had grasped and was holding on to me. I had the sensation of movement without moving. The motion picked up until it was unbelievably swift. It was like sitting on a flatbed train as it sped along the railroad track, the wind rushing against my whole body with a power that was almost enough to knock me over.

Suddenly, the train began to slow, the energy decreased, and I was left alone in the blackness of my mind. I looked into the darkness. All was quiet, except for a low humming. I found myself in a dimly lit room, seated before a plain wooden table. My seat was a simple, stiff-backed wooden chair.

Across the table from me sat the initiator. "It's time for you to be given your gift," he said in a soft voice. "What do you wish as your Divine Inheritance?"

"A flower," I replied, somewhat to my surprise, but with great intensity in my heart. Instantly, a flower appeared on the table. It was the crocus that I had bought. "That's me," I thought again. The crocus was just beginning to peep out of the earth in the little pot.

The initiator looked into my eyes. "What do you want the flower to do?" he asked.

"I want it to bloom!" I replied, in a sudden burst of inspiration, almost shouting for joy as I spoke the words. Instantly, the flower grew by several inches and opened its petals. It was like a luxuriant tropical plant, bursting with energy.

"You've moved past working with pain," the initiator intoned. "You're now working with love, joy, and freedom. You will learn most from the field of play. You know now that you are Soul—not the little self, that pallid thing that always doubted its abilities. Claim your Divine Inheritance. It is yours!"

I opened my eyes. The initiator sat smiling in front of me. "Well," he asked, "would you like to tell me about it?"

"I understand now," I replied. I spoke slowly, as if coming out of a fog.

"What do you understand?"

"I understand why I was so nervous today. It was the negative part of my self. I see now how it functions. It's like a trap. First comes the bait. It can be any action on my part, no matter how insignificant. To Soul, it's nothing. Then the jaws of the trap snap together. That's the guilt mechanism. It operates like a reflex action. It's the truly destructive part of the self, which undermines our consciousness of ourselves as Soul. This guilt factor held me back until now. It was the idea that I was not worthy!" I felt as if I was soaring as I spoke.

The initiator smiled and leaned closer to me, looking deep into my eyes. "We're now speaking from a very high level of consciousness," he said. "Listen to me closely. The whole thing of feeling not worthy is over with. It's done. We've left it in a little pile here on the hotel carpet. The maid will clean up in the morning and it will be gone."

I nodded. "I feel like I've just come out of a cave," I said in a hushed voice. "The guilt trap was yesterday. Now it's a whole new ballgame."

"You just said it. It's a game! It's having fun. If you're not getting fun out of your life and out of your initiation, you're not doing it right."

The initiator's words moved through me to a deep level of understanding. I felt a sense of protection, as if I had a large buffer zone around me. I felt loved. I felt in balance. I felt that I wanted to give to others.

"Thank you," I said.

"Don't mention it," the initiator replied. "I'm just doing my job. Besides, I got something out of it, too."

"Oh, I doubt that," I replied, in what I thought was a self-effacing manner.

Without any warning, the initiator got to his feet and posed like a gunfighter poised to pull out a pair of six-shooters. His large body loomed over me like a menacing shadow. "Are you calling me a liar?" he boomed. "Then draw, mister."

I was taken aback, unaware of what I had done, yet even the sudden aggressiveness of the initiator did not penetrate my new-found serenity. I remained seated, without flinching, calmly and quizzically observing his performance, and trying to assess its meaning.

"I'm trying to tell you not to impute motives to others," the initiator explained, sitting down again. "You do that all the time."

"I was just trying to…"

"Don't rationalize," he cut in, "and don't apologize. You were apologizing all over the place today. One of the things you're going to have to deal with now is the Law of Silence. Don't be judgmental about other people, don't impute motives to them, don't criticize them, and don't offer unwanted advice!"

"OK. I see," I said tentatively. It was becoming clear to me that, despite the bliss I was experiencing, there were some limitations to this new state of consciousness. I was still operating on the basis of some of my old mental habits. This would require careful monitoring.

The feeling of guilt was gone, however. Even if I made mistakes, I felt as if I could observe and evaluate them with an almost serene detachment.

"It's not a guarantee," the initiator explained. "You're still going to do stupid things, but now you can look more objectively at them, without attaching to them any negative value or blame. Still, you can always fall back into old patterns of thought. You have to be on your guard the whole time, so watch out! The power of your initiation will continue to bring you the gift of the Divine Inheritance. The gift will take many forms, but it's always a gift of love."

I felt emboldened to ask a question. "What's the difference between love and power?" I wanted to know.

"Is love a kiss, or is it a smack in the kisser?" he asked rhetorically, throwing a mock punch my way. "This isn't a dichotomy to be resolved. Regardless of the form in which you receive this gift of love, your task is to just be yourself. Be happy, enjoy life, and maintain a loving attitude toward all life. That is all."

"My biggest fear coming here today was that I would not have an understanding initiator," I confided to him. There were tears in my eyes as I spoke.

"I'm glad that I could be that for you," he replied, putting a hand on my shoulder. "When you become an initiator, I know you will be an understanding one, too. There's a world out there. It's not a world of limitation, but one of possibilities and opportunities. The initiation is only a beginning. If you thought that you'd be forever content once you received it, you have a surprise coming. You have to go from here. You've been given a gift, and now you'll want to give back to others. The joy you will experience comes from giving."

He got up to leave the room, indicating a pen and paper on a desk in the corner. He explained that he was giving me some extra time to write down my thoughts and do one more contemplation. I was then free to depart when I felt ready. I shook his hand as he paused in the doorway. "Be good to yourself," he said in parting, "and remember that you don't have to apologize for anything!" When he was gone, I took up the pen and paper and wrote:

This is what I have sought all my life. I have looked for it in the dark corners of the earth, in the muddied rain upon the streets, and in the creaks and uncertain gloom of alleyways, but it was nowhere to be found. Only when the time was right was the gift presented. Then, I was like a beggar invited to a feast and showered with love and warmth, and like that beggar, I was incredulous, wondering if I was really experiencing this, if it was really happening. Was it true that God loved ME? Was it true that there was no blame, no sin, no action for which I could be called unworthy? Could it be that God loved without reservation all ITS creatures, regardless of their rash acts, their impetuousness, and their selfish concerns? Was it true that under the sun there lived the race of man, and over all dwelt a God, a Force, a Protection that was loving, that was LOVE itself? Then, if this was true, wasn't it best simply to smile, to work in silence, to betray no one with an ill-considered word, to show, merely by example and gratitude, one's love for life? To know that one was truly blessed, that God, in ITS infinite love, desired only what was best for ITS creatures—wasn't this the Divine Inheritance?

I then sat in contemplation. As soon as I closed my eyes, I found myself in an unknown location with the Living Master. Before us was an immense field of yellow and purple crocuses. The Master pointed to a spot in the field and singled out a cluster of blossoms. "You are that flower there," he said, his finger identifying the fragile plant. I examined it closely, as I might scrutinize my own face in a mirror. The Master then pointed out other flowers to me, identifying each with the name of someone I knew. We were all flowers in that universal field of life.

Next, I found myself seated at the same small, plain table. The Living Master sat opposite me. The crocus was on the table between us, just as it had been when I had been with the initiator. Again, it began to grow, but this time, it kept growing until it went through the roof of the hotel and reached into the sky. I climbed up as if it were a magic beanstalk, entered the clouds, and reemerged above them. Finally, I hoisted myself onto the gigantic petals of the flower and stood within its strange, smooth walls. They were perhaps twenty feet high, with huge stamens and pistils sprouting from the middle like modern sculptures, loaded with pollen.

Suddenly, there was an immense roaring sound overhead. I looked up to see a huge yellow bumblebee, the size of a Volkswagen, hovering above me. It landed and began collecting the pollen. I ran for cover, slid down the stalk, and resumed my seat across from the Master.

"What was the meaning of that experience?" I asked.

"That's how the experience of your initiation would seem to the uninitiated," he said.

After my contemplation, I left the initiator's hotel room and took the elevator down to the conference, overwhelmed with the feeling that life was utterly new and the world was full of opportunity. It was as if a door had suddenly opened, and I found that I had been living in a cramped, stuffy room. With one step, I was out in the fresh air. Life smelled of confidence and affirmation. Even my steps on the hotel carpet seemed more buoyant. I could hardly believe that I was viewing the same world that I had lived in before.

As soon as I arrived downstairs, a man at the reception desk called to me. I had met with him earlier, and mentioned I was planning on spending the night and was interested in sharing a room with another person to save expenses.

"You were looking for someone to share a room?" he asked "Well, I've found someone for you. She's right over there." He pointed to a stunning young woman with long dark hair at the other side of the lobby. Having noticed his signal, she was already advancing toward us. She wore a short black skirt, white blouse, tailored jacket and pumps, and carried a flight bag slung over her shoulder. As she introduced herself, her perfume struck me with the force of uninhibited sexuality. I tried to mask my astonishment. Only a moment ago, I had been thinking that life was entirely new and filled with opportunity. Now it was presenting me with living, breathing proof. Could this possibly be a coincidence, or was it directly related to my initiation?

We agreed to share a room. I helped her unload her baggage from her car. Then, since it was already evening and the conference had adjourned for dinner, we agreed to go out for something to eat. We found an Italian restaurant not far from the hotel. The lights glowed with a soft golden hue, and there were blood red candles on the tables. As we talked, I sensed that she was a longtime member of the League. She exuded independence and self-sufficiency, along with the hint of charisma that I had always noticed were traits of the members of the Brotherhood, as the high initiates were called. At the same time, she showed a great deal of curiosity about me, which was both flattering and discomfiting. I wasn't used to women paying attention to me, and felt defensive about revealing my age or lack of achievement in life.

After dinner, instead of going back to the hotel, she proposed a short walk in the city. The idea was a little crazy, as cold as it was, but I was agreeable. We came to one of the tallest buildings, a favorite of mine, and took the elevator to the observation tower. When we got to the top, the area was entirely deserted. We huddled together, fighting against the stiff wind, the exhalation of our mingled breath coming out in sharp bursts like puffs of smoke. "Are you a Brother?" she suddenly asked me. I looked at her uncomprehending for a moment. I wasn't used to that term being used in conversation, nor had it yet sunk in that I was now a member of this fraternal circle within the League. "Are you a high initiate?" she prompted me.

"Yes. Yes, of course," I replied, finally cognizant of what she meant.

"I thought so," she said, looking at me with a penetrating gaze, still puzzled by the hesitation in my response. We gazed together at the cityscape, constantly changing before our eyes, and I felt the infinite possibilities of the moment. This was the Journey to the East about which Hesse had written—an endless procession of Souls moving toward the Source of All, and at their vanguard, the Brotherhood of the League. I realized that I had yet to adjust to the idea of being a member of an elite inner circle, and felt the urge to conceal the fact that my initiation had only taken place that day, as if that would make me the object of my companion's condescension.

When we got back to the hotel, the conference had concluded for the day. We went up to our room. We each chose a twin bed and began to get ready for the night. I got into the T-shirt and shorts in which I was used to sleeping, and turned the bathroom over to my roommate. She emerged in a nightgown. "What do you think?" she asked, in a coquettish tone of voice. I shook my head. She disappeared into the bathroom again and re-emerged a minute later in a T-shirt and short shorts. "How's this?" she inquired. I indicated my approval. We slid under the covers of our beds and lingered a while, with the lights in the room still on. "Do you like women?" she suddenly asked.

"What kind of question is that?" I replied. "Of course I do."

"I was just wondering."

Her question left me feeling that I must be coming across as extremely undemonstrative, but I didn't know what to do. Reaching up by the head of the bed, she turned out the light. We were left with only the lights of the city shining through the picture window. Suddenly, she got out of bed. "Come here. Take a look," she said. I got out of bed and stood next to her. We gazed out again at the starry night. "It's cold," she murmured. "Come over here by the heater!" She sat down, huddled in the corner, and warmed her hands over the vent. I did likewise. Our bare feet were touching and our hands were inches apart as we held them over the heating duct. I anticipated at any moment a greater display of intimacy on her part. Suddenly, however, the heater turned inexplicably cold, and she scampered back into her bed. I reluctantly followed suit. I lay on my back for a while, staring at the ceiling, unable to come to any sense of what I should or should not do. After a while, I fell asleep.

I awoke sometime in the middle of the night and sat bolt upright with the overwhelming conviction that I had been a fool. How could I have tamely gone to my separate bed, with this beautiful young woman who had relentlessly flirted with me all evening only a few feet away? I sat forlornly in bed, watching her sleeping figure. Finally, I touched her gently, and she woke up. "What's the matter?" she asked.

"I can't sleep." I had a stubborn look on my face, as if to say that I was determined to fend off any of her palliative suggestions.

"Well, come to bed," she said, finally, with a resigned tone in her voice. She opened the covers for me and I gratefully crept between the sheets. She turned on her side, away from me, advertising her intention to sleep, while I snuggled timidly at her back. Finally, she began to question me, as she had earlier. "How long have you been a High Initiate?"

"Today," I replied, reluctantly. "That is, yesterday, just before we were introduced. I had just come from my initiation. That's why...maybe...I'm acting a bit strange. I don't usually act this way. What I mean is that everything is different. The world is different. I'm different. Everything is beautiful. Don't you see it? Surely, you understand!"

She sighed deeply. "How old are you?" I told her my age, which must have been greater than she anticipated. "Oh, my God!" she exclaimed, in shock. "You're kidding me."

"Why should I be kidding you?"

"But you're so...so immature!"

"Immature? Well, maybe I am," I replied, defensively.

"Look, all I really want to do is to get some sleep," she said, in a tone of irritation. "I don't know what you thought, but I didn't intend anything else."

"That's OK," I replied. "I understand." Without any further prompting, I slipped noiselessly out of her bed and returned to my own. Lying there in the darkness, I wondered about the strange miscommunication that had occurred between us. To what extent would I have made the same immature impression on her under normal circumstances, and to what extent was it because of the initiation, which had caused me to feel reborn, even childlike? Maybe the way I had cuddled next to her had turned her off. If so, however, wasn't she judging me by all sorts of expectations of how a man should act? She was a High Initiate, as well. She must have gone through something similar in the wake of her initiation. Was it truly possible to experience that same innocence and wonder, and then lose it? Perhaps I had made an utter fool of myself, but I didn't care. If my timid advances had not appealed to her, that wasn't my concern. I felt I had been true to myself. I had acted on my feelings, the best way I knew how. I retained that sense of wholeness, well being, and self worth that had been imprinted on me the previous day. Amid these reflections I once more fell asleep.

The next morning, she was already dressed and on her way out the door when I woke up. I insisted that we talk about what happened. "What about it?" she replied, coldly. "It happened, that's all. It's over and done with. You just wanted some companionship."

"Yes, that's right."

"I understand. The only thing I would recommend in the future is that you take greater responsibility for your actions. Don't make assumptions about other people."

I remembered that the initiator had said I tended to do this. "I guess you're right," I conceded, "but I think the same goes for you."

"Why? Did you think I was flirting with you?"

"Of course you did," I replied, without hesitation. "What about the way you asked me to come to the window? What about the way we sat by the heater together? What about the way you asked me what you should wear to bed? What about the way you asked if I liked women?"

She was blushing now. "OK, you made your point," she exclaimed in a frantic tone, wringing her hands as she got up to leave. "Now just leave me alone." She literally ran away from me toward the door.

"Look, no hard feelings," I said in a soothing voice, as I tried to keep up with her.

"Fine! No hard feelings!" she snapped. She rushed out of the room and down the hall.

My overwhelming impression about all of this was that, despite the fact that she was a more experienced high initiate than I was, she was the one who was upset. Perhaps the situation was meant to be as much of an object lesson for her as it was for me. The fact that I was fresh from my initiation made me an even more potent instrument of her instruction.

I caught sight of her briefly two more times. The first was at the hotel checkout counter, at the end of the conference. She had just paid her bill and was going out with her bags. She brushed past me without a word and entered the elevator. I was standing directly in front of the elevator door, waiting for an elevator going the other way. The door to the elevator that she had entered remained open for a long time. I watched and listened as a man greeted her.

"How did it work out—sharing that room?" he inquired.

"Oh, great," I heard her lie to him.

"I'm glad to hear it," he said effusively. "I told you it would work out, didn't I? Aren't you glad I suggested it?"

Her discomfort was palpable as the man prattled on. She was clearly aware that I was gazing directly at the two of them the whole time. The elevator doors slowly closed like theater curtains on a scene. It struck me that this performance was meant especially for me. I was being shown in the most explicit way the means by which a spiritual lesson was being administered to this young woman. She was being taught to recognize certain assumptions that she habitually made about life or other people. What mattered for me in this was only that I understood that all initiates of the League were the recipients of such instruction, regardless of their rank or seniority in the Brotherhood.

As I left the hotel to start my journey home, I glimpsed her one more time. She was walking across the street to a nearby restaurant, all alone, in the face of the blistering cold wind. I felt an urge to follow her for one more conversation, but then thought the better of it. She would only resent the gesture. She needed to be alone to sort out the meaning of the experience for her, just as I had to do for myself. I thought about the initiator's warning that the High Initiates were continually tested, and that they needed to carefully nurture and protect the state of consciousness that was their Divine Inheritance, yet I was so full of bliss that I felt invulnerable.

When I got back home, I walked around testing my new senses. My steps were light with anticipation. Every sight, every breath was a blissful experience. I bubbled with energy. In each meeting, every eye contact, I felt potential. I was aware not only of a difference in myself, but in others. I felt the light not only in my eyes, but saw it in *their* eyes, as well. They had every bit as much presence, as much beingness, as I did, but they didn't seem to be aware of it. They acted as if everything was normal!

I found that my inhibitions were greatly reduced. I went around speaking to every girl I met. I felt that I was filled with love, that I needed to make the most of every opportunity that came along. If I did, I was sure that I would soon find someone special. I bumped into one of my best friends at the university, a young Indian woman named Sreemati. I knew that she was married, and had never been overtly attracted to her, but now I couldn't help stealing occasional glances at her. I smiled, and she smiled back, very sweetly. She was a doll! In my exuberance, I blew her a kiss. We walked down the stairs together. Suddenly, she seemed agitated. "Please don't be offended by what I have to say. If my husband were to see what you just did…he's very conservative. He just wouldn't understand. I have to ask you please not to express yourself again the way you just did. Please!"

After that, I became more careful in my actions, but the high from the initiation had not entirely worn off. One evening, I sat down to do my contemplation. I found myself sitting at the same table that I had seen during my initiation. The crocus was in my lap, looking quite tall and erect. The Living Master sat across from me. On top of the table was a voluptuous dancer in skimpy attire. She pressed her body against mine in a deliberate attempt to arouse me. I responded by trying to embrace her. Eventually, the Master had to separate us.

"This is no good," he said. "You only want to do what you *have* to do. You're trying to take a shortcut, to get what you want in the least amount of time and effort. That way, you'll never get anything!"

A number of weeks went by. Finally, one day, I came across a tomboyish girl hanging out on the curbside near the house where I roomed. Her name was Judy, and it turned out she lived right next door to me. She was far younger than I was, a student in the local community college, and in no way beautiful, yet I was attracted to her. We soon became inseparable. We were like children together. We had a way of kidding each other and making each other laugh that I had never experienced with anyone else before. I believed that in one stroke I had thrown away all my preconceptions about love.

Judy's mother, on the other hand, was a seedy-looking, unappealing woman. Her mother's boyfriend was a drunk, and her brother was a pimply teen with a Howdy Doody face. The boyfriend was always sitting on the stoop of the house with a six-pack of beer, and Judy would escort me past him, lead me upstairs, and play her Garth Brooks albums for me in her rumpled room. I, in turn, would take her to my own upstairs room just across from her house, and we would make love by the window, within sight of her family members next door and down below. I believed that I had found true love. It didn't occur to me that, in my choice of a partner, I might still be taking a shortcut to love just as the Master had warned in my contemplation.

Chapter 4

Falling Apart

"Spiritual insights tend to wear off. Knowing this, the Master has intentionally placed doubt in the seeker's mind. If, because of the subtlety of what he is experiencing, he can't accept what is going on within him, he may leave the path, asserting that it is of no value to him. If he persists, however, the chess game continues, move by move, until he has achieved a greater understanding of the Force."

—Andreas Leo, *The Face of the Eternal, Book Two,* 20, 31

My secret relationship with Judy continued for over two years while I pursued my graduate studies, but eventually the League came between us. A local chapter existed right in Huntington Park, and I immediately joined in their meetings. To my dismay, however, the members were far from my idea of spiritual seekers. In the corner of the room sat a woman fat as an ox, with stubble on her chin and a suspicious and querulous voice. Next to her was a sallow couple, the woman's face petty and vindictive, the man's bigoted and self-righteous. A dowdy spinster, gossipy and vain, often dominated the proceedings. There were members with whom I was more in tune—young, intelligent, and broad minded—but seniority belonged to the pettiest and most tyrannical. The area director—a tall, dark-complexioned man with a charismatic presence—seemed in love with himself and his own authority. Moreover, he consistently picked what seemed to me to be the least competent and trustworthy individuals as his lieutenants, apparently in order to bolster his own power and sense of self-esteem.

My big mistake was bringing Judy to these meetings. Although normally attended exclusively by League members, they were, in principle, open to the public. We sat next to one another like a pair of lovebirds. Judy never said anything during the proceedings. Sometimes we would press closer to one another, in wordless comment at some opinion expressed by one of the participants. Although not vocal, Judy was perceptive about human nature, and I trusted her instincts. She didn't seem to think any more of the local League members than I did. Eventually, I got involved in the politics of the group, supporting the complaints of some members who felt, as I did, treated like outsiders. My relations with the local leadership deteriorated steadily, and, despite my status as a high initiate, I found myself barred from their organizational meetings.

Finally, one day, I was summoned to the home of the area director. I was quite sure that the subject would be a disciplinary one. I brought Judy with me, but she waited in the car while I went in to talk to him. My apprehensions were fully realized. He sat down with me, and went over a long list of complaints that had been lodged against me by members of the group. The most universal complaint took me completely by surprise, however. It concerned Judy's presence. People had complained of our holding hands, as well as the occasional touches and nudges with which we communicated. Our behavior, they said, was lascivious! This shocked me, for in my mind there was nothing remotely immodest about our behavior. I felt we were like two innocent schoolchildren, and assumed everyone else would see us in the same way.

I was especially reprimanded for my inattention at the meetings, as well as the way in which I would sometimes smile skeptically at people's pronouncements and turn to Judy with a wink and a nod. The members had noted all this, and duly submitted their complaints behind my back. When the area director saw me to the door, Judy's head ducked under the rim of the car window, as if she were hiding from sight. It occurred to me that the very childlike quality that so endeared her to me must have confirmed her, in his eyes, in the role of a provocateur.

From that point on, my relationship to the League community deteriorated rapidly. Judy ceased to come to the group meetings, but she had not been particularly interested in them in the first place. Feeling unfairly treated and resentful that no one had spoken their feelings to my face, I became more rebellious. Finally, the area director came to a meeting and gave a speech about the damaging effect of people who were too independent minded and did not appreciate the importance of cooperation and harmony within the group. After this, I found it practically impossible to show my face at the League meetings again. At the last one I attended, no one greeted me. On the few occasions that I met fellow League members on the street or in shops, they looked at me queerly, as if I was deformed.

Once I encountered a tall, dark-haired woman in a doctor's waiting room. I must have stood next to her for a considerable time as she talked to the doctor's secretary before I recognized her as a League member whom I had known quite well. "Don't you remember me?" she asked, in an ironic tone.

"Of course I do," I replied, trying to cover up my confusion. In fact, however, I had forgotten her name. She seemed amused at my discomfiture. I felt like Hesse's narrator when he finally realizes that he has lost his way and is no longer worthy of inclusion in the Brotherhood of the League. My connection with the Order seemed to have been reduced to a small pile of mental debris. The grand experience of my high initiation was nothing but a dim memory. I was beginning to understand the warnings that had accompanied the initiation, and the struggle necessary to maintain one's footing on the Path.

At the same time, my relationship with Judy attracted a wider circle of critics. I took Judy up to visit my mother in her summer cottage in Maine, and while my mother was very solicitous to Judy, I heard that in conversations with other people she had dismissed our relationship as something not to be taken seriously. Back in Huntington

Park, I got into a confrontation with Judy's mother's boyfriend one day, as he sat drinking beer on the porch. Unaware that my relationship with Judy was anything but platonic, he questioned my masculinity in a vulgar fashion, and Judy had to restrain me from resolving the matter with my fists.

Although I clung to Judy more stubbornly than ever, determined to remain uninfluenced by the opinions of others, this social pressure had an effect on me in the long run. Eventually, I developed a fanatical crush on a French professor at the university. A dark, romantic-looking creature, worldly and sophisticated in her manner, speech, and dress, she was an utter contrast to Judy. I was scheduled for a series of tutorials with her, but they turned into futile sessions in which unspoken words and feelings oppressively filled the room. When I finally declared my feelings, she refused to proctor my exam, and I took to obsessively haunting the corridors that led to her office—all this without a word to Judy about what was going on.

Judy was changing, as well. When we first met, she attached herself to me completely. I encouraged her to be more independent, and gradually she began to take my advice. The friends she chose, however, were callous, working class kids with whom I had nothing in common. My fixation with the French professor was an added indication that Judy and I were mismatched. One night, Judy had told me she was going out with her friends. The time dragged on, past the middle of the night. I became distraught, imagining the worst scenarios. Finally, I received a call from the police. My fears were confirmed. A member of Judy's clique had driven her to his house, invited her in, and then sexually assaulted her.

After that, I knew I had to let Judy go. I felt that, although she had been the victim of the attack, in some way she was psychologically complicit in it. I suspected that this was her unconscious way of declaring her independence, which she couldn't bring herself to do directly. Choking with sobs, I told her that I didn't think I would love anyone else again the way I had loved her. I refused to return her school ring, which she had given to me, or to accept the college ring that I had given to her. I tried to tell her that I was not abandoning her, but was giving her back her freedom. I knew, however, that she didn't understand, that she interpreted my action as a sign of cowardice, wounded pride, and failure to stick up for her. Maybe she was right.

During this time, the League was rocked by the excommunication of the President and former Living Master. A new Living Master had been appointed about a year previously, but the former Master had retained the League presidency. A power struggle ensued, and when the new Living Master gained control of the organization, the former Master and now ex-President attempted to abscond with the membership lists. Although I was consumed with my personal problems and was only barely aware of these events, I received a letter from the former Master, pleading his case. I was amazed that with merely a glance at the letter, I was able to gauge the state of consciousness of the writer, which I estimated did not even approach that of a novitiate. I sat down and wrote a reply. In my letter, I thanked the former Master for his guidance in the past, but made it clear that I could no longer support him.

That the matter was a cut-and-dried one for me probably had to do with the fact that, due to my general estrangement from the League community, I had already rid myself of most of my attachment to the previous Master. Subconsciously, however, the adjustment was not so easy. After sending the letter, I felt sick and developed a high fever. For three days, I was in a delirium. I tossed and turned in bed, hardly aware of where I was. Just before the fever broke, I had a truly nasty dream. I found myself in a deep basement or cavern, the walls covered with a mixture of plaster, whitewash, and lime. I noticed a single lamplight burning, darkly illuminating the face of the former Living Master. His eyes were a hideous green with no expression in them at all. He was making all sorts of facial expressions indicative of power, but there was no power in him. His own realization of this seemed to be accompanied by a sense of desperation.

Below him, on the floor, was a small cage of wood and wire mesh, with something crawling about inside. The former Master stooped down, picked up the cage, opened a little door in the front of it, and took out a large rat. Holding it high in the air by its tail, he looked at it hungrily, as if intending to eat it. When the fever broke, I realized that the dream, appalling as it was, served the function of severing what remained of the deep emotional attachments that I had built up toward the former Master. His downfall proved that no individual was immune from spiritual failure.

Still, we had a new Master who had taken his place. There was a sense of continuity. The former Master's disgrace did not shake my trust and faith in the League, but it produced a subtle shift of allegiance. Although I was unaware of it at the time, I believe that these events caused me to establish a relationship not with the new Living Master, but with the Force itself.

I did have some dream experiences that involved the new Master, which confirmed in me the sense that I was in accord with the direction in which he would be taking the League. In one such dream, I found myself at a League conference, where the new Living Master was autographing books. A multitude of people waited in line to get close to him. As I waited with them, I glanced at his face, and saw that he wore an expression of sadness and boredom. The dream was telling me that the cult of personality had no interest for the new Living Master.

After receiving my degree, I moved back to Belle Harbor and got a part-time teaching job at the university. There was still a core group of League members left from the early days, and this enabled me to feel accepted again within the group. Professionally, however, I couldn't get anywhere. I looked high and low for full-time teaching jobs, with no luck. I secured a short-term contract with the university in Belle Harbor, but it was not renewed, and the following year I was forced to accept a job at a small Catholic college about forty minutes' drive southwest of town.

My salary at this college was so meager that I was getting into greater debt each week that I worked. The department head was a diminutive woman with dark, sympathetic eyes, and a warm, motherly personality. During the job interview, she held out the possibility that a full-time position would open up the next term, and this was my main incentive in taking the job. Sometime in mid-semester, I got a sudden phone call from her.

"Would you be interested in teaching again next term?" she asked. A brief moment of pleasure changed to chagrin when she explained the details. She was proposing a substantial increase in my teaching duties—the equivalent of full-time and a half—but with no increase in pay. It was the kind of offer that would have been of interest only to a graduate student who needed some experience to put on his resume, not a proposal that would seriously be made to someone who had already earned an advanced degree.

"I'm sorry we can't offer you more, but we're operating under severe budget restraints," she explained. "I realize that the offer may even seem insulting to you."

"It IS insulting," I blurted out.

"I understand," she said in a sympathetic tone, maddening in its utter lack of sympathy.

"I'll have to think it over," I replied, without enthusiasm. "I'll let you know within a week." I not only resented the demeaning offer, but also that she expected me to make a split-second decision. She was treating me like a corporate recruit when it came to the manner in which I was expected to negotiate, but like a child in terms of the salary that I was being offered.

Caught between the twin prospects of unemployment and underemployment, I felt that I was carrying an intolerable weight on my shoulders. Countless times during the ensuing week, I thought to myself that it would be better to make a complete break with teaching than accept the humiliating offer. Then I would panic at the thought of being jobless, and would consider accepting the position. Finally, on the day I was supposed to get back to the department head, I received an e-mail message from her.

"This is just to let you know that I have someone else interested in the position," she wrote. "If I don't hear from you by today, I'll assume that you are not interested." I immediately called her office, but she was not in. Numerous frantic calls throughout the day produced no result. When I finally got in touch with her at her home in the evening, she told me that she had already offered the job to someone else.

"Why couldn't you have waited until you heard from me personally?" I complained.

"You sounded so ambivalent when I made the offer to you over the phone, I assumed you weren't interested," she replied.

I was devastated by this turn of events. There was something particularly cruel, unfeeling, and heartless about my misunderstanding with the department head. While I had assumed that she was simply giving me time to make up my mind, she had been shopping around for another candidate to cover herself. I not only had to endure the humiliation of her offer, but had ended up groveling at her feet for the job when it was already out of reach. All the resentment I had built up about my limited job prospects now boiled over. I spent the rest of the semester so angry that I avoided the department head, afraid that if I encountered her I would fly off the handle.

The last day of the term finally arrived. I had already turned in my grades, and was preparing to make my departure without a word of good-bye to anyone. I stood in the hallway, engaged in a last conversation with a student, when I saw the department head passing out bunches of yellow roses to departing faculty members as a gesture of appreciation for their work over the semester. Unable to disengage from my conversation with the student, I couldn't avoid her approach. She came up to me and wordlessly handed me a bouquet of the yellow roses, beaming at me as she did so. I glanced into her eyes for just an instant, and saw only the most benign, impersonal love. Her obliviousness to my feeling of desperation only fueled my anger.

I said good-bye to the student. Then I walked down the stairs, carrying the roses in my arms. Without any fanfare, I exited the building through the main door, got into my car, and drove away, never to return. I had only a single thought in my mind. I wanted to find a deserted stretch of road, stop my car, put the yellow roses in the middle of the road, and run over them. Then I wanted to take a photograph of the mashed bouquet as record of the event. Since I didn't have a camera with me, however, I first had to drive all the way back home to retrieve it. By the time I got there, the roses had inexplicably wilted, as if poisoned by my resentment.

Things had gone equally badly in my personal life. At the beginning of the semester, I had moved into a house owned by Ray Hardcastle, a League novitiate. The house was a beautiful suburban place with a garden in front and a wide lawn in back. I had the entire upper floor to myself, with a large bedroom, study, and bath. Ray was in the final throes of a nasty divorce. When he asked if I was interested in renting the upstairs, it seemed like a good idea. For a couple of months, things went well. Ray gave me the run of the place, and all I had to do was listen sympathetically to his occasional bitter complaints about his wife.

One day, Ray approached me and said, "Look, my wife has half title to this place. I'm worried that if she finds out I'm renting the upstairs to you, she'll make trouble for me. Would you mind if I don't charge you any rent until my divorce is finalized?"

"Fine," I thought to myself. If Ray wanted me to live there rent-free, I wasn't going to complain. I was practically broke, anyway, so this came as a welcome development. I shrugged off the nagging thought that nothing in life is free, figuring that lonely as Ray was, I was perhaps contributing something by way of my mere presence.

Around this time, I met a pretty co-ed in a foreign language class I was auditing at nearby Eastern University. She had hennaed hair, a number of silver rings on her fingers and thumb, and wore baggy jeans along with a fake leopard skin coat—a 'retro' look that reminded me of my own college days. I hung around with her after class, and managed to ask her out.

"Sure, why not?" she said. "Give me a call next week."

Buoyed by this encounter, I went back to Ray's place and called a mutual friend of ours named Dee Hughes, who frequented the League meetings, to tell her about my prospective date. I expected that she would be happy for me, but I got just the opposite reaction. She gave me a stern lecture about how I was a typically shallow male, always chasing after women half my age. "You're in a negative pattern," she said. "You're never going to find what you're looking for with these co-eds. It's just going to be the same thing over and over again."

As soon as I got off the phone with Dee, I went downstairs and started complaining to Ray about my conversation with her. Ray was a tall, gangly, bespectacled fellow. He had a way of moving his head from side to side involuntarily as he listened to me, as if by these movements he could compensate for some psychological discomfiture. "I don't know what got into Dee," I said. "She was preaching to me. She thinks I'm some kind of dirty old man! I'll be damned if I'm going to turn my back on an opportunity to get to know this girl just because of what she says," I told him.

"So you're going to go out with her?"

"I might bring her over next week," I said. "I'll let you know in advance. If it's inconvenient, just say the word."

The next day, I came home to find the following note from Ray on my desk:

> I'll try to be as clear and up front with you as you've been with me. It's a free world and you have freedom of choice. If you want to continue staying here, you must respect my position. I simply have too much food on my plate to be able to deal with women and romance right now. If you want to stay here, you must think of it as a monastic experience. If this doesn't meet your needs, you must follow your own path.

"What's with the note?" I asked Ray angrily when he got home.

"It means just what it says," he replied. "I don't want you bringing your girlfriends around here. I'm going through a divorce. I'm not into all sorts of women coming and going."

"What do you mean, all sorts of women? I'm talking about an occasional date, maybe."

"You can do what you want on your own time. Take her out for dinner or a movie. Get a motel room. But don't bring her around here."

"That wasn't part of the deal when I moved in," I argued.

"When you moved in I thought you had a different kind of lifestyle."

"What does that mean? Did you think that I was a monk? I have an occasional female visitor and that makes me immoral?"

"She's a young girl."

"She's an adult!" We were nose to nose. I thought he was going to hit me. I walked out the front door, as he yelled abuse at my back.

The atmosphere in the house had changed so abruptly that I decided to camp out in my mother's apartment. Luckily, she was on vacation in Florida at the time, and wasn't due back for another three months. I therefore had the place to myself, at least temporarily. Meanwhile, the chaos that had ensued in the way of my meeting with the young coed only served to fuel my fantasies about her. I thought there must be something very powerful at work here if the mere mention of a date with her sent both Dee and Ray off the deep end. After our next class, we went out for coffee together. When it got late, I offered to drive her home. As soon as we were on our way, she immediately asked about my personal life.

"I've had a couple of girlfriends in the past year," I told her. "They were both a lot younger than I am. That's about it. What about you?"

"Actually, I'm still seeing someone," she said. "But I've been planning to break up with him for a while now." She spoke of her current relationship as if it was a casual appointment, after which she could fit me right in.

"How do you feel about dating someone older?" I asked her.

"Oh, it's no problem. My present boyfriend is older than you."

I was surprised at this, and somewhat pleased. True, I hadn't been prepared for the fact that she was still seeing someone, but the directness of her display of interest was encouraging. I stopped the car in her driveway, and we sat there somewhat awkwardly. I drew a little closer to her. "How about a kiss?" I asked, impulsively.

She drew back slightly. "Uhh, I don't think so," she said.

I was crestfallen. "Why not?" I asked, in a childish tone.

"I just don't think I'm ready for that."

"I see." I was struggling to recover my balance.

"I'd still like to get together sometime," she said in a placating tone.

"Yeah, sure. OK," I replied, entirely deflated. I dropped her off feeling awkward, unable to look at her directly.

I drove home wondering if maybe Dee and Ray weren't right, after all. Maybe this was all one loud wakeup call for me. Perhaps these events were telling me that there was something wrong with my basic attitudes and assumptions. If not, why had I felt so defensive with Dee? Why did I feel that if I didn't get to first base with this girl, my pride would prevent me from facing Dee again? A week went by. I tried calling the young co-ed on several occasions, but either she wasn't home or she wasn't answering her phone. Finally, I wrote an e-mail message, telling her about my current difficulties, and apologizing for coming on too strong.

Meanwhile, I decided to have it out with Ray, but our last encounter had been so potentially violent that I dreaded talking to him alone. I finally called Dee to ask if she would go with me.

"I'm not taking sides," she said. "I'm neutral."

"I know. That's fine. I just want you around so that Ray doesn't go haywire. He won't, as long as someone else is around. You just have to sit there and not say anything."

"OK," Dee agreed. "I'll come with you."

On the way over, I told her that I hadn't been paying any rent.

"Ray's not accepting rent is his way of controlling you," she suggested.

"You mean, he wanted to make me feel indebted to him, so that he would be in a position to dictate to me in other respects?"

"Something like that. He knows you're hurting financially. That's your weak spot. Maybe you can pay, but the prospect of saving some money is attractive. That's the way Ray is. He uses material things as an inducement to get what he wants from people emotionally."

When we got to the house, we found Ray in the dining room, sitting behind the table, a dim light behind him. His back was ramrod straight, and his head bowed like a penitent vulture.

"Ray, we have to talk," I said. "If I'm going to continue to live here, I feel we just have to go back to the way things were when I moved in. I'll start paying rent again. Other than that, I don't think we need to live by any rules except mutual respect."

Ray was eerily quiet. He looked haggard and dissociated, his head bobbing rhythmically up and down. He said he wanted to play us a tape, got up, and fumbled with a tape player and some cassettes. The tape was a barely audible recording of his wife talking on the phone to a psychic whom she used to consult. Ray had often claimed that his wife had said incriminating things on this tape. It was impossible for me to distinguish anything that was being said on it, however. There was nothing Dee or I could do until the whole bizarre performance was finished. When the tape concluded, I tried to get him back on track.

"Do you feel I owe you any back rent?" I asked him.

"No. But if you want to stay on, you'll have to pay rent again, and no guests."

"Well, then we're back to square one."

"Then I want you out now. Or I'll throw your stuff out on the street!"

Anger started to well up inside me. "Fine. I'm going to call the police. This may be your place, but you can't threaten to throw my stuff out like that. There are laws that protect tenants, you know, and I'm still a tenant here. I've always been ready to pay my rent. It was your choice not to collect it from me." I got up and headed upstairs to make the call. Ray became frantic. He was paranoid about the police. He started running around the house in an aimless manner, as if hunting for some kind of weapon to use against me. Dee stood up, alarmed. She hadn't anticipated the situation getting so out of control.

"It's OK, Ray," she said. "He's not really going to call the police."

"Oh, yes I am," I called from upstairs. I was already talking to the desk officer on the phone when both of them entered the room. At that point, Ray gave me two weeks' notice, and I agreed. As soon as he had backed off and gone downstairs, I left with Dee.

"It's not your fault," she said. "That's just the way he is. You can't deal with him. You're better off moving out."

I started moving my belongings out of Ray's place and into my mother's apartment. To avoid Ray, I went over to the house during the weekdays when he was at work. After several days, I had managed to get most of my clothes, books, and important papers. With still more than a week remaining before I had to be out entirely, I went back to remove some of the heavier items, and found that Ray had changed the locks on the doors. When I called him up, he said that if I wanted the rest of my stuff, I would first have to pay all the back rent I owed him.

"If you think I'm going to pay you now, after the way you acted, you're crazy," I replied. "I don't feel I owe you anything!"

The next day, I filed a lawsuit in small claims court to recover my belongings. When my mother called from Florida to check in on me, I told her what had transpired. Instead of being sympathetic, however, she got on my case for not being more active in looking for a new job.

Strangely, what bothered me most among all the things that had recently occurred was not the blowout with Ray, the hassle of moving out of his place, the fact that I was soon to be out of a job, or my mother's disapproval of my passivity in the face of looming unemployment. No, it was the female student. She was all I could think about. A few days later I got a reply via e-mail from her giving me a polite brush-off. She unequivocally ruled out anything but a platonic friendship. Still, I couldn't let it lie. I had to call her up and have it out with her. This time she answered the phone, probably not suspecting that I would be so persistent. "Did you change your mind about me as soon as I asked you for a kiss?" I wanted to know.

"I'm afraid so," she admitted.

"There's no way we can just pretend it didn't happen?"

"No. I've made up my mind," she replied.

I had shown a brief flash of unwanted emotion, and based on that she had rejected me out of hand. I felt helpless in the face of that verdict.

After I hung up with her, I called Dee again, and complained to her. “Why do women get to make all the decisions? Why are men powerless in the face of their whims and assumptions? Why can’t she suspend her judgment and give me a second chance?” I asked her.

“You’d stand a better chance if you accepted her terms,” she stated.

“What does that mean? If she says she just wants to be friends, I take her at her word. Are you implying she doesn’t mean what she says? I can’t agree to just a platonic relationship when I’m hoping the whole time that she’ll change her mind.”

“Then you’re not going to get anywhere,” Dee replied.

PART TWO

The Basis of Self-Deception

"Self-awareness entails carefully examining one's motives and actions. Man's spiritual development cannot proceed if it is based on self-deception. He must learn for himself who he is and what he is not."

—Andreas Leo, *The Face of the Eternal, Book Two,* 42, 62

Chapter 5

The Way Life Works

"The essence of a spiritual path lies in gaining a fresh view on life. If a person's way of living does not grant him freedom in the most sacred sense of the word, he must try to find a way to regain a feeling of satisfaction and contentment."
—Andreas Leo, *The Face of the Eternal, Book Two*, 37

After my conversation with Dee, I felt that I was in a hole so deep there was no direction left but up. I was looking for even the smallest sign that my life could improve. My mother was due back from Florida in another month, and so far, I had made no progress in finding a job or a new place to live. Meanwhile, I had the task of buying a used car for her, since the one she had was no longer reliable. Setting my mind to this project, I called a League member named John Weber, and mentioned my problem to him. He asked me what kind of car I was looking for, and I told him that I liked Toyotas.

"I've got a cousin who's going overseas right away and wants to get rid of his car," he said. "It's got less than 100,000 miles on it, and a brand-new engine."

"What kind is it?"

"It's a Toyota."

"You're kidding me," I said in wonderment. "That's just what I'm looking for."

"The only problem is he's driving into town tomorrow and won't be here until evening. If you want the car, you won't be able to drive it away until the next day."

"That's OK. I'm not in a hurry," I told him. I was delighted by the apparent ease with which my search was proceeding. "Is this amazing, or what!" I exclaimed enthusiastically.

"That's the way life works," Ben replied, with the optimism typical of many League initiates.

I smiled deprecatingly to myself at this platitude, so at odds with my own experience. When had anything ever gone right for me? Still, on this occasion, I was strangely hopeful that things would indeed work out.

The next day, I called Ben. He reported that his cousin was slightly delayed, but would be there that evening. He was planning to make dinner for the two of them, and invited me over to share it with them. "I'm cooking steaks," he said. That sounded good, so I accepted. I arrived just as Ben was filling two plates with the steaks, home fries, and salad. He opened a bottle of wine. His cousin had not arrived yet, so we sat down together and dug in to the meal. As we ate, he regaled me with stories of his experience as an electronics salesman in Canada.

"Selling is all about sizing up the customer," he said, "making them comfortable. If they come into the store, they're ready to buy. You just have to lead them to the merchandise that suits their needs."

"I can tell you're a good salesman, Ben," I remarked.

"Sure, I sold you on the steak dinner, didn't I?"

I was getting an uncomfortable feeling about his cousin with the Toyota. The evening passed, and he hadn't shown up. Ben got on his cell phone. "My cousin's still in Chicago," he announced. "He's going to Detroit tomorrow, and will be here in the evening. It'll be just one extra day's wait."

The next morning, I called again. "I talked to my cousin just now," Ben said. "He won't be able to give up the car for another week. His other car is in a repair shop."

I wasn't surprised at the news. I had been feeling for a while that the deal would go sour. I had allowed Ben to sell me on the Toyota the same way I had let him sell me on the steak. His nature was to size up people according to what they desired, and then tell them what they wanted to hear. I wasn't angry with Ben, only with myself. The situation made me aware of my lack of self-reliance. I had been left dangling on a string because of my desire to get a "good deal." I was less interested in Ben than in what he could do for me. At least I had gotten a steak dinner, so I had no reason to complain. "That's the way life works," I thought ruefully.

Shortly after this, I attended a workshop sponsored by the League in a neighboring town. The workshop was entitled "Coping with Change in Your Life." In one of the exercises, each participant was offered a piece of paper with three magazine cutouts pasted on it. Each piece of paper contained a different set of pictures. I received a sheet on which were pasted images of a smiling couple, a set of keys, and a can of soup. The participants were each asked to say something about the images on the pieces of paper they had chosen. When the facilitator turned to me, however, I was unable to say anything. The truth was, the pictures dumbfounded and terrified me. I couldn't even give a name to the fear they represented.

When I closed my eyes briefly in contemplation, it immediately occurred to me that the pictures symbolized the three most basic aspects of life. The loving couple stood for emotional fulfillment: intimacy, partnership, and love. The keys symbolized stability: material possessions, home, job, and career. The can of soup represented the ability to provide for one's basic physical needs. The shock that the pictures produced in me came from the realization of how far away I was from achieving any of these things.

"It's important to accept responsibility for change in one's life before this can occur," the facilitator told the group. As she spoke, I wondered whether, despite my feeling that I had struggled to achieve these things all my life, I had really tended to deny them to myself. Had I automatically assumed that they would come to me on their own, and therefore not made the proper effort? Or was I operating on the assumption that I would never achieve them, and therefore choosing a self-destructive path?

I tried to imagine what the facilitator meant when she talked about accepting responsibility for one's life. The thought that my lack of success was entirely due to my own choices was a numbing one. If the responsibility was my own, and I had created my own lack of success through my own thought and my own will, how could I overturn such a monumental pattern of belief?

The next exercise was an imaginative technique called "The Fear Room." One was supposed to visualize a foggy room, then clean the mist out of it, and see what was there. I visualized the accoutrements of domesticity—a music console, a kitchen, a rug, an easy chair, a long shelf of books, a dog on the rug, and a wife beside me. The thought came to me that this was something I had never permitted myself to imagine. With this came a feeling that sunk a shaft deep inside me. Then came tears.

My recent experience with Ben, coupled with these workshop exercises, caused me to review my entire life experience. I had to acknowledge that, despite the spirit of adventure that had drawn me to Andreas Leo's teachings, I had not led an adventurous life. I had charted my path along an introspective course, more interested in living according to spiritual precepts than in worldly success. At the same time, however, I somehow expected that all my needs would be met, just as I expected a Toyota to fall in my lap. Why, I wondered, during all the time that I had been a student on the Path, had I received no clue that I was going the wrong way? What was the value of the League teachings if they hadn't provided me with the necessary perspective to change the course of my life?

I decided to call my friend Lynne Silva, who worked at a nearby health food store. Since she was knowledgeable about alternative medicine, I had gone to her for advice about certain health problems in the past. She was also a League spiritual aide, however, trained to listen to people with spiritual problems. I dropped in at the store around noon and talked her into going out to lunch with me at a Thai restaurant just down the street. When we sat down, we looked at the menu and both ordered the same dish—shrimp and vegetables.

"It's great to see you," she said. "How's your health these days?"

"Well," I began, "that condition I've been struggling with for so long cleared up not long ago. That's the one bright spot in my life. As you know, I spent years going to doctors and alternative practitioners, but nothing really helped. Then just recently I found a cure. I had been suffering from a simple mineral deficiency. What I don't understand is why I had to go through all those years of discomfort. What was the meaning of that experience? Why did the answer elude me for so long, and then present itself so suddenly?"

"It's not strange," Lynne replied. "That's the way life works."

"What do you mean?" I asked sharply, struck by this echo of Ben's remark.

"I mean that life isn't a matter of outer experiences alone. Experiences flow from higher conditions, or conditions within ourselves. Have you heard the expression, 'As above, so below?' Everything that exists in this world is a reflection of a subtler reality. In our daily lives, we run into obstacles. We have periods of ease and enjoyment. Some people put forth a great effort to apparently little effect, while others fall into success like pigs in a mud hole.

"As someone who works in the health business," she continued, "I can often tell which people have the capacity to be cured. A degree of flexibility is required, and often the cure doesn't come until they've turned some kind of a corner in some other aspect of their lives. For instance, let me ask you a question. How long have you been in the academic field, including the time you worked on your degree?"

"A long time."

"Was it the same period as your health problem lasted?"

"Approximately, yes."

"What happened? Are you still teaching?"

"No. I've given it up for now. I've come to a dead end. I can't go any further with it."

"Did your cure come at about the same time?"

"Yes."

"So what does that tell you?"

I nodded, already anticipating her reasoning. "I have to admit, it's quite a coincidence."

"It's not a coincidence," Lynne replied. "Life has nothing to do with predictability or unpredictability, with good luck or bad luck, joy or suffering. Instead, it poses certain problems for us to solve, without indicating the nature of the problem or its solution. If the source of the problem is still inside us, then it continues to create the same conditions. As soon as we discover the solution, everything shifts, and we get a new problem to solve.

"The truth is," she continued, "that we're spiritual beings. What we really are exists outside of time and space. We're creators of our own circumstances. Where, however, do the circumstances that we create get started? Quite honestly, almost every cycle that you set in motion is the effect of something else. What you have is a chain of effects masquerading as causes. This chain of cause and effect really doesn't exist in time and space. That's why we can't look for the cause of a condition in a linear fashion. The real task is to look at what we're carrying inside ourselves at this moment. We have to be able to recognize at any given point in time whether we're acting on the basis of something that's an effect of a previous action, or in accord with our pure spiritual nature. In large measure, most of us live from effect."

"And a true spiritual Master lives from cause?"

"Yes. What exactly does that mean, however? It means that every cycle that gets set in motion by that individual has its origin in the heart of God, and not anything else. It simply happens because there is an impulse for it to be created. A true spiritual Master has learned to be a clear and open participant in that process."

"What about the rest of us?"

"People who are in training to become spiritual Masters (and that's not necessarily everybody on the Path) are still learning. Any true spiritual path will have three essential components. First is the company of a Living Master, to enable the individual to move in consciousness to the higher planes of existence. Second is the initiation into these higher states of consciousness. Third is the daily discipline of the spiritual exercises. In the company of a true Master, you get to cross the border. He's a guide with the authority to lead people into these higher states. With the initiation, on the other hand, you go from being a visitor to a citizen. You no longer need someone to get you across the border. Finally, by means of the spiritual exercises, you get to practice this type of movement daily.

"If you look at a particular event in your life and ask yourself, 'What led me to do that?' you can follow a sequence of events back through time," she added. "Then, however, you can view the whole sequence, and look for the common theme. By this means, you get to a point where you see that there's a fundamental assumption about life in general, about yourself, or about your relationship to others, or to the Path itself, that is creating this repetitive cycle of conditions in your life."

"My main concern, at the moment," I told Lynne, "is to discover the reason for my lack of success in life. I have another concern, however, and that is to understand the relationship between my lack of success and my membership in the League. Somehow, I feel these two problems are connected with one another. When I joined the League, I understood that it was a path of spiritual growth. I've never had any doubts about it in this respect. On the other hand, I've never had any faith that it could help me with the practical matter of living. It never promised that it would bring me wealth, love, or even happiness. The consequence, however, is that for me, the League has become a path of failure. I don't mean that there's something wrong with the League itself, but perhaps there's something wrong with my relationship to it. I've used it to justify and even aid me in my lack of success."

"You could be right," Lynne replied, not very helpfully.

"On the other hand," I asked, "what does spirituality have to do with achievement? What does it have to do with finding a career, love, or even happiness? For some people, the path to God may include these things. What if my path does not? What if achieving these things is at odds with my spiritual goal? Then there's no sense in asking for them, is there?"

Lynne shrugged her shoulders sympathetically. "I can tell you one thing," she said. "This is not about you. Our purpose is to be of service, and being of service means being of service anywhere, not merely where we THINK we can best be of service. You've worked for several years to get a full-time academic job. You thought that that was where you could best be of service. Maybe you were wrong, however. You might be of greater service somewhere else. You have to be open to that possibility."

I looked down at our plates. Lynne had finished everything on her plate, while I had mainly just picked the shrimp off the top and left the vegetables. In an instant, I saw a parallel between the food left on my plate and my attitude toward life. "I don't think I'm a lazy person. I've worked hard the last few years. Maybe I've been too picky, though," I confessed. "I haven't wanted to settle for anything less than a certain kind of job. I realize that life isn't going to be all shrimp and no vegetables, but can't I at least expect to find a job that will make me happy?"

"Not necessarily," Lynne replied. "Often, a job is just a job."

"I don't know if I can live that way," I replied, disheartened.

"You can be of service in whatever situation you're in."

Now I was truly chagrined. That wasn't what I had wanted to hear. My greatest fear was that I would be stuck doing something for which I had no enthusiasm. I had worked at many dead-end jobs in my younger days, and they had been much harder on me psychologically than physically. I felt I needed to do something creative, something that required vision and inspiration. Without that, life didn't seem worth living.

"I don't know if I can be happy doing something I don't feel passionate about," I told Lynne. "It's not that I don't want to be of service, but I feel it's an utter necessity for me to find out how I can BEST be of service. I feel as if this awareness is buried somewhere deep inside me, and that I have to make a tremendous effort to bring it to the surface."

"In that case, you're right to persevere in your quest," Lynne replied. "You should hold on to that vision of your deepest spiritual desire."

I was grateful to Lynne for this last remark, but was still confused. I needed to follow my heart's desire, yet I couldn't dismiss the vegetables I had left on my plate. They told me that beneath my picky attitude was a fundamental fear of life that I was stubbornly refusing to face.

"I still don't understand what's wrong with me," I persisted. "Why don't I have any vision of my future? Why is there no stability to my life? Am I simply sabotaging my efforts? Am I failing to take responsibility for myself? Why can't I achieve even the most modest trappings of a conventional life?"

She smiled. "Have you ever simply considered," she asked, "that you're not destined to live a conventional life?"

I accompanied Lynne back to the health food store. A young woman was waiting for her. "This is Marcia Diamond," she said. "She's a new member of the Brotherhood from upstate who's helping me out a little today. She's had some experiences that you might find interesting. Why don't the two of you talk, while I attend to some business?"

Marcia and I were agreeable, so we sat down in a small lounge set up for employees in the back of the store, while Lynne went inside her office to get some work done. Marcia was a willowy young woman who sat with her back arched, her dark hair accentuated by a costume jewelry tiara and matching earrings that appeared homemade.

"I like the look," I told her.

"Thanks," she replied, in a lively voice. "If you don't have much money, you have to find ways to be creative."

I got the strong sense that she was a person with a story. "Tell me a little about yourself," I asked her. "What's the most important experience you've ever had in your life?"

"I was very ill," she replied, immediately launching into a complex tale. She explained that over the past two years after her parents died, she started getting sick and then progressively sicker. She didn't know what was going on and went to many different doctors, including specialists in neurology.

"I was seeing this doctor once a week," she said, "and every time I came in, he said I had a new illness in another organ of my body. Another doctor said I had leukemia. He thought I was going to die. I gained a lot of weight, and no one could come up with a diagnosis. The point came where I could no longer walk. I suffered excruciating pain every time I stood up. I had repeated dreams that when I tried to walk I'd fall down. I started having severe emotional problems, as well. I was beginning to become suicidal. As a student of the League teachings, I knew that if I committed suicide, I'd have to come right back in another life, but I really wanted to die. I felt a tremendous amount of fear and guilt. 'What did I do to let myself fall into this state?' I thought to myself. I had no money. How was I going to pay for my treatment?"

Marcia recounted how she went to an outpatient clinic, but since she had no insurance, all they did was give her painkillers and send her on her way. Eventually, she ran out of money, and her landlord kicked her out. She was in contact with a friend throughout all of this. Eventually, she called the mental health clinic. She had no place to go, so they brought her there. She owned a walker, but they took it away because they thought she could use it as a weapon.

"There was a woman on the floor," she related, "who knocked me over as I was walking toward her. My bones were very brittle at that point. I lay there for heaven knows now how long. It was just the most horrible thing to be in a mental hospital. It was wild!" She laughed. "They had no idea what to do with me, so they dismissed me. Still, I didn't have any place to go. I was homeless, and about sixty pounds heavier than I am now."

I tried to imagine this slender young woman carrying an extra sixty pounds, but found this quite difficult to visualize.

Marcia added that they finally diagnosed her illness as Cushing's syndrome, a hormonal imbalance in which the body overproduces cortisone, a steroid. The cause was a tumor in the adrenal gland.

"I was wandering around the street with my walker," she recounted, "and the police picked me up. They took me to a place called Tent City, which is where all the homeless people go. I was there for another night. No one knew where I was. My sister, who is an initiate of the League and lives in Canada, was in touch with a number of our mutual friends, one of whom worked as a volunteer in the homeless shelter. They found me there. My sister was shocked. She put me into a hospital, and I was there for four months. They did a couple of biopsies. I had millions of tests. When they found the tumor, I had to have surgery. All the time I had no idea where I was going to live afterwards, or how I would pay for the treatment.

"Then, because the bones get really soft, I had to have reconstructive back surgery. They put two metal bars in my back. I can't stand needles, and every day I had needles. They take your blood a million times a day. I was on so many different floors. One night, a mentally ill person in the bed next to me was talking to invisible entities and screaming. This was after I had my surgery, and was unable to move. She came over and started 'playing' with me. They tied her down, but she broke loose. It was nightmare after nightmare."

Her account was absorbing. Looking at her fresh face, I found it hard to believe that she had been through so much.

"Finally, they took me to another hospital for rehabilitation," she said. "I had to learn to walk all over again. They really push you. When my time was up there, I still had no place to go. I wore a body brace for four months. I could hardly get up by myself. They found a place for me, which was an assisted living facility for homeless people. The place was dark and smelled of urine and cigarettes. I lived there for almost a year, until last July. But, you know, now that I'm over the experience, I'm happier than I've been in my whole life."

"What do you think it was all about?" I asked, struck by her optimism.

"I think it had to do with what I was willing to go through to get to a certain state of consciousness," Marcia replied.

"Not everyone has to go through hell to get to a different state of consciousness, do they?"

"No, but in my case, I had to let go of so much that had accumulated inside me. If that was the only way that it could be done, then it had to happen that way. It makes you feel thankful. Being in a place with a lot of mentally ill people and people on drugs, you realize how responsible you are for your own circumstances. These people have given up their free will. They've relinquished their own responsibility. There were a couple of women there whose husbands had passed away. They were still in denial about it. One of them had apparently been very wealthy. Her husband had left her, and she had been totally disconnected from reality ever since. Another woman's husband had died, and she was still asking, 'Where is my husband? Have you seen him?'"

"Years ago," I recalled, "I had a dream in which I went insane. It was not a recall of a past life, nor merely a reflection of fear. They say that sometimes if you go through something in a dream experience, you can avoid having to go through it in the waking state. I think that was the situation in my case. Through the dream, I received the same understanding that you did through your experience—that insanity is essentially a matter of giving up one's free will and responsibility for one's own life."

"Yes," Marcia agreed. "You're responsible for your own state of consciousness, for everything that you create. I guess that could be a scary thought for some people, but it's actually a very wonderful thing. Everything is a learning experience."

I thought of Marcia's willingness to accept whatever experience had been necessary for her to go through. I didn't know if I had the capacity to be that accepting of life. Our conversation at an end, I found myself sitting wordlessly with her in the employee lounge, just appreciating her silent company.

At this point, Lynne came out of her office. She talked to Marcia briefly, and sent her on a brief errand. Then she sat down with me again. I recounted what Marcia had told me of her story. "I'm glad you introduced us," I told Lynne. "Even though she's gone through a much more difficult experience than I have, the questions she's had to ask herself are the same as mine: 'Why is this happening to me? What is the meaning of this experience?' I asked her what her illness meant to her, and she said that she felt it had something to do with simply being willing to go through that type of experience. But I wonder if there's more to it than that."

"Well, what she said is not quite accurate," Lynne replied, "because the choice of going through it or not was taken away from her." She chuckled. "For six years, she was in denial about her illness, until it caught up with her. She was flat on her back in a body cast and couldn't move for months because her bones were deteriorating in her spine. They were breaking with every movement. Doctors had to piece the whole thing together with metal rods.

"It's strange how life works," she continued. "It's like a powerful river. If we fight against its current, we'll exhaust ourselves in fruitless struggle. If we surrender, however, we'll find that we have a limited freedom of movement—more movement than we perhaps imagined, and certainly far more than we would have if we continued to try to swim upstream. Life will give you an experience, and you can choose to learn from it. If you choose not to, however, it's eventually going to get a little harder. Finally, you come to a point where it says, 'Okay. Now you have no choice. Here's the experience, and you've got to deal with it.' Of course, she could have died. She DID have a choice to live through the experience, rather than die from it."

"But then she'd probably have to go through it again in another life," I commented.

"Yes. It's been an amazing transformation. It's funny. Something that you run from so hard is actually the one thing that transforms you. You get to the point where there's nowhere to run and nowhere to hide. Marcia could have actually died, because she was running so hard."

"So you're saying that there was an inner problem corresponding to her illness?"

"That's right. Do you remember I said, earlier, 'As above, so below?' Her illness stemmed from abuse on the part of her father. It was very deep, but it began to surface. She kept pushing it down, instead of dealing with it. Then it manifested in this physical illness. She went into denial about that, too. For six years, she ballooned up. She didn't even look like Marcia. Actually, she became almost a duplicate, physically, of her mother."

"Because the mother had enabled the father in his abuse?"

"Yes. Marcia was just punishing herself. That's why the disease was so physically debilitating. For almost eight months after the surgery, she couldn't go to the bathroom without assistance. The pain was excruciating. For at least five months, she just lay flat on her back, looking at the ceiling. Cushing's disease not only softens the bones, but also affects the hormonal balance in the body. Once that got adjusted, she could heal physically. Now she's able to start looking at the cause of what took her down that road to begin with. It's often so with victims of abuse. That's the key word—victim. It's hard for some people. I've been blessed because I came into this lifetime with the knowledge of who and what I am, and I've never been a victim."

I had little clue as to what Lynne meant when she said she had never been a victim. Frankly, it had sounded to me like she was boasting. Although I had never been through an experience as severe as that which Marcia had endured, I identified with her. When she suggested that people needed to accept responsibility for their situation in life, I presumed that she was talking in fatalistic terms about the necessity of experiencing her illness. Lynne shocked me, however, by implying that Marcia might not have needed to go through that experience if she had earlier uncovered the layers of denial about her history of abuse. The illness was an effect of the denial. Lynne was implying that it was not necessary to take responsibility for the effect if one did so for the cause.

I could follow the logic of this type of analysis in relation to Marcia, but not, however, in relation to myself. Lynne's precepts rang true, yet remained curiously abstract for me. How could I apply them to my own problems? What did they have to do with my lack of luck in getting a deal on a Toyota? Why did the Toyota incident appear to me so symbolic of my own life? Why did I identify so strongly with Marcia's experiences? Why did I feel so threatened by optimists like Ben, who viewed life as an endless procession of miracles? What, in fact, was the nature of my dissatisfaction with life? These questions, considered singly, were like the peeled layers of an onion, almost translucent, ready to yield an interpretation. Taken together, however, they remained like the onion as a whole, opaque.

CHAPTER 6

A DISCOVERY OF ONE'S OWN SEEKING

"God never designated an exclusive path for man's spiritual liberation. He gave many the power to lead Soul back to its true home."
—Andreas Leo, *The Key to the Science of the Soul*, 10

SHORTLY AFTER MY conversations with Lynne and Marcia, I was on the Eastern University campus inquiring about jobs, and met an instructor who suggested that there might be a part-time position still open for the fall term. Since I didn't have a better option, I swallowed my pride and applied for the position, hoping that returning to teaching wouldn't bring back the health problems that had so mysteriously vanished during my hiatus. I got the post, and, with my resentment about my poor career prospects diminished, I was determined that I would do the best that I could, regardless of the circumstances. Meanwhile, my mother had returned briefly from Florida only to depart for her seasonal vacation in Maine. My lawsuit against Ray successfully forced him to allow me to retrieve my belongings, and I had the rest of the summer to find an apartment of my own.

The lingering effect of my spat with Ray, however, inhibited me from attending the local League activities in Belle Harbor. I was aware of the pettiness of my feelings, and tried to master them. I showed up on a few occasions at the local center, and suffered Ray's presence without complaint, but the irritation remained. The atmosphere at the center was dispiriting, and I began to feel as out of place there as I had in Huntington Park. At the same time, changes were occurring within the very structure of the League. The new Living Master had set out to remold it along the lines of a world religion. A temple had been constructed, worship services established, and new books written that drastically simplified the League teachings so that they could be understood by virtually anyone. Outwardly, I went along with these changes, but privately, they troubled me.

If the Science of the Soul was something apart from conventional faiths and the League was built directly on this foundation, how, I wondered, could it now call itself a religion? Andreas Leo, in his writings, had clearly differentiated between the Science of the Soul and religious teachings. God, he had stated, was neither old nor new, neither great nor small, neither shaped nor shapeless. Having no opposite, IT was what opposites had in common. The Science of the Soul was the purest of all teachings, and the original fountain from which all faiths sprang. So staggering was it in its simplicity, Leo had declared, that once grasped, it would confound the intellect. Religions, on the other hand, were the product of intellect. They inevitably gave a shape to God in some form or other.

What set the League apart from other groups, in my view, was the very fact that it was not a religion. True, League doctrine involved certain assumptions, tenets, and principles, but as a spiritual path, it involved much more than that. To find a spiritual path, the individual first had to become the seeker. He had to ask himself questions such as "Why am I here?" "Where have I been?" "Where am I going?" Then he had to meet with a spiritual master, teacher or guide. Once this connection occurred, he was put on a course of study and given certain practices and techniques to follow, the purpose of which is to link him in gradually increasing degrees to the Force that sustains all life.

Behind League doctrine, in other words, was a system of instruction, and the tenets of the League had to be considered in this context. For instance, one such tenet was that the world was never without a Living Master—that individual uniquely empowered by God to lead

Soul back to its true home in the spiritual worlds. The Living Master was thus the key to liberation. The wandering Soul, making its way from birth to birth, might be required to pass Its long and tiresome course for millions of years, unless he met with the Living Master and accepted him. The Master would link him, via the Force, with the great stream of Life, and there would be no further births or deaths for him.

Clearly, it was possible to turn the Science of the Soul into a religion. I had done so, and observed others do so. In my early years in the League, I created a whole system of morality for myself out of Andreas Leo's reference to the passions of the mind and their reciprocal virtues. My non-religious, permissive parents simply assumed that I would grow up with a sense of ethics. They never lectured me on right and wrong. It was perhaps inevitable, therefore, that I would take the League teachings and turn them into a system of morality. One day, I brought an acquaintance of mine over to my apartment, and started lecturing him on the five passions—lust, anger, greed, attachment, and vanity. A few weeks later, I encountered him on the street. "Hey, are you still in a League of your own?" he called out. I realized from his mocking tone that I had made a fool of myself. I was thus not only skeptical of conventional religions, but also of the tendency of League members to create religious doctrine out of Andreas Leo's teachings.

One day, I was in a bookstore and came upon an illustrated book on the Mormon temples, with beautiful color illustrations of the most historic and grandiose. The ambition, wealth, and creativity poured into these buildings impressed me, as well as the individuality of their design and the sumptuousness of their interiors. Most of all, however, they reminded me of the new League temple that had just been completed. I felt that there was a similar intention involved in its construction, and that reflected some commonality between the League and the Mormon Church. I was curious, so I called up a local representative of the Church to get more information. A few days later, I received a call from a young woman who introduced herself as Sister Coggins. She offered to meet with me and answer any more questions I might have. We set up an early evening appointment at a community center near the Eastern University campus.

When I arrived, Sister Coggins greeted me. She was a young college-age woman with a shy grin, dark hair pulled back tight over her head, and sparkling eyes. Her companion, Sister Ruff, was the same age, but more authoritative in her manner, with a round face and dark hair that went down to her shoulders. They walked down the hall, entered a wide lounge, and sat down on two sofas, the two women next to one another, and I facing them.

"Do you mind if we start out with a prayer?" Sister Ruff asked.

"Not at all," I replied. I closed my eyes, as I normally did in contemplation, while Sister Ruff said some words of appreciation in a soft voice. I felt a tingle up my spine and over my shoulders that I associated with the presence of the Force.

"Did you feel it, too?" I asked once the prayer was over.

"Uh, huh," Sister Ruff nodded her head energetically in the affirmative.

"That interests me," I said. "We're not of the same faith, but we both felt the presence of Spirit in each other's company. I wonder if you felt the same thing as I did."

"Probably," she replied. "Those are feelings of the Holy Ghost. We feel peace, joy, happiness, calm. Many people feel a touch of emotion. It's different for everyone, I think. That feeling is our Heavenly Father letting us know that He's there, that He's hearing our prayers, and answering our prayers."

I told them about my admiration for the Mormon temples, and asked them about the difference between a church and a temple.

"Temples are used for sacred ordinances of an eternal nature," Sister Ruff replied. "For instance, we believe that marriage is eternal. When a marriage takes place in a temple, we say that you are sealed in time and in all eternity."

"And this isn't true of a marriage that takes place in a church?" I asked.

"Not in our opinion. In a church ceremony, they say: ''Til death do you part.' In such a case, the marriage is only one of convenience in this lifetime. It's not a marriage for eternity. If everything we do is directed toward this life, then we haven't much faith in the life hereafter."

"So do you believe that in the next world we will have a body similar to the one we now have, and will be able to sit down and have a conversation, just as we're doing now?"

"Yes. We believe that the afterlife is a world of materiality, but glorified materiality," Sister Coggins stated.

What Sister Coggins and Sister Ruff said made logical sense, given their assumption that marriage was a holy sacrament and the afterlife simply a continuation of one's present life. For this reason, they viewed the normal Christian approach to marriage as debased and even sacrilegious. While I could see that this would bring a deep sense of sanctity to human relationships, it differed considerably from League doctrine, which was much more individualistic in its orientation.

The League taught that the true nature of the individual was Soul—a spark of God, eternal and indestructible. Soul accumulated experience over many lifetimes until it was ready to meet with the Living Master, consciously connect with the Audible Life Stream, and ride that wave back to the Godhead. The journey of Soul was thus a procession of countless lives on earth spent in many guises, lands, and cultures, speaking different languages, worshipping all manner of deities, inhabiting bodies of alternating sexes and various races, and practicing innumerable professions. The true nature of Soul went far beyond the notion of one's family ties or bonds of love with particular individuals. Nevertheless, I told them in diplomatic fashion that I was intrigued by the Mormon concept of extending one's relationships into the afterlife.

"Personally, I think it makes sense," Sister Ruff replied. "We come down to this earth, and our Heavenly Father knows that we're going to come down here, and that we're going to love our families. Most parents would give their lives for their children, and I think I would give up my life for my parents. I love them very dearly. To have that just end at death doesn't seem very merciful. To me, it's reasonable that our Heavenly Father would allow our sacred and wonderful relationships to last forever, and not just while we're here."

"What happens to non-Mormons who have not had their marriages sealed for eternity?" I asked. "Are their future lifetimes spent seeking a partner they didn't have in this life?"

"Well, we also believe that after we die, we go to the Spirit world and continue to learn about the plan of our Heavenly Father," Sister Coggins explained. "That's where there are other missionaries, people like us, who teach people the Gospel."

"If, after we pass from this life, we go to a world in which we're still working to learn God's plan, then there must be prophets and teachers that are helping to give people God's word and an understanding of God's plan in that world, as well," I suggested.

"I think our spirits will be the same, and therefore the prophets and teachers we have had on earth will also be the same," Sister Coggins commented. "When we die, our bodies go to the grave, and our spirits go to the Spirit world. We're the same person, or spirit, and whatever knowledge we've gained here, we'll be able to take with us into the next life. We also believe that we have lived before we were born. We had a pre-mortal existence. We don't remember anything about it, because if we did, we would have no reason to be here. Salvation is a returning back to the presence of our Father in Heaven."

"What do you think is the most crucial determinant for achieving salvation?" I asked.

"Definitely our Savior Jesus Christ," they both replied. "We have to accept Him as our savior," Sister Ruff added.

"When we prayed together and felt the presence of Spirit, or the Holy Ghost, is that feeling, for you, the evidence of your relationship with Jesus Christ?" I wanted to know.

"Yes," they answered. I immediately felt that this answer anticipated a question that I had been debating whether to ask.

"You have just said that feeling the presence of the Holy Spirit is evidence of your relationship with Christ. If I feel that same presence, then I must have a relationship with the same thing that you identified as Christ, even if I call it by some other name."

"What do you think that means?" Sister Ruff asked me, when I voiced this sentiment.

"I think it means that Spirit is everywhere, and is not restricted to any particular religion or spiritual group," I replied. "We both feel the same presence in our hearts. We just call it by a different name. It's the identical phenomenon, whether it's called the Cosmic Force or the Holy Ghost."

I asked if we could do another prayer together, to wind up our meeting. This time, Sister Coggins led the prayer. As she did so, I felt the Force sweeping over me with a gentle power that brought tears to my eyes. I emerged from the interlude smiling, dabbing the corners of my eyes with my knuckles, slightly embarrassed about my display of emotion. I thanked them for the time they had taken to meet with me, and walked out into the summer evening feeling refreshed, invigorated, and grateful for having made their acquaintance.

This experience, while uplifting, sparked a wave of doubts in me concerning the League. I had always assumed that the League represented the highest, most direct path to God. Most League initiates, I suspected, were just as convinced of this as I was. Why else would people choose to remain with a single path if they didn't feel it was superior to others? If the Mormons experienced the same Force in their lives that we did in the League, what was the real difference between us? Was it simply a matter of doctrine? Did it really matter that they believed a marriage could be sealed for eternity, and we didn't? What did a doctrine or set of beliefs really matter, when what was important was cultivating that presence of Spirit?

Andreas Leo had written of the League as the source of all religions. Another way of stating this, however, was to say that every religion was a manifestation of the League. I was beginning to see this doctrine in a new light. When Leo spoke of the League, was he referring to the organization in its present form, or more generally, to a universal structure of which the present League was just the latest incarnation?

Where was the true League to be found? Was it in the outer organization, or was it somewhere much deeper, hidden in all life, transcending all cultural boundaries, trademarks, and doctrines? I went home, opened one of Andreas Leo's books, *The Shining Path Letters*, and read the following passage:

> All religions, doctrines, and philosophies spring from the Cosmic Force. It is the heart and soul of life. The most important discovery of one's own seeking occurs when one finds that all life contains this Force and begins to see it in everything. (207)

I felt that I had just made such a discovery. For the first time, it occurred to me that the League was not necessarily the highest, most direct path to God, but simply one path among many. Although this thought was shocking to me, it left me curious. Was it necessarily such a terrible conclusion? Was the loss of faith in the League's exclusivity such a tragedy? If that loss included a portion of one's own vanity and self-importance, was it not a potentially joyous loss, and an even more important gain?

Not long after my encounter with Sister Coggins and Sister Ruff, I saw an advertisement at a new age bookstore in downtown Belle Harbor headlined "An Evening with Richard Albert." The event was to take place at the Putnam Center, on the Eastern University campus. I asked the girl at the counter if any tickets were still available.

"Twelve dollars for the talk, a hundred dollars for the reception afterward," she replied.

"I'd like to do an article on it," I said. "Is it possible to get a pass to the reception?"

She gave me the name of someone else to contact, and, after going through the proper channels, I was delighted to receive a free ticket for front row seating, as well as for the reception.

It was a Friday evening. The Putnam Center stage was decorated with three impressive Tibetan Buddhist wall hangings suspended from tall metal stands. In front of these was a small table with a brightly colored flower arrangement, a microphone, and single leather chair. I wondered, since the event was billed as a conversation between two people, why there was only one chair. I received my answer as soon as Richard Albert was introduced and emerged in a wheelchair. He was a patriarchal figure with long white hair, a white moustache and dark glasses, incongruously dressed in brown corduroys, casual hiking shoes, and a windbreaker, as if for a walk in the woods. The life of this former Harvard professor of psychology, an associate of Tom Lurie, Ralph Michener, and Allen Gutenberg, author of *Be, Hear, Know* and many other books, had assumed the stature of myth in American culture.

"I'm a strokee," Albert began haltingly. "I'm not only in a wheelchair, but I also forget words, which means it's hard for me to lecture. If I forget the word, there are periods of long silence. You can use the silences. Don't use them to wonder if I'm going to get the word. Instead, find a way to surf the silence. Why don't you join me now, and surf right into the deepest space within you, which is silent awareness."

The simplicity of Richard Albert's words and the humanity of his condition immediately touched me. Closing my eyes, I felt myself going deeper and deeper into the heart center, feeling the love within. I was so happy with this sense of peace that I would have preferred to have simply remained in silent contemplation. Eventually, however, Albert resumed his talk. As he picked up the thread of his life experience, his words began to flow more easily.

"Mushrooms and LSD showed me another reality than the one I had been taught existed," he said. "Aldous Huxley gave Tim Lurie and me *The Tibetan Book of the Dead*. We used that to model psychedelic experiences. I was having experiences that were at the edge of ecstasy. They were something so real for me that I said they were like home.

"I started reading *The Tibetan Book of the Dead*, and right in the middle of the book was a description of the acid trip I had the previous Saturday. Then I started to read the Tibetan literature and the Hindu literature, and they were like maps of my consciousness. We were using these chemicals and plants, but we really didn't know what to do with them. I was a psychologist. The drugs, the mushrooms, the LSD experiences did not correspond to Western psychology. If I took a 'trip' on Saturday, and then gave a lecture to my psychology class on Monday, the most important thing was what happened to me on Saturday, yet it was not my role to impart that to my students.

"I had been in India in the late '60s and came back for my mother's funeral. They were laying her gravestone at the cemetery. I was dressed in a potato sack, with a beard, long hair, and lots of beads. My father was on the board of his temple. The rabbi had never seen someone who looked like I did. After the ceremony, he took me by the elbow and propelled me forward. He wanted to know what I had been doing. I proceeded to tell him about my trip to India, my guru, the miracles…all that sort of thing. We were leaning against two tombstones.

"'I had a similar experience,' he said. 'I was in theological school, reading the Bible. I took two No-Doz tablets, the book fell away, and I was right there in the middle of the scene.'

"'You must have shared this with your congregation,' I replied.

"'No,' he answered. 'I've never told anyone but you. That was a mystical experience, and I'm a priest of a folk religion.'

"The man's role forced him to skirt his mystical experience with his congregation, just as I had to do in my lectures," Albert commented. "I was born a conservative Jew, but I never felt that teaching gave me any purchase on my spirituality.

"After the mushrooms and the LSD," he continued, "I tried to figure out what was going on with my consciousness. I went to the East because I felt if they had these maps, they must have readers of the maps. I decided to go to Nepal and India. I was in Katmandu, when an American sat down at our table in a restaurant. He was going to walk through India and visit Buddhist temples, and asked me to go with him. It was dark out, and the stars seemed so close. My mother had just died, and I thought about her. I had a new Land Rover, and the guy said, 'Wouldn't it be nice if I could go and see my guru in this Land Rover?' He wanted to stay in India, where his guru would have connections for him to get a visa. I was so Buddhist then. He was going to see a Hindu. I felt hijacked. I didn't want to go.

"We arrived, and he greeted his guru. I was standing back. I wanted to have nothing to do with the whole scene.

"This old man who was his guru looked at me. 'You came in an expensive car,' he said.

"'Yes,' I replied.

"'Will you give it to me?' he asked. I had seen fund-raising before, but this was ridiculous. This young fellow was looking at his guru and saying to him, 'If you want it, you can have it.' I was steaming mad.

"The guru sent us out to get some food, brought us back, and invited us to sit down. Then he spoke to me. 'You were walking under the stars. You were thinking of your mother.' I was a psychologist, and that just blew me away. I looked in his eyes, and realized if he knew about that incident, then he knew everything. He was looking at me with such love. Imagine—loving such a one as me! Later, they told me that he had arranged for the whole meeting. He had sent the young man to get me. He busted my mind, and then he busted my heart!

"My guru was the first person I met who loved me unconditionally, because he recognized my Soul instead of the fact that I was a professor, and all that stuff. My life had taken a turn. I had been going along the high road of the Western academic enterprise. When I went to see my guru, I stood back from the rest of the people around him. I thought to myself, 'I'm not going to touch his feet, because I don't touch people's feet.' Two days later, I was angling for his foot. I was jealous of people who had his foot. I wormed my way to the front row, put my hand out, and he pulled his foot back under the blanket. That started a whole thing, a game of spiritual cat-and-mouse.

"I don't know what impelled me toward Spirit, but from the time I met my guru, I felt that he was blessing me. He showered grace on me, because my *sadhana*, my spiritual path, was through the guru's blessing. When I was driving down the street and would find a parking space, I would think, 'Aha, he's watching over me.' I was focused on a very limited level of grace.

"More recently, I was trying to write a book about aging," Albert continued, "and my editor told me that my writing was shallow. I was sixty-five. 'I feel age,' I thought to myself, 'but I'm not really an aged person. She must be right. What can I do that will put me in the position of an old person in this culture?' Just then the stroke occurred. I was taking care of my father, who was ninety. All of a sudden, I looked at my hand. It was his hand. I was walking like him. He used to sink slowly down in his chair, and say, 'Ahh… There we are!' as if he had just taken a long journey.

"After I had the stroke, I said to myself, 'My guru must be looking the other way, because this can't be grace.' Maharaji's grace… Stroke…Maharaji's grace…Stroke. I put these two things together.

"I was so used to having Maharaji's grace. Everybody around me was thinking, 'Isn't that terrible. Richard Albert has had a stroke.' Stroke… Grace… Stroke… Grace… Stroke…

"There was a period of about two weeks when I felt a flickering of my faith. It was a very cold period. That lack of faith was terrible for me. Then I started to put the two together. The stroke made me much more silent. Silence is space for God. In the end, I called it terrible grace. I would say of God, 'He is wielding his terrible grace.'

"By thinking of it that way, there was room in my consciousness for my guru, and he became my companion. He died a long time ago, but he was an imaginary companion—a wise, compassionate, loving, humorous, rascally companion. That companion helped me deal with the stroke. Now I go to stroke conventions. The stroke has put me in touch with people who need my faith."

Albert ended his remarks at this point. I felt myself deeply moved by his story. Here was a man whose devotion to his guru had brought him to a high state of consciousness. Yet, for years now, he had been on his own, without his guru. He had suffered a stroke, gone through a crisis of faith, and found renewed purpose in a humble form of service. In his period of deepest doubt, he had continued to examine and question his experiences. This persistent self-scrutiny allowed him to see the higher purpose behind his experience, and find his way back to faith.

A number of questions from the audience followed. A young man asked if it was necessary to have a guru. "There are only so many gurus," he observed. "How can there be enough to go around?" The question struck me as loaded with assumptions. Perhaps there were more gurus in the world than the questioner imagined. Some gurus might be able to serve large numbers of people. Then again, how many genuine spiritual seekers were there in the world? Certainly not everyone's destiny was to find a spiritual path in this lifetime.

Richard Albert was diplomatic on this issue—overly diplomatic, in my opinion. "The guru is only one path," he replied, "and there are so many paths." At the same time, he admitted that he was saying this with trepidation. I could understand that he did not wish to imply that it was necessary to find a guru, in order to avoid offending those who had not found one, yet in this he seemed to avoid expressing his true opinion.

League doctrine, of course, stated that one needed the guidance of a Living Master. I was therefore skeptical of Albert's response to the questioner. As a League member, I believed that any true spiritual path had to have three essential components—the company of a Living Master, the initiations, and the spiritual exercises. Even if the League was only one path among many, even if there were other paths with these same components, it was still necessary to find such a path. Even as I was thinking these thoughts, I was aware of my own feeling of superiority to the questioner because, as an initiate of the League, I had found such a path, and he had not. Moreover, even Richard Albert no longer had a Living Master, so didn't that put me in a superior position to him, as well?

I wanted to ask Albert whether he felt it was necessary to have a living guru. Clearly, he still felt an attachment to his own guru who had passed on many years ago. Could an attachment to a departed Master take the place of a Living Master? I also wanted to ask him if he was now the guru himself, but that would have been a tactless question. Then I put the two questions together, just as Richard Albert had put together "Grace" and "Stroke." I thought of an answer. If Richard Albert were now the guru himself, he would have no need of a Living Master!

After the talk, I loitered in the reception area. There was an expensive buffet set against the back wall. They wheeled Richard Albert in and placed him in the center of the room. Only a few stood waiting to talk to him. When my turn finally came, I approached him, gently took hold of his left hand, and looked into his eyes. It was like looking into the deepest well of Soul, a vortex of pure love. His gaze held my eyes in locked embrace. I couldn't break that gaze or avert my eyes. It would have been like turning down a beautiful woman's invitation to dance. The smile on Albert's face broadened, and he sighed deeply. The rhythm of his breath was like that of a Hindu deity, creating upon exhalation, destroying upon inhalation, and re-creating with each new intake of breath. His smile was that of a god.

I was now convinced that, whether he chose to acknowledge it or not, Richard Albert was his guru's successor. Like his stroke, the guru's grace had been bestowed upon him an abrupt and incomprehensible manner. I thought of the puzzlement, the bewilderment that he had expressed about having found his spiritual path. No matter how much he might wonder at the fact, this state of consciousness had been bestowed upon him. He was the guru, despite himself, despite any idea he may ever have had about himself.

"The ego thinks it makes choices, but it does not," Richard Albert had said, answering an earlier question from the audience. "The choices are made for us by a higher Power, or a higher part of our selves." Whether he had made a choice, or simply accepted a fate that was laid out for him, he was now the bearer of the same love his guru had bestowed upon him. He was the prisoner of that love, the bestower of that love. This was his *sadhana*, his spiritual path.

After we had gazed into each other's eyes for too short an eternity, he asked me about my own spiritual path. I told him about the League.

"I know of it," he said, in a disparaging tone, suddenly becoming quite human again. "I, myself, have never followed any single path. Nevertheless, the League seems to have provided you with a beginning."

I shrugged off Richard Albert's condescending comment about the League, and clung to the hope offered by League doctrine, that liberation was not possible without the guidance of a Living Master. The sneaking suspicion began to dawn on me, however, that this was a limited viewpoint. Hadn't Lynne Silva said that many on the Path were in training to become spiritual Masters? If this was true, didn't it ultimately entail freeing oneself of all tutelage, and becoming one's own Master, as Richard Albert had done? It was impossible to deny that Albert had achieved a rare state of consciousness. He was immersed in love in a way I couldn't fathom. How could I believe that the League represented the ultimate path, when this individual was living testament that there were other, uncharted ways to a higher consciousness?

Chapter 7

Guidance and Acceptance

"Consciousness can be defined as that awareness in man which is independent of mental activity."
—Andreas Leo, *The Face of the Eternal, Book Two,* 62

During this period, I had gotten involved with another young woman. I met her in the company of some friends at a restaurant in a downtown hotel. She was at the other end of the table, looking at me with a mischievous smile. At the conclusion of the meal, she sat down next to me and we immediately started talking and laughing together in the most natural manner. Her name was Monica, and her laughter immediately made me aware that I was attracted to her. Within an hour, we were sitting on the hotel balcony together, my arm resting on top of the seat behind her. When she laughed, she threw her head back until her hair touched my arm, and I felt the sudden thrill of potential intimacy.

We went out numerous times, and she clearly enjoyed the flirtation. One evening, we went to an outdoor café together. We were having a fine conversation, punctuated by much laughter. She made a clever remark, which I picked up on. "Oh, you're really quick," she said.

"Yes, I'm quick," I replied, with an air of self-satisfaction. She broke into hysterical laughter, and I laughed with her. "I don't even know what I'm laughing about," I said.

"We won't get into that yet!" She laughed even harder. Now the double meaning had sunk in. She was clearly flirting with me, making sexual innuendoes. Her words implied that she was contemplating a closer relationship with me. My hopes soared.

That night, we said goodbye on the sidewalk outside a restaurant after dinner. I felt the moment had come for a kiss. I stood there modestly, and let her give me a peck on the cheek. Then she ran across the street with a wave of her hand and a coquettish shrug of her shoulders. The following evening we said goodbye at the door of her apartment, and I got merely a sisterly hug. Suddenly, it just seemed wrong. She was clearly putting me off.

The next time I talked to her on the phone, it was like a negotiating session. Would she come over to my place? Would she call if she were going to come? Would she call if she weren't going to come? I didn't want to sit around waiting for her all evening. She had the last word, however, and I lingered in the apartment to hear from her. I really didn't expect her to call at all, but she did, around the middle of the evening. She wanted to go out on the town. "I was planning to see someone else, actually," I said.

"Can I go along?" she wanted to know. It was plain that her main reason for seeing me wasn't my company. She just wanted an excuse to go out. That was the last straw for me. "I guess I'm just in a bad mood," I explained weakly.

She immediately caught on. "You mean you don't want ME to come along. Fine. When you're in a good mood, call me," she said, and hung up.

I was convinced that Monica was not interested in me except as a superficial friend. Otherwise, she would have wanted to see me whether I was in a "good mood" or not. I prepared to go out alone, but before I could leave, she suddenly appeared at my door. She was disheveled and upset, and told me that someone had just made unwanted advances to her on her way over. I was unmoved by her story. After offering some polite condolence, I confronted her about our relationship.

"I'm not your type," she declared. "I just want to be friends."

"Well, I want something more."

"Why can't you just ACCEPT the way things are?" she asked. "I think you're mean for not wanting to continue our friendship."

"And I think you're mean for leading me on."

"I realize I did. I'm sorry about that. I apologize for giving you the wrong impression, but you wouldn't be happy with me. I'm just trying to protect you from being disappointed."

"I'm already disappointed, so you're not protecting me from anything," I replied. "I think you're the one who is trying to protect yourself. You're the one who's afraid. You're afraid of developing feelings for someone who's different from what you imagine for yourself."

She suddenly turned very cold. "I could never have been serious about you," she said, "because I would have made my mind up about it a long time ago."

"What do you mean by that?" I asked.

"Whenever I meet a man that's 'right,' we just kiss right away, and it takes off from there. Just the fact that we're having this conversation right now means there's no hope for us. I would never have a long conversation like this with someone I was serious about."

"What's wrong with having a conversation?" I objected.

"You don't understand. Since I've been here, I've already slept with two other men."

I was shocked, but I tried not to show it.

"I sleep with men," she added, shrugging her shoulders.

"If you have a lover, why aren't you with him right now?"

"Why should I always be with him?" she replied.

"I don't get it," I told her. "What's so important about your relationship with me? Why are you even here? If you're so serious about this other guy, then you should be with him. What's so special about this guy, anyway? Why did you choose him?"

"My heart told me to choose him," she said.

"I don't think your 'heart' had anything to do with it," I answered.

When she was gone, I felt that I'd been a complete fool to assume that she was living as chaste a life as I was. At the same time, it was naïve of her to think that after leading me on the way she did, I would still want to be "friends" with her. Couldn't she see that that was the ultimate slap in the face for a man? She must have been seeing me as much as she had been seeing her lover. When it came to choosing between us, however, it was no contest. She chose the sexual relationship. She chose what gave her the greatest pleasure. Did she really use her "heart" in choosing a partner? If so, what did I use? I had a heart, too, didn't I? Wasn't I attracted by much more than her outer appearance? Didn't I feel a connection like electricity that flowed between us? I assumed that she felt the same thing, but maybe she didn't.

Maybe she felt that connection with men all the time. Maybe it was a completely ordinary experience for her, and a rare one only for me. Maybe the difference between us was simply in the degree of access that we had to that kind of experience. She was seeing from the viewpoint of someone who never had to be without intimacy. She could have sex whenever she wanted. She was probably propositioned multiple times a day. Why shouldn't she take advantage of that?

It occurred to me that life was like a game of cards. We had to play the hand we were dealt. Some people had strong hands, others weak ones. It was as simple as that. Some people lived lives full of intimacy, while others didn't. Some ran around having sex all the time, while others lived dry intellectual—or simply materialistic—lives. Intimacy was a commodity, an unequally distributed form of wealth. All the time I had been going around like some kind of reformer with the idea that life should be fair, that people should be equal, that everyone was entitled to as much intimacy, sex, or love as everyone else. Life didn't work that way, however. My idea that it should was absurd!

The trouble with me was that I wanted to play the game of love, but didn't understand how it worked. I was sitting at the table with a poor hand and no chips, resenting the fact that it was a game at all. I was protesting that it was not fair, and trying to change the rules so that the player with the losing hand would win! The world wasn't going to change its rules for me, however. I had to adapt to the world.

This whole thing wasn't about Monica, or even about women in general. It was about the whole world to which I couldn't adapt, yet which I couldn't change. I shuddered to think of the clumsy way I had courted Monica. I hadn't really wanted her as much as I simply wanted to be like other people, and to have what they had.

"Why can't you simply ACCEPT that I'm not attracted to you?" she had said.

Acceptance—yes. That was the key. I had to accept life as it was. I had to accept the world as it was. I had to accept that Monica had sex the way I had a glass of beer. It wasn't my place to speculate about her motivation, lifestyle, or the state of her heart. I had no one to blame for my pain but myself. The real pain wasn't in being denied sex or intimacy. It was the pain of being a fool, of living in a fantasy world, of insisting on seeing women for something other than what they were. They were just people, after all, living with their own assumptions about themselves, the world, and other people—most probably just as false as mine!

Shortly after this, I received a rare call from a League representative inviting me to give a brief talk at an upcoming gathering in a neighboring town. The subject was "Relying on Guidance in One's Daily Life." I agreed to come, and set my mind on preparing a talk. The problem was that I had nothing to say on the subject of Guidance. In fact, I knew nothing about Guidance. All I knew was that a voice within me was telling me that I had to accept my limitations. That was the only thing I wanted to talk about. I sat down, quickly wrote down my thoughts, and afterwards felt a great sense of accomplishment.

Another local League member named Emily Cole called. She was also planning to go to the meeting, and asked if I could give her a ride. Since my car was in the shop, I suggested that we take a bus together, and she agreed. Emily was a young woman who worked as a supervising nurse in Belle Harbor's largest hospital. She had straight brown hair, a forehead etched with delicate lines, and an authoritative air about her. After transferring at the central station, the local bus route ran through a series of small neighborhoods whose streets curved back and forth in serpentine fashion. At each intersection, the bus took a new change of direction. Eventually, we lost any sense of where we were headed. We got off at the next stop, crossed the street, and waited for a taxi. Emily was visibly agitated by the delay, and suggested I had been negligent in not getting the proper directions. I watched her take a few deep breaths and close her eyes. There was a brief fluttering of her eyelashes, indicating that she was doing some type of contemplation. Finally, a taxi came, and she calmed down.

We arrived at the meeting just in time. The League representative greeted us at the door. Most of the League members were already seated in the lecture room when we entered. Their faces were largely unfamiliar to me. The League representative introduced me and invited me to step before the group. I had the strange sensation of standing at the bow of a ship, aware only of what was directly before me. I thanked the group for inviting me to be a guest speaker, and told them how glad I was to be able to attend. Then I launched into my address:

"We have been speaking about Guidance, but I want to speak about Acceptance: accepting the world as it is, other people as they are, and ourselves as we are.

"I don't believe that we have the power to change these fundamental things. We don't have the power to change the world. We don't have the power to change other people. We don't even have the power to change ourselves in any fundamental sense. We can only change our thinking, our viewpoint, our attitude, the way we react to life. If we're in a negative state of mind, it may be the result of our reaction to the world, to other people, to something in ourselves or to our circumstances. All these things, however, are simply symptoms of a lack of Acceptance. THIS we can change!

"We come into the world with certain attributes—strong in some areas, weak in others. We have certain tools to work with in this life, with certain limitations built into them, and THAT is what we cannot change. Life is like a game of cards. We have to play the hand we're dealt. You may think, 'How cruel, how unjust. I wish that I had a better hand. I wish the rules were different. I wish that every person at the table had the same hand, or an equal hand!' It doesn't work that way, however.

"If we're on a spiritual path, we will be tested in our acceptance of this precisely where we are most vulnerable. There is always something that we feel is so important we can't do without it—something we want, something we want to keep, something or some way we want to be—and that's probably exactly what will be taken away or denied us. The purpose, however, is only to build up our spiritual strength.

"We must become very meek and very humble—as meek and humble as the smallest, most insignificant thing in the universe. Only when we accept our limitations, will we paradoxically gain greater freedom, power, and responsibility.

"One can find people living in this world at every conceivable level of awareness. People all have the equality of being human beings, yet there is literally no way to know another person's state of consciousness. You may look into the face of your neighbor, and you may see the face of God mirrored in their face, while they may look into your face, and see just a face—or even the face of their enemy!

"You may think, 'How cruel, that there is no mutual understanding. How unjust, that people are operating on such different assumptions.' It is NOT cruel, however, nor is it unjust, for to each according to their state of consciousness!

"Guidance, I believe, cannot operate without Acceptance. Once you have found Acceptance, it doesn't MATTER whether you go left or right, up or down, or forwards or backwards. The world is simply open to you, and you are open to the world. THEN—only then—you are ready to be guided.

"Acceptance is the fundamental problem that all of us must face. We have to learn, individually and collectively, to accept what is here and now. We need to accept the people living around us, and accept ourselves, together with our limitations, because if we don't, we will not know ourselves. We will not know our place in the universe. To know oneself is an individual's first spiritual duty! If we don't know ourselves, we'll go on living in a dream world from here to eternity, and no amount of asking, praying, or relying on Guidance will change that!"

As I delivered my talk, I looked into the faces of those present. Most were attentive, and some even appeared moved by my words. After the meeting, several of the people went out of their way to congratulate me on my remarks. A young woman spoke of the considerable distance she had to travel to be there that evening. "Now I realize why I made the journey," she said. "Your talk was exactly what I needed to hear." Her face was shining as she spoke. On the way back with Emily, I brought up the subject of my talk in a rather self-satisfied manner. When I mentioned the idea of Acceptance again, she jumped all over me, however.

"I don't think you got the point," she said. "The subject of the meeting was 'Receiving Guidance in One's Daily Life.' It had nothing to do with Acceptance. For instance, when we were waiting for the taxi earlier today, I asked inwardly for a taxi to come. If I want to get from point A to point B, I always ask in this way. That's an example of Guidance."

"That's ridiculous," I said, rather harshly. "Even if you didn't ask, what makes you think the taxi wouldn't have come anyway?"

"That's just a rationalization," she said.

"Personally," I replied, "if I want to take a cab from point A to point B, I simply do all the practical things to put myself in the position to arrive at my destination on time. I go to the taxi stop with plenty of time to spare. Then I just wait, and have faith that I'll get where I want to go. In most cases, the taxi comes. If it doesn't come on time, then I'm late. I accept that, and make the best I can out of the situation."

"Typical male ego," she huffed. "You men are too proud to ask for help. You'll only do so when you've exhausted every other resource."

"I don't know what male ego has to do with it," I replied in an irritated fashion. "Are you trying to say that women have some kind of monopoly on spirituality? Of course I wait until I've have exhausted every other resource. As far as I'm concerned, that's just a matter of common sense. Why should I ask for guidance when what's going to happen is going to happen anyway? As far as I can see, asking for every little thing only causes one to go up and down in one's expectations. If you don't expect anything in the first place, then whatever you get is gravy!"

"But you're supposed to be detached from the outcome," she replied.

"Well, if you're supposed to be detached from the outcome, why ask at all?"

"It's practice for the 'big' things," she said, rather lamely, I thought.

"If I ask to get from point A to point B, and the cab comes—fine," I concluded. "But maybe the next time it won't. If I built my faith on such a foundation, it would surely crumble."

"Your experiences are in accordance with the thoughts you form," she replied. "If you don't believe that you can find what you're seeking, you probably won't. No wonder you haven't had any success in your life!"

That remark cut deeply. "If you have to pray every time some little thing goes wrong," I shot back, "you're showing that you are dissatisfied with your present situation. How, then, are you an example to anyone?"

At this point, the argument settled into a tense standoff. I was bitter. No sooner had I found a new attitude of acceptance toward life, than my viewpoint was assailed as a false one. Emily's presence now irritated me profoundly, and we said little to one another for the rest of the trip. As I reflected on our argument, I felt that she had struck a nerve. When I said that if I built my faith on her notion of Guidance it would crumble, I had admitted that my faith was weak and would not survive a test. Was I crippling myself by my lack of faith? Was my realization about the importance of Acceptance just another illusion?

I had an opportunity to get some answers to my questions at another League event only a few weeks later. The occasion was a talk by Lee Nakamura. Lee was the author of two books, *Meetings with the Masters* and *The Searcher*, which had gained him considerable prominence among members of the League. "What distinguishes people who listen to their inner guidance from those who just think they do?" he began by asking. "The answer has to do with energy and stability. If you're going to base your life on something important, base it on something that's not going to change. Scientists speculate that if an atom were taken apart, we would find no matter at all—just energy. Let's say that God is powering this energy. Whenever we make a decision, it's either taking us toward the source of this energy or away from it."

After his talk, I sat down to dinner with Lee and a number of other League members. "How can people tell if their guidance comes from a genuine spiritual source?" I wanted to know.

"Generally, you look at what they are doing," Lee replied. "What are their actions? Are they helping people or not? If people are really in touch with life, they'll be happier and give more love to others. The very essence of this energy wave I talked about is love. What can be more loving than that which is keeping us alive? To know if you're in balance or not, ask yourself if what you're doing is helping you and other people gain some kind of love, in a survival sense. Is it making your life better? Are you contributing?

"When people complain, you don't even need to listen to their words. Just look at what they're doing. Look at the way in which their energy is flowing." He laughed. "I think sometimes we get fooled by the content or the context of what people are saying, rather than looking at what they're actually doing. In the case of people who are in a negative state of mind, you know there's something wrong with them, but there's a weird logic to what they're saying. It actually sounds good. If you get away from trying to understand their train of thought, however, and just look at their actions, you'll see which way the energy is going. Are they robbing you of your energy, or is what they're saying making you feel better or more empowered?"

"In your talk, you also connected the principle of decision-making with stability," I remarked. "I felt that was quite an important point. I always see two sides to everything, so I have a hard time making decisions. Every time I'm faced with this crisis of decision-making, I feel very unstable, like I'm walking the razor's edge. You said that one decision will take a person toward God and the other will take one away from IT. That's exactly what makes the decision so hard for me. If I ask other people for advice about my predicament, they tell me, 'It doesn't matter what your decision is. Just go ahead, make the decision, and you can always revise it.' Of course, they don't have to live with the consequences."

"The trick in making decisions," Lee replied, "is that, in every situation, you have to make a choice of which action is in line with the Force and which is not. The problem is how good you are at identifying this. This involves skill. Now, my take on the spiritual exercises is that the more time you spend practicing getting in touch with Spirit when you do your contemplation, the easier it is to recognize it in daily life.

"I have this ongoing conversation," he continued. "I imagine the Living Master, and ask him what I should do—this or that? I've found that I have to break it down to yes or no answers. I'll either see the Inner Master or hear his voice. Sometimes I just see him either nodding or shaking his head. It's a fifty-fifty chance, and I'm not always right. So I go with the choice I think he's indicating, and wait to see how it plays out. If the decision I've made benefits not just me but everyone else, I know. Then I just have to remember the next time another situation comes up what it felt like when I asked the Inner Master: 'Yes or no?'"

"So this technique has a lot to do with memory."

"Yes. It entails remembering what it feels like when that inner voice speaks to you. If you fail to pay attention and remember, then you just keep going through the same thing over again, or worse, you reduce the League to superstition by thinking that the Inner Master will take care of it. In that case, you've relegated the Inner Master to the role of a caretaker, continually giving you the same information. That's when people start saying things like: 'The last time, the Inner Master told me to use this fork instead of that fork.' From then on, instead of checking with your inner guidance, you just use the same fork."

What Lee was saying reminded me of my objection to Emily's

method of asking for guidance. I had been wary of relying on such a technique purely out of habit. Richard Albert had mentioned how he used to look for a parking space, and in finding one, felt that his guru was watching over him. His comment had been that this was a very limited view of grace.

"I think what happens in a lot of religions," Lee added, "is that people start believing in things without really knowing. Only the Soul body has the ability to know and recognize love. All the other bodies are machines. The reason we can recognize love through our emotions, our physical body, or our minds, is because Soul is operating through that body. For instance, if I ask the Inner Master for an answer, and receive one, it can only be perceived by Soul, via the mind. If you just use your mental body to pick up an answer, it relies on logic, and logic is always based on past experience. As soon as the mind gets hit with a situation that it has never encountered, it falls on what it knew before. The dogma that we find in many religions simply represents a shared past experience for that body of believers.

"The trick is to recognize when your decisions are coming from the Inner Master, and when they are not. Again, like any other skill, the more experience you have recognizing when you're making decisions that are connected with the Force, the better you get. We try to encourage people to use this technique in the smallest details. Most of the time people only turn to God when they have a big decision to make. Our theory is, unless you practice all the time on the little things, how are you going to be able to rely on the Inner Master for the big decisions in life?"

I was reminded again of my argument with Emily. "Asking for the little things is practice for the big things," she had said. A moment ago, I thought Lee had come down on my side of this debate. Now he appeared to side with Emily. I was confused.

"To ask inwardly for help with every little thing has just not been my style," I confessed to him.

"I tend to ask inwardly all the time," Lee replied. "Someone told me that they don't like to ask the Inner Master directions because they're afraid they're going to wear it out. But how can you wear it out?" he chuckled. "I don't look at the Living Master as an individual. I conjure up the image of him, but I view him more as a thing that connects me to the Force. So no matter where I am, I'm always asking this thing: 'What is it that you want me to do?'"

"I think my hang-up is that if I were to ask for something specific, and then it didn't happen, I feel that my faith in the process would be in jeopardy," I explained.

"Well, I don't necessarily ask for anything specific. I always ask 'What do you want?' instead of asking for what I want for myself. I do it even when I eat. Now it's like a running conversation. 'What should I eat now? When do you want me to stop?' Sometimes I'll just get an impulse that says, 'That's enough.' At other times, I'll say, 'I don't know if this is really coming from my inner guidance or not. I'll just eat some more and see what happens.' If I get sick, I think back and say to myself: 'OK. The next time I hear that voice or have that kind of feeling, I'm going to pay attention.'"

I realized that Lee was making an important distinction. When he asked inwardly, he asked Spirit for what IT wanted, not for what HE wanted. This went to the heart of my skepticism about asking for guidance. It wasn't a question of lack of faith, nor of a dichotomy between guidance and acceptance. It had to do with the manner or technique with which one communicated with the Inner Master. I had felt all along that in asking that my personal requests be fulfilled, my faith was misplaced. This was what I objected to in Emily's attitude. In asking for help in getting from point A to point B, she was asking for what *she* wanted. This was putting faith to an unreasonable test. Lee's technique, however, did not rely on asking that one's personal wishes be answered. It consisted only of engaging in an inner conversation.

"I'm always asking, always in dialogue," Lee was saying. "I figure the Inner Master is my teacher, and he's trying to lead me to self-mastery. The more I can follow the minute details of what he's trying to teach me, the quicker I'm going to learn it. What's the point of just scheduling the lessons of life for a certain time, or taking a long break from learning anything? If life is teaching you all the time, you might as well be receptive all the time. I figure when I'm always asking, I'm not going to wear out my inner guidance. To me, that is the essence of being a co-worker with God. It's a matter of asking 'What do you want me to do next?' You're allowing yourself to be used by Life itself. Most of the time I have no idea why I'm doing what I'm doing, but I've learned that when I'm in harmony with the Force, good things tend to happen.

"Big decisions are made up of a million little ones. The more correct little decisions you make will determine how successful you are at making big ones. That's why I tend to ask for guidance regarding the minutiae of life, because when you put them all together, that's your life! You can master the decision-making process by breaking down big decisions into little ones."

"The problem is, when I'm faced with decisions, I feel that the choices have the same weight," I said.

"To the mind, they will," Lee responded. "The mind wants to eliminate all the wrong answers. Every time it makes a mistake, it sends you the message that you blew it and that you're a horrible person. Instead, you have to just realize that it was not the correct decision, and try something else. I think that's really what the Masters are trying to get us to do—to get us to look at our mistakes without beating ourselves up for making the wrong decisions.

"When I first began to study the Science of the Soul," Lee added, "I was too afraid of making wrong decisions. It took me years to begin to get over this self-judgment and fear of making mistakes. The more I get over that, the more clearly I think I hear what the Inner Master is saying to me. When people make a wrong decision, it's usually because of their 'want' or 'should' rather than because of what 'is.' I think the test of real Mastership is how to see the 'is,' rather than our 'want' and 'should.' The 'wants' always distort the choice. You have to be objective to see the answers, and the only way to learn that is by experience."

In the wake of my conversation with Lee, I reflected that Guidance and Acceptance were like two sides of a dialogue that continually took place within us. Our concern with Guidance reflected our feelings of desire and obligation, our "want" and "should." Our concern with Acceptance was our way of coping with frustration, with having our "want" and "should" denied. Beyond this dialogue, however, was a higher form of both Guidance and Acceptance, which consisted of engaging in a direct communication with the Force. In that interchange, there was no difference between Guidance and Acceptance. The ego was like a middleman who broke down transactions into benefits and costs. Once we ceased to bargain with the Force, however, the middleman was out of a job, and we were in a position to receive directly. No matter whether we got from A to B on a given day, no matter whether we had a winning hand or a losing one in the game of love, we were always in dialogue with the Force, and always receiving from It.

CHAPTER 8

THE LAST WALL

"Man can't change anything in his life, although he thinks he can. The sooner he learns that his powers are minuscule, the sooner he will be directed toward God. Then he will meet with the Living Master, who will assist him in reaching the heavenly realms."
–Andreas Leo, *The Face of the Eternal, Book One,* 23

WITH MY MOTHER'S return from her vacation, I found an apartment of my own, but this put a renewed strain on my finances. Eventually, I made a few attempts to look for another part-time job in order to supplement my income. It was with this purpose in mind that I paid a visit to the local community college. The job inquiry was fruitless, however. It was a cheerless gray day, and I was depressed. As I walked back to my car in the parking lot, I noticed the groundskeeper, Isiah Askew, his left hand sticking out of the window of his truck, waving at everyone and no one.

I had first laid eyes on Isiah a number of years before, when I had taught at this same community college. I used to come out of the Student Center building after my classes were over, heading for the parking lot, and he would be there, puttering around the shrubbery or driving around in his red truck, waving to all the students, and exclaiming in his high-pitched voice, "Amen! Amen! How are you?

How are you doing? Wonderful weather, isn't it? Lord, what a beautiful day!" It didn't matter if the sky was gloomy and overcast, the wind chill was below zero, or that no one paid attention to him. He kept waving and chirping, "Amen! Amen!" I couldn't understand how anyone could be so cheerful. I thought the man must be crazy.

This time I stopped. He was wearing custom fitted overalls with the words "Goodwill Ambassador" stitched into the right breast. I greeted him, grasping his gloved hand, and peered into his eyes. They were narrow and squinty, yet they sparkled with the luminosity of stars. I felt a twinge of envy and self-consciousness that he could be so happy. He asked me what I was doing, and I told him I had been inquiring about an extra job, and was about to go home.

"Already?" he asked. "It's just the middle of the day!"

"Well, I'm going home for lunch, and I'll look some more in the afternoon." I lied. The truth was, I couldn't stomach any more job-hunting that day. For the moment, at any rate, I was much more interested in talking to him. I asked if we could get together, and he told me, sure, as long as I set it up with his boss. I promptly did so, and a few days later, I met him in the lunchroom of the Plant Operations building. He was full of questions about my line of work, where my office was, and so forth. I explained to him that I shared an office with a number of other lecturers, and that I really didn't have the prospect of a full-time job.

"Really?" he made an incredulous face. "A nice handsome man like you can't get a real job?" He could hardly believe it.

When I tried to turn the direction of the conversation toward him, he shifted uneasily in his chair. "It's seven minutes after noon," he said. I could tell that referring to the time was his way of telling me that he didn't want to talk about himself. "I always look at the time when someone wants to go into my details," he explained.

"Well in that case, I've got some things that I wrote down," I said, pulling out a sheet of paper. "Maybe we can just discuss some of them. They're reminders of certain principles I'm trying to practice. The first one is: *Love the situation you're in.*"

"Well," he said, responding eagerly to the change in my approach, "love is something that people will not and cannot understand. Love is more than talking. It's action and doing what is called for. Like when you met me and we started talking, that brought you more understanding of what I stand for. You felt that love in so many ways you didn't even understand it."

"I think I know what you're saying," I replied. "I saw you two or three years ago, when I was teaching here, but I never said anything to you. The other day, however, I saw you again. This time, I thought, 'He looks so happy. There's got to be something to it. This time, I'm not going to just go my way. I'm going to stop and talk to him.' If I understand you correctly, you're saying that love is action. In my case, that action consisted of stopping to talk to you."

"That's it. When an individual stops to talk to you, you almost know where that person stands. A person who is intentioned with the right kind of love is there to help you. When you have that love, you're going to share that love."

"When you stop to talk to people, you find out about them," I added. "I didn't know what you were about because I didn't talk to you. You could have been crazy, for all I knew."

"Thank you," he replied. "You know that many people view love as crazy because they don't understand. When you have it, no one can take it from you. They may try to get ahead of you or put boundaries on you, but that love is still going to be stronger than ever. What you have to do is get the right motive. That's always been in my life, during all of my thirty-five years of service here. I've tried to help, to encourage, and to do my very best. I thank the Lord for the power he gave to me. I'm not educated like lots of people are, but I always tell people, 'It's not what you have, it's what you do by what you have.' There's a lot of educated fools."

"I have a Ph.D. and other degrees, but they haven't gotten me anywhere," I confessed.

"OK. You know why? It's because you dwell on what you have. You've got to dwell on what you don't have. All those degrees that you have, you look back at them. You're attached to them. But if you look to what you don't have, it will eventually come your way."

"I've got another thing I've written here," I replied, "and it says exactly the same thing that you just said: *Be grateful not for what you have, but for what you don't have.*"

"That's the answer right there."

"That's a revolutionary idea, Isiah. I'd say most people don't think that way, though."

"Because they dwell on what they have, and not on what they don't have. That's the reason why many people today don't have respect for anyone but themselves. They feel that they are better than you or me."

"In other words, everyone is thinking: 'I am what I have.'"

"Right," Isiah proclaimed. "And that's the worst thing that anyone can meditate on."

"I agree with you." I said. "All these degrees are like a kind of brainwashing. They make people think that they have this, or they are that. You get a degree next to your name and you go around saying, 'I am so and so. Here's my degree. That's me!'"

"Right," Isiah insisted. "That's me, and I'm better than you are! Look at what I got on the wall. Look at that doctorate degree! That's where the sadness comes in, my brother."

"Like you said, the sadness comes when people dwell on what they have. What we don't have is about a million times greater than what we have, because what we have is such a tiny portion of what can be," I suggested.

"That's right," Isiah agreed. "We have something, but it's more than you can even explain. We have something when we know how to respect and be respected. That's what education can't understand. You have to think on that. If I got all this here and don't respect you, I'm nothing. I am somebody only when I respect you. I can't meditate on what I have. I've got to meditate on what I don't have. When I meditate on what I don't have, I can't even explain it sometimes, myself. When my sister or my brother comes up to me, asking for advice, I don't speak just to be speaking. I try to speak by the power of God. And that's something that neither you nor I can understand."

"I think I get it," I said. "What we have is only what we can understand about ourselves. What we don't have is everything that we don't understand about ourselves, which is far greater."

"You got it. People don't understand this man here," he said, referring to himself. "'How can he speak so well? How can he speak the way he speaks, and I got all this on the wall, and he don't have nothing on the wall?' A man can only give so much. Through the spirit of God, however, he can give it all. That's why it's not about what you have. It's about what you don't have. That's why people don't understand this man here, and never will."

"I agree," I replied. "You're so much more than your education. You're a man, just like me. How are you in any way less than I am? It's impossible. All men are created equal, right?"

"Every man is created equal by the power of God. But in the eyes of education, I'm not created equal, because I don't have what that other person has."

"That's right," I admitted. "But no matter who we are, what we don't have is so much more than what we have. It makes much more sense to be grateful for that. Why dwell on what you've achieved, or what you are right now? Look ahead, to what you can be."

I glanced at my list to see if any other quotes might spark Isiah's interest. "This one says: *When one door closes, another door opens.*"

"Surely," Isiah nodded his head. "When one door closes in your mind, there's another door that's gonna come open if you're able to wait on it. It may not come when you want it, but it'll come just at the right time. If you can't be yourself, you'll never know what future lies before you. You have to come to the knowledge of what God has given you, and no man can take that away. Don't be what you have. Be what you don't have. When you're being what you don't have, it may not be what you went to school for, but sometimes it may be a lot better than what you went to school for."

"That's what I'm thinking," I replied. "If I stuck to the things I went to school for, ten years down the road I might not like my life at all."

"Right," Isiah agreed. "You might be in the psychiatric home right here down the road, with all your degrees. It's the mercy of God, however, showing you through your tests and your trials that there's always a blessing near. There's always a blessing nearer than you think."

"Here's another one," I said: "*Don't waste time trying to change reality.*"

"That's what I'm saying right at this moment," Isiah responded. "Changing reality is changing yourself. You can try to change by trying to please other people around you, but you won't be able to do it to save your neck. People may look at you with a smile. They may be smiling at your face, but they don't always understand you. You have to stand up and focus on what you are. Forget about what you have, and focus on what you don't have."

"OK. Here's one last one: *Accept the world the way it is. Accept people as they are. And accept yourself as you are.*"

"That's a good point. You've got to accept it all to make yourself what you are. If you accept the world as it is, other people as they are, and yourself as you are, then you ARE somebody. Focus on being yourself. That's what counts. When you're not focused on what you have, but focused on what you don't have, then your reality is coming stronger. When it comes your way, you'll receive it. You can have the whole world, and you've still got nothing. But if you focus on what you are, that's where your blessing is."

I came away from my conversation with Isiah marveling at the profundity of his attitude toward life. His phrase, 'Don't dwell on what you have; dwell on what you don't have' was still reverberating in my mind, as was his last dictum, 'Focus on what you are.' There were two distinct ideas represented by those statements: what a person HAD, and what a person WAS. Isiah's point was that a person should focus on the latter, not the former. He was talking about beingness, rather than status in society. We were conditioned to think that we were the sum of our education, and that therefore we could only do certain things or go in certain directions in life. We were conditioned to think that what we didn't have was worthless and what we did have was everything, but actually the opposite was true. What people had didn't amount to anything, and what they didn't have was everything.

I had felt unlucky for so long because of all the things I didn't have, or hadn't achieved—a decent income, savings, a place of my own, a social life, an intimate relationship, status, recognition, and accomplishments. I thought I was among the poorest of the poor. Now I began to consider my poverty as wealth. I wasn't tied down by anything. My life was full of possibilities. How many people my age could still see their lives as works in progress? There was much value in that. Isiah had never acceded to what other people thought of him. He had an entirely different vision of himself, and if you had the eyes to see, you could discern that he had grown into that vision. There was great courage and wisdom in that choice. It was like looking up at all the stars in the sky and saying, "I AM THAT!"

If I was bowled over by the force of Isiah Askew's personality, the next person I was to encounter in the course of my spiritual research was even more impressive. I became interested in Jerry Schaefer after having read his book, a small volume of reminiscences, anecdotes, and homespun wisdom that I picked up in the local authors section of a Belle Harbor bookstore. Schaefer was a former newscaster familiar to long-time residents of the area through his career as an investigative reporter on the local ABC affiliate, Channel 7. A recovering alcoholic, he presented himself as a purveyor of no-nonsense spiritual insight. I called him up to see if he would talk to me, and he agreed, proposing that we meet at a Starbucks in a nearby suburb.

I arrived at the appointed time and spent a few minutes sizing up the customers, seeing if I could guess which one was Jerry. Finally, I spotted him just entering the establishment. He greeted me briskly and ordered a chocolate chip cookie from the counter, while I carried a couple of plush chairs into the far corner of the place to ensure a maximum amount of privacy.

I told him about the kind of writing I was trying to do. "The most important thing is to be aggressive," he responded. "Just let it hang out there. Put your issues into it. Write the things that you feel, and see what happens. If it's aggressively done, that means there's passion in it."

"Thanks, I appreciate that," I replied. The word "aggressive" had a positive connotation for me, especially in relation to spirituality. "A lot of qualities go into spirituality, but one thing it takes is a certain degree of courage," I added.

"A great deal of courage, actually," Jerry responded. "The scariest thing we look at in our lives is ourselves. When you look into the mirror and something has happened—something that may be considered something terrible—it takes courage to say, 'OK. I'll hang tight. I'll feel this feeling that I've buried previously, with faith that I'm going to come out on the other side feeling much better about myself.' That's really the goal of spirituality—to be at peace with oneself. I look at things now, when so-called 'bad' things happen to me in my life, and I think of them as having no other reason to happen other than for my good."

"That's a great attitude," I commented, "but it's surprising how elusive such an attitude can be, no matter how serious we are about living the spiritual life."

"Why," he asked rhetorically, "do I choose to believe that when negative things happen, they're happening for my good? When positive things are happening I recognize them as good things. I don't have to worry about them. They're not stealing anything from me. But when bad things happen to me—even something as simple as somebody cutting me off on the road—if I believe that good things will happen as a result of what is occurring to me right now, I stop myself from feeling self-pity. If I feel sorry for myself, the next step is that I get angry—'Why me, damn it?' Then, all of a sudden, I'm caught in the resentment trap, which leads back to anger and self-pity. I become the dog chasing its own tail. All of which steals my happiness."

"I understand what you're saying," I replied, "and I try to practice it, but still there are so many times that I find myself feeling angry."

"You know why that is, don't you? You're human."

"If that recognition were just turned on all the time…"

"Practice makes perfect," Jerry stated simply.

"Yeah," I agreed, "but there's no telling how long it's going to take some of us."

"It's going to take some people longer than others. For instance, you see this chocolate chip cookie I'm eating?" he asked. "I'm eating this because I want to. I want it because it gives me pleasure. Perception is the most important thing here. If I perceive that you're doing something to harm me, hurt my feelings, or wrong me in some way, my perception tells me that's not pleasurable. It also says, 'Get angry, get impatient, get intolerant.'

"Now, you can say to me, 'Gee, I really feel bad for you,' but you can't feel my feelings. Nobody can feel another person's feelings. If we believe that we're powerless over the people and things in this world, but that we are powerful over ourselves, then it's an easy job. All we have to do is to make the choice. Am I going to stay angry, impatient, or intolerant because of some jerk? Am I going to let him live in my life rent-free? No. I'm going to say, 'Check it, Jerry. Look in the mirror and you're going to see the problem,' because I AM the problem. You're the problem when it comes to your feelings, and I'm the problem when it comes to mine.

"For instance," he continued, "I was at the bank the other day. A woman came up to me and said, 'Hey, does that book of yours say anything about husbands?'

"I said, 'Yeah. The first sentence says, 'Look in the mirror to see the problem. It's not your husband.'

"The woman looked shocked. She said, 'What do you mean?' Then we talked a little about it. We talked about accepting responsibility for your own feelings.

"I'm eating this cookie because it gives me pleasure. If it didn't give me pleasure, I could choose not to eat it. No one forces you to have your feelings."

I had completely forgotten about his reference to the chocolate chip cookie until he unexpectedly came back to it. Jerry was saying that eating the cookie was a choice, just as our emotional responses were choices. Everything we did was the result of a choice. There was something amazing about the simplicity of this. Our responsibility didn't extend to things other than ourselves, but for our response to life it was total. In other words, we could NOT control what happened to us, but we COULD control how we felt and acted in any given situation.

"So the power of choice means working in the most positive way with whatever you've got on your plate at the moment?" I asked him.

"Precisely," he replied. "All you have is this moment. This is it. If you have breast cancer, that's it. That is what's happening today. That's what you're dealing with. If you hide it, if you don't want to tell your husband about it, if you're worried or scared about it, what you're doing is avoiding what IT is. That, in turn, will create a hundred-fold more elements of fear in your life. Fear is the most destructive force, in terms of stealing your happiness."

"I was hiking the other day," I said, "and I got into an area where there were a lot of mosquitoes, and they were biting me. And I was thinking..."

"Those little bastards..." Jerry interjected.

"Yeah," I replied. "But I was also thinking, 'What would happen if they didn't itch?'"

"Well, you wouldn't know you were being bitten. You'd ignore it."

"So what would happen to our resistance? People would allow mosquitoes to bite them, and we'd have them swarming around all over the place."

"Well, now hold on a minute," he replied. "We're bitten by a lot of bugs that don't itch. I'll tell you what's interesting in what you've said, however. You mentioned resistance. Resistance is a big problem. We are not in this universe to resist it. Resisting is trying to control a situation because of fear. If you could go through life without trying to control another person, place, or thing, and just go naturally with the flow of the universe, it would make you available to all the wonderful things the universe presents to you on a moment-to-moment basis."

When I expressed wonderment at his philosophical attitude, he responded vociferously.

"Am I peaceful all the time?" he asked. "Hell, no. I get irritated. I get angry."

"You do?" I responded. He had me believing that he was a total master of himself.

"Sure," he replied, "but then I say to myself, 'OK, Jerry, you get pissed off over this stuff. How long do you let it bother you?' The answer is, 'As long as I choose to.' The most important aspect of spirituality, for me, is the ability to choose how long I want to be angry, stay upset, or allow another person to live in my life rent-free—whether it's the guy who cuts me off on the freeway or the President of the United States."

"There were a couple of stories in your book that were just like experiences that I've had in my life," I said. "You told this one story about a guy who has everything go wrong for him, and then says, 'That's it, God? You call that a hit? Can't you do any better than that?' I had an experience just like that years ago when I was studying Arabic in Egypt. Everything had gone wrong for me there. It wasn't an easy place to be, in the first place. I had various health problems at the time. I had an operation, nearly lost a finger, broke up with my girlfriend, and managed to get on the wrong side of just about everyone I knew there."

"And were you grateful for that?" Jerry asked with an inquisitor's intensity.

I laughed. "No. At the time, I wasn't particularly grateful. I was saying, 'Why me?'"

"But when you almost lost your finger, you could have said, 'Gee. That was only my finger. That could have been my own life!' Life is how we look at it, at that moment."

"I agree, but I was a long way from being able to have that kind of outlook. At any rate, one day I was walking down the street, and came to a covered market that had a sewage gutter up above near the roof. I was just in the process of saying 'Why me?' when I got a load of raw sewage dumped right on my head."

"Perfect! And I hope you looked up and said, 'No shit!'"

"I said something that was the equivalent of 'Can't you do any better than that, God?' Except I said it in Arabic, and there was a little extra irony to that."

"That's great. When something becomes so utterly painful, one must remember that God gives us the gift of pain in order to bring about change. That's an absolute, because we're complacent people. We don't like change. We like our own little niche and our own ways of doing things. Change is scary. If you stop to think about it, however, you change because of fear, and after that, you're no longer afraid. Fear is what enables us to survive. You don't run out in traffic with a car coming at you. If you see a guy in a trench coat on a dark night and there's something in his hand, you don't go up to him and say, 'Hey, got a light?'"

"So if you're afraid, but you're doing something about it, you're OK?" I asked.

"It's OK as long as you're not running away from that fear. That's also 'doing something about it.' Instead of running away from it, run toward it. Embrace it. Stop the resistance. You'll be amazed what happens."

"The question that's in my mind," I told him, "has to do with the direction in which I'm running. Am I running toward my fear, or away from my fear? I want to do what I want to do, but am I more afraid of doing what I WANT to do, or of doing what I DON'T want to do? If I'm afraid of doing what I DON'T want to do, is that what I should be doing? It's confusing." I was thinking that the prospect of trying to conform to other people's ideas of what I should be doing with my life was in direct conflict with my deepest feelings. I didn't know, however, of which alternative I was most afraid.

"Why don't people do what they want to do?" he asked me pointedly. "Because they're afraid to. One of the great things about alcoholics is they jump into the pit of fire and then say 'Now what do I do?' For instance, when I was rebuilding my house, I reached a point where I didn't have the carpenters lined up, didn't have the plumbers lined up, and part of me was saying, 'You can't start anything until you've got everything in order.' That was the old picture, the picture that said, 'Everything's got to be perfect.' Well, I got off of that and said, 'What will be, will be.' I told the crew to go ahead and demolish the house, and they took down everything. All that was left were studs—no rooms, just studs. I knew I had nowhere to go but up. That's when I started worrying only about what was happening right here and now."

Jerry's analogy struck a chord in me. I felt that I was almost at that point in my life where there were no rooms, just studs. I was just waiting for that last wall to be demolished.

"This is important stuff," Jerry said, bringing me back to attention. "We're all born with this wonderfully healthy ego, the one that says 'Good job, Jerry. You really feel good about yourself,' or 'Thank you, God. It's great to be alive.' The moment we come into this world, that wonderfully healthy ego starts to become diseased. Those folks who give us their love and guidance—our mothers, fathers, brothers, sisters, teachers, and friends—also give us their character defects, the stuff they haven't fixed. That's the root of our disease. How many times have you heard, 'I don't want to be like my father or my mother?' It's important to create new pictures in your life—new, healthy pictures.

"Part of this problem is perfection. I refer to these as old, unhealthy pictures. Now, to get new pictures, generally what you need is some kind of jolt, a slap in the face. In my case, it was the gift of alcoholism. That was a terrific gift, because it gave me the opportunity to say, 'There are ways in this world other than black and white. I can look at things in many different ways.' What I did then was to start to form some new pictures."

I felt that Jerry had nailed my problem. Lynne Silva once told me that I had to change in order to come into harmony with what I wanted in life. The problem was identifying what I wanted, without mistaking it for what other people wanted for me. My mother, for instance, was clearly worried about my future. My sister, in turn, resented me for not earning enough to enable me to assume my "proper" responsibilities. What was my greatest fear—settling for a job that satisfied their expectations, or finding out what I really wanted to do? If Jerry's suggested course of action was to do what I wanted to do, and at the same time what I was afraid of doing, the implication was that I was afraid of what I WANTED to do. The notion that I was afraid of doing what I DIDN'T want to do was a red herring, tossed at me by my family members.

"Some people would view this idea of doing what you want to do as an escapist attitude, particularly when it comes to choosing a profession," I said, thinking of my mother's typical criticism of my impractical attitude toward life. "They would say it's not responsible."

"Well, ask them what they do for a living," Jerry replied. "Then ask them if they're happy. Ask them to define happiness."

"Don't people have to discipline themselves by doing what they don't want to do?"

"Oh, absolutely, they do, but is that why a person chooses a profession—because of discipline? In that case, they're doing a disservice to themselves and the people they work for and serve. You shouldn't choose a profession because you think that's what you're obligated to do. You should choose a profession because it's what you want to do."

I was getting a real therapy session from this man. Even if I was an adequate teacher, I knew in my bones that teaching wasn't what I really wanted to do. Why, then, was I still doing it? I had spent years working on a Ph.D. mainly because my father was a college professor, and I thought I had to follow in his footsteps. I allowed my family to exercise an entirely unacceptable amount of influence over me, by substituting their habit patterns for my own imagination and initiative. To trace back the root of the fear, to identify the precise nature of the ego disease that I had inherited from them, was not something I could do in an instant. I was aware, however, that for most of my life I had a mistaken idea about myself. I thought I was an adventurous person, when I wasn't at all. I had been meekly trying to live up to other people's expectations all the time.

"Well," Jerry replied, when I expressed these thoughts to him, "just remember that expectations, nine times out of ten, will lead to disappointment. Don't feel bad about disappointing those people, and their expectations of you. The secret is to be true to who you are. If you're not happy with your situation, the question to ask yourself is, 'Why am I doing this?' And the answer is, 'Don't.' Do what you want to do."

Jerry had taken control of the conversation from the start, and although I had tried to guide it in certain directions, he had constantly dug new channels that I hadn't anticipated. That was all right, though. In a way, it felt good not to be in control. That was Jerry's whole point, really. It wasn't possible to be in control of life, only in control of one's response to life. For years, I had thought that everything in my life had to change, but that wasn't necessarily true. Maybe I just needed a change of attitude.

I came away from my conversations with both Isiah Askew and Jerry Schaefer awed by their powerful sense of certainty. They were among the most secure, self-assured individuals I had ever met, yet unlike Richard Albert they hadn't traveled to India, found a guru, or even joined a spiritual group. All the time I had spent in the League had not given me that sense of confidence. The whole notion that the League was some sort of elite spiritual group seemed laughable to me now. It had insulated me, rather than exposed me to the reality of life. I felt that my time of thinking about spiritual issues in theoretical terms was ending, and the time for acting was at hand.

PART THREE

The Great Social Lie

"The great social lie is that we must be the same as others in the human race. Once the spiritual student commits himself to the Path, all the energy that he has used in exercising his ego is withdrawn. At this point, he realizes that he has nothing left to prove or to lose. He only has to be true to himself and live free of all things."

—Andreas Leo, *The Face of the Eternal, Book Two*, 29, 31

Chapter 9

The Weight of the Halter

"The introverted spiritual seeker uses the inner senses to experience the divine Reality. The extroverted seeker perceives the same world as other people do, but the objects in this world are transformed, for the Force shines through them to illuminate the senses."

—Andreas Leo, *The Face of the Eternal, Book One*, 170

I NOW BEGAN scrupulously recording my conversations with the people I encountered, particularly those outside the League. I felt liberated talking about spirituality with people like Isiah Askew and Jerry Schaefer, and suffocated doing the same with members of the League. The jargon, pattern of conversation, and ideology of the League members was familiar, while that of outsiders was both more stimulating and less threatening. To go outside my own spiritual community was simultaneously a challenge and an escape.

The problem was that as soon as I began to take my writing project seriously, I completely lost interest in my daily contemplation. This was troubling to me, for the spiritual exercises constituted the most fundamental discipline and obligation of a League initiate. The assumption was that by neglecting the practice of one's daily contemplation, an individual would ultimately sever his connection with the Living Master, lose his spiritual moorings, and abandon the Path. The threat he faced was nothing less than spiritual failure.

On the other hand, there was something refreshing, even liberating about freeing myself from the discipline of daily contemplation, as if it had become repetitive, something I did out of habit. Lee Nakamura had used the analogy of always choosing the same fork to eat with as an illustration of how relying on past guidance could reduce the League to superstition. I found myself asking the Inner Master what I should do, as Lee had recommended, and the answer that I got was that the writing was more important for me at this time. I found that writing forced me to examine myself to a greater degree than I had ever done before. This was particularly noticeable in the process of revision. Revision was a never-ending process. I likened it to combing a cat in summer. I always found some flaw or lack of perspective, no matter how many times I repeated the process. This made me highly aware of the constant need to develop a greater perspective on myself. If the process of writing was prodding me to adopt a higher viewpoint, wasn't this the essence of a spiritual exercise?

Whenever I looked at what I had written, I focused particularly on the way I used the word "I," trying to gauge what impression the word made on the reader. What state of consciousness was represented by that word? Should I write from the viewpoint of the seeker or the knower—of someone looking for spiritual knowledge and experience or of someone who already possessed those qualities? While it might be presumptuous to try to write from a point of greater understanding than I possessed, if I didn't adopt such a higher viewpoint, of what value would my writing be to potential readers?

One night, I had an obscure but suggestive dream. In the dream, I was having a conversation with a member of the League about the way I used the word "I" in my writing, and demonstrated in a comical way that it could have different meanings by drawing three successive pictures on notepad. The first drawing was a picture of an "eye." The second was of a hand with the thumb up, indicating yes ("aye"). The third was of an egg (in German, "Ei"). The scene suddenly changed to an idyllic setting. It was near sunset, the sky turning colors—blue, pink, and gold—the deep shades varying somewhat, with the modest majesty of mountains in the background. A vessel approached, moving almost by itself. It had a flat surface, like a float or barge, raised only a few inches above the water. As it drew closer, I saw that a figure sat upon it, whether human, ghostly, or Godlike, I couldn't be sure. Finally, the impression of a spiritual being emerged—perhaps a member of the invisible hierarchy of the League. The being spoke:

> This is what you have to know. A Master needs his own identity. Define it clearly in your mind. See it! Give the Master his own name. He is the Master, and his name should be invoked instead of "I."

The dream seemed to indicate that in order to write in a way that would be of value to other people, I had to write as if I was a Master. I had to revise my own self-image from that of a seeker to that of a knower.

Shortly after I had this dream, I was hanging out at a Greek restaurant downtown, when I noticed a young woman enter, buy a cup of coffee, and leave. She was in no way extraordinary in terms of her outer appearance, but something about her magnetically captured my attention. I watched through the window as she sat down on a bench in front of the restaurant window and gazed at the passersby on the sidewalk. I paid my check, exited the restaurant, and boldly sat down beside her. We started up a conversation, and I was immediately impressed with her intensity, as well as with her sense of relaxation and ease.

Still a high school student, Athena Marcus was already a martial artist, cross-country runner, and horse trainer, as well as a talented writer and musician. As we talked, I thought of William Blake's famous aphorism: "Energy is beauty." Here was something worthy of investigation. What gave her that energy, intensity, and awareness? Did her martial arts training have something to do with it? When I found out that she attended a weekly class with her parents at a nearby martial arts studio, I arranged to meet with her and her family at the same restaurant on the following Saturday, right after class.

I arrived to find Athena seated with her parents, Lauren and Steve Marcus. Wedging a chair in at the periphery of the small table, I began by asking them how they would define the martial arts to someone like me, who knew nothing about the subject.

Steve explained that the martial arts had evolved from a pure, combat-oriented, self-defense technique to a method of self-improvement and cultivation of the self—physically, mentally, and spiritually. "All the arts that we study are forms of *jiu jitsu*, which means fighting arts," he explained. "Eventually, a shift occurred in Japan from the *jiu jitsu* arts to what became *do*. This word comes from the Chinese word *Tao*, meaning the Path. In other words, the martial arts came to be used as a path to self-awareness and self-enlightenment. In the Japanese culture you can use anything—the tea ceremony, or calligraphy, for instance—to reach the same goals of self-awareness."

"Are you saying that any activity can be used as a spiritual exercise?" I asked.

"Sure," he said. "Any activity can be used as a mirror to examine ourselves. The martial arts force you to look at yourself on a deeper level. When you're doing *judo* or *karate*, you're trying to improve your technique, constantly becoming aware of your failings or weaknesses. You can choose to not see them, or pretend they don't exist. If you have the correct attitude, however, you look at them as offering you a chance to improve."

"A lot of times you'll go through the same mistakes over and over again," Athena interjected. "You'll ask yourself, 'Why is this happening?' You may not get the answer right away, but eventually it will come, and in surprising ways. Sometimes it's hard to notice. It may just seem that you've taken another step along the path of maturity. You may not necessarily experience any sudden, startling revelations. It's a lot more subtle than that."

"It's not just a matter of doing it physically or mechanically correctly," Lauren added. "I've had to figure out that I needed to develop a feeling and sensitivity for what I was doing."

"Once a martial artist reaches a certain level, whether in *judo*, *aikido*, or *kung fu*, he has certain abilities to move and balance," Steve said, "In *karate*, we focus on linear power and force—kicking and punching in straight lines. In *aikido*, the stress is on circular motion, redirecting that linear force in spherical motions. Yet, *aikido* also needs to have force in linear fashion, and *karate* needs to flow in a circle, as well. So they start from seemingly contrary positions, but at the higher levels these principles blend together."

Steve went on to explain that the Japanese tradition of martial arts drew heavily on Zen Buddhism. The qualities of inner reflection were important, both spiritually as well as physically. "If you want to improve yourself," he said, "you have to be able to look at yourself honestly. The whole idea is that it's an individual quest. It's different from the Western monotheistic tradition that puts God at a level above man, and results in man always trying to please God. Instead, the Buddhist tradition teaches that divinity is within you, and your task is to discover it."

I commented on the balanced energy that I sensed they all possessed. "That's one of the things that you really work to achieve," Athena replied. "In the ancient times, back in Japan, you would have to spend many hours per day training in martial arts, and then you'd have to learn to balance that with the rest of your life, with outside chores and family duties. The whole thing is about achieving an inner balance within yourself that helps you to cope with that life outside the martial arts center, or *dojo*."

"Can the martial arts be likened to contemplation techniques?"

"Absolutely," Steve said. "The *kata* forms that we practice, at the highest level, are considered moving meditations."

My conversation with the Marcus family corroborated my own thoughts about writing and the spiritual exercises. Initiates of the League tended to refer to contemplation and spiritual exercise interchangeably. When I took the trouble to investigate Andreas Leo's writings, however, I found that they weren't defined the same way at all. The term "spiritual exercise" was meant to indicate any practice that promoted the movement of the inner consciousness.

"Contemplation" had a much more specific meaning. It signified a particular type of spiritual exercise, during which the attention was focused on a specific spiritual principle, thought, or idea, or upon the Living Master.

If writing could be considered a type of spiritual exercise, was it a fair substitute for my daily contemplation? Was I just using this activity as an excuse for my lack of discipline, or was I exercising a higher type of discipline? Contemplation was more than a discipline. It was a tool to maintain, refresh, and renew one's connection with the Force. I had always felt it produced in me a sense of balance, but I was now skeptical about this feeling because despite it, I hadn't been able to make positive choices in my life. If anything, it had rendered me too passive. I actually craved the feeling of being out of balance, because in this state I felt more active, more impelled to get out into the world, and become a greater participant in life. Instead of relegating spiritual exercise to a tiny portion of the day, life became a continual attempt to maintain balance, and thus the very act of living was rendered a spiritual exercise.

If anything that could produce a shift in consciousness, awareness, or perspective was a spiritual exercise, and the injunction of the League was always to remain faithful to one's practice of the spiritual exercises, rather than contemplation, was I really failing in my spiritual discipline? The more I thought about this, the more convinced I became that I was not. The problem was that few League members would have accepted my logic. Despite what my own inner guidance was telling me, I was still unsure to what extent I could get away with failing to practice the daily contemplation. I decided to call Lynne Silva for advice. "I'm not sure I want the safety of contemplation any more," I said to her. "I don't even want the sense of balance that it offers. My life has been too static, too motionless. If I have to abandon my practice of contemplation to throw myself into a crisis, then so be it."

"I think you have the right idea, Lynne replied. "Spiritual crisis is not the same as spiritual failure. It can be productive. It can invigorate us and lead us in new directions. Sometimes we need crisis to have spiritual growth. Simply adhering regularly to one's spiritual discipline isn't necessarily a ticket to salvation. A person who makes their contemplation exercise simply a routine or habit could get the idea that this is all the discipline they need to do in life, whereas this is far from the truth.

"Of course," she concluded, "the idea that you can simply substitute writing for your contemplation may also be a false assumption, in the long run. There may be a point when you realize the need to come back to it. The most important thing, however, is to be true to yourself. If you're doing your contemplation out of a sense of duty, obligation, or even fear of the negative consequences of not doing it, that's not a proper reason to do it. Rules apply mainly to beginners on the spiritual path. You're not a beginner any more. You're ready to make your own rules."

Paradoxically, just at the time that I was abandoning my contemplation, I decided to apply for a position in the League hierarchy. Perhaps this was consonant with my desire to throw myself into a crisis. In any case, I felt I had a good relationship with Dan Koster, the president of the area Board of Directors. He seemed to take my application seriously, and told me he would get back in touch with me about it soon. Weeks went by, however, and I never heard from him. Eventually, I found out through the grapevine that someone else had been given the position. The rejection itself didn't bother me, but the fact that Dan hadn't bothered to let me know hurt deeply. He was one of the most conscientious people I knew. It was completely out of character for him not to follow through on a promise or commitment. Had the area director sandbagged me? Was that the reason Dan wanted to avoid giving me the news directly?

This wasn't my first taste of volunteering for a position in the League hierarchy. A few years before, I had applied to apprentice for the position of communications coordinator. The area director had told me that it was up to the current officeholder, and that I would hear from her in a couple of weeks. I never heard from either of them, nor did the director even thank me for volunteering. I also applied several times for the position of spiritual aide, but never received so much as an acknowledgment of my application.

That's the way it was whenever I dealt with members of the League hierarchy. The area director and her various appointees didn't seem to know how to treat other people, to make them feel welcome, or to let them know that they were part of the community. Other members had shared similar impressions. They reported that the area director filled the state hierarchy exclusively with her friends and cronies, conveying the impression that such appointments were political rather than spiritual. The area director didn't seem interested in diversity of points of view, or in change of any kind, but rather in stability, reliance on structure, and the goal of turning the League into a safe, predictable organization. Under her leadership, the state organization had become a tiny bureaucracy filled with a few self-important people who believed that they constituted some kind of spiritual elite.

Was it any wonder, then, that morale was poor, activities had virtually ceased, and the organization was not attracting new members? It didn't take a genius to see that we were top-heavy with high initiates, that the average age of initiates was increasing, and that the message presented by the League no longer appealed to young people. The current President and Living Master had once noted that when the level of participation in an area went down, the cause was often with an individual in the hierarchy who was blocking the Force. I suspected that this was the problem in our area, but even if that were true, what could I do about it?

Years ago, I had been present at a meeting of League high initiates, which was chaired by the area director. There was a good deal of discontent at the time, in response to which the area director gave a little speech about his job, how much paperwork it involved, and how thankless it was. "If anyone wants this job," he concluded, "they're welcome to it." Of course, everyone just sat and stared at him. No one had any thought of standing up and volunteering. The incident stuck in my mind, however. I finally decided to test what the area director had said. I wrote to the head office of the League, and volunteered for the position. Eventually, I got a letter back saying that my request had been forwarded to the area director himself. Either my application hadn't been taken seriously by the head office, or the area directors were given the courtesy of vetting their own replacements. If the latter was the case, was it any surprise that some of them hung on to their positions year after year?

In the final analysis, what had I done except embarrass myself? What kind of bizarre fantasy had caused me to volunteer for the job of area director? I wasn't practicing my daily contemplation. My notion of writing as a spiritual exercise was one that most League members would have considered a mere rationalization for lack of discipline. I no longer attended activities at the local center. I was suspicious of the League's transformation into a religious organization, and critical of the message it presented to the public. Yet, I somehow aspired to leadership in that same organization! I was either suffering from vanity or insanity.

My feelings of resentment in response to this bureaucracy and stagnation contrasted with the sense of excitement and adventure I had felt when I had first joined the League. I was hanging on by my fingernails to some sliver of remembrance of what I had experienced years before. Above all, I felt a sense of loyalty to the ideals that had first attracted me to the League. That League was still inside me, still a part of me. At the same time, I was aware, deep inside, that all my complaints about the League were connected with my continuing discontent with my own life. I knew that I was projecting all my personal dissatisfaction onto the League, and that if I could only find some measure of personal fulfillment, all my dissatisfaction with the League would likely disappear.

In this frame of mind, I paid a visit to the Flaming Heart Center, located on the old north side of town, on a blustery Sunday morning. The Center offered teachings of one of the ancient Tantric lineages—part of a non-monastic, non-celibate school of Tibetan Buddhism. I had come to attend a public teaching with the American lama Sangsu Rinpoche, formally recognized as a *tülku*, or incarnation, of a great Tibetan *yogin* from the last century.

I had little idea what to expect. The entrance hall was already hung with dozens of coats as I came in. The meeting hall, decorated with colorful Tibetan wall coverings, was packed with over sixty people, most sitting cross-legged on the floor, some in chairs against the back wall. The lama entered, his palms pressed together, fingertips pointed upward in a traditional Tibetan greeting. He was dressed in a broad, white skirt, with a maroon sash slung over his shoulder. The assembly bowed and began a chant that lasted for five or ten minutes. Some had liturgical books open before them, but most sang the Tibetan words by rote in remarkable unison.

Lama Sangsu opened the meeting, his manner relaxed and informal. He began his discourse by quoting a well-known aphorism from the Sufi tradition: "One should gauge the quality and level of one's activity the way a good camel driver gauges the weight of the halter. If the halter is too heavy, the camel will lie down and not get up or walk at all. If the halter is too light, the camel won't listen to any directions."

He illustrated this principle by recounting the history of the Tibetan saint Milarepa, who began his spiritual search by choosing the swift and seemingly facile Dzogchen path, but found that he could not master it. He then took up the far more physically demanding Marpa path, in pursuit of which he was given tasks of mythic proportions, and thereby achieved enlightenment. Lama Sangsu's point was that a so-called "light halter" would not work for some people, and a "heavy halter" would not work for others. "Each person," he explained, "has a 'soft limit' and 'hard limit.' If you never go beyond your soft limit, you will not progress, but if you go beyond your hard limit, you will be hurt, and feel crushed or ashamed about your constant failure.

"Those who never go beyond their soft limit relax into their habits, and sink into their slovenly, animalistic nature. Those who go to the opposite extreme tend to be people who want to be admired for their spirituality. Given that we are all camels, metaphorically speaking, we tend to limit ourselves both with our 'soft' and our 'hard' behavior. Most of us do both. In certain areas of our lives we won't go beyond our soft limit, and in others, we insist on punishing ourselves by going beyond our hard limit.

"All external events can be taken as the communication of teaching,"

Lama Sangsu continued. "Over and over again we have to assess what we're doing. We ought to be shocked at our ability to rationalize our own behavior. All fingers should point to ourselves. When people undermine their whole life by trying to do what they are unable to do, it's annoying to see. Our whole culture is designed to make us forget what our potentialities are. The constant stimulation represented by this cultural production is endless. Disengaging from its influence is the first step to putting you in greater touch with yourself."

After the teaching was over, I went up to Lama Sangsu, introduced myself as a member of the League, and asked if I could meet with him. He agreed, and the next Tuesday we arrived at the Flaming Heart Center almost simultaneously. A female student accompanied him to help open the room. We sat down cross-legged on meditation cushions in the middle of the otherwise empty meeting hall, with pleasant incense wafting above us. "I'd like to return to the subject of your teaching on Sunday, specifically the Sufi aphorism about the camel," I said.

"This is actually used in a series of instructions for teachers," Lama Sangsu replied. "The idea is that if you lay a halter upon your students that is too heavy for them, then they won't be able to function at all, and they'll become despairing. On the other hand, if one has no discipline at all in one's life, then the mind wanders about randomly without any ability to tell that it's wandering. In our particular tradition of sitting practice, it's a very delicate matter, in the beginning, to even recognize what distraction is. If we have no discipline at all, we can spend our whole lives distracted without even realizing that we're distracted. Once we try to rest our attention on one thing, let's say within concentrated sitting meditation, then suddenly the mind goes crazy because it's like a mad elephant that's never been staked to one spot before. The mind doesn't actually go crazy. It's always been crazy. We just never realized it before.

"You therefore have to be careful not to burden people with too much, not to tell people that they have to take on all kinds of disciplines that they're not capable of taking on, which are beyond their ability at that phase of their practice. Sadly, in some groups this happens on purpose. You cause the person to feel broken and incapable, which is a very good thing if you want to exert control over other people. First, you make them think that there's something their life depends upon achieving if they're going to be worthwhile human beings. Then you make sure they can't achieve it. They depend on you, or on your system of teaching, for the achievement of the thing. No other teaching will do it. If you make almost every natural impulse of a human being sinful, then you'll be sure to make all people feel sinful. Then they'll need to rely on whoever is the purveyor of that which relieves them of their sins."

"That's serious if you're actually in a group in which that's occurring," I commented.

"Oh, yes," he nodded. "You can find people with a high degree of realization, with a mediocre degree of realization, as well as downright mean and nasty people in almost every spiritual tradition. A well-functioning group will almost necessarily include some people with strong aberrations, because spiritual life is meant to help those people. Most groups are mirrors of society. The group doesn't control the psychodynamics of any individual, but each individual contributes to the dynamics of the group as a whole. The group develops an ethos, an overall *Gestalt*. Groups and their members are like a river and the banks of the river. The banks shape the river and the river shapes the banks.

"Are you familiar with Herbert Marcuse's *One-Dimensional Man*?" he asked. "His analysis of technological society is that it shapes the apparent needs of people, and then people are bound by what they feel to be their needs. You can find groups whose function is the fantasy that they're all very spiritually advanced. Therefore, they never apply any discipline to themselves, so they never discover that they're not."

"So every spiritual group is actually attuned to a halter of different weight?" I asked.

"That's correct," Lama Sangsu replied.

"In the League, we do only twenty minutes of contemplation a day," I said. "But you're doing—well, I don't know how much you're doing, but you're doing a lot!"

"A lot," he agreed, and we both laughed.

"My impression is that the Tantric tradition of Tibetan Buddhism employs a looser halter than the more widely recognized monastic and celibate Sutric tradition in Tibetan Buddhism, at least in terms of the outward observances that you are required to perform," I added

"This is an issue of great debate within Tantric lineages," Lama Sangsu replied. "Tantric practice has far fewer external regulations. It has internal vows, however, that are extremely difficult to follow. Monastic rules, such as 'Don't have sex, stay away from money, and never drink alcohol,' are easy to follow. There are two hundred and thirty-seven of these rules for average male monastic practice, a few more for females. That's a lot of rules, but they're all very clear-cut. Do this. Don't do that. It's easy to tell when you're in violation of a rule. Either you're having sex or you're not having sex, drinking alcohol or not drinking alcohol. The Tantric view is fundamentally different. It has nothing to do with renunciation, but rather with transformation. Certain activities are fine as long as they are done as transformative Tantric practice. Being able to discriminate in this respect is difficult, however. It's easy to say that one is having sex as transformative Tantric practice while just indulging in grasping, clinging desire."

"So it's difficult to judge or evaluate any group," I said. "To external appearance, a group may offer a very loose halter; there may be a lot more going on under the surface."

"At least for some people," he replied.

"In the League, for instance, one of our guidelines is to be at all times an example of joy and happiness to other people. Well, Jesus Christ! That could be a very big discipline."

"Exactly… Jesus Christ!" Lama Sangsu joined me in laughter.

"You said on Sunday that we give ourselves a short halter in some things and a long halter in others. You said that we have a 'soft' limit that we do not exceed in certain areas of our life, and a 'hard' limit that we exceed all the time. Have you ever felt that you're only a mixture of extremes—completely lazy in certain areas and beating yourself up in others? You look at one aspect of your life, and you think you're being too lazy. Then you start seeing it from a different perspective, and you're no longer sure. Maybe you're being too hard on yourself. An analogy would be the act of touching a hot stove. For a brief instant, it feels cold. The hot feels like cold, and cold feels like hot. Does that make any sense?" I asked.

"It makes absolute sense," Lama Sangsu agreed. "In our particular lineage, we believe that this is greatly aided by having a teacher, and usually by having more than one teacher. We have a saying in our tradition: 'You have one lama in your heart, many lamas in the world.' This means that you have one teacher who you feel has gone significantly farther than you on the path and has great clarity, insight, and ability to understand you and your situation. Then, you also learn from many other teachers within the lineage and within the world, in general.

"If you don't know whether you're being lazy or pushing too hard, you might go to your lama or guru," he continued. "Generally, a good lama doesn't tell you 'You're being too lazy.' If you're experiencing a lack of clarity on a particular issue, it's not that you need an external answer. If you're simply given an external answer, it becomes a crutch, and it takes away from you the very important process of learning how to have the clarity for yourself."

My conversation with Lama Sangsu had given me a greater perspective on the League. To begin with, it seemed to epitomize the "light halter" path. Compared to the amount of time Lama Sangsu spent in meditation, the twenty minutes a day required for the spiritual exercises didn't seem to require a great deal of discipline. A spiritual path was a lifelong program, however. Even if the discipline demanded only twenty minutes a day, it had to weather all kinds of storms in one's personal life. That was not always easy. The great Tibetan saint Milarepa had failed at the "light halter" Dzogchen path. The demanding Marpa path was actually easier for him. Despite its apparent ease, the path offered by the League was not a simple one.

As Lama Sangsu noted, rules were easy to follow. Left to our own devices, we tended to find rules to impose on ourselves, and even extended those rules to others. Since there were practically no rules in the League, many initiates ran around creating rules for themselves and for others. This was part of the process of spiritual growth. The League was a testing ground. Those for whom spirituality was a matter of rules and guidelines would serve a role in maintaining the outer organization. Those who could not fit their spiritual sensibility into such a mold, however, would have to look deeper and farther for their own rules, their own discipline, and their own truth.

This was the true source of my conflict with the League hierarchy. Whatever the League organization was, whether it was a useful instrument in the Divine cause or not, was irrelevant. It was my testing ground, and I was compelled to throw myself against its unforgiving structure in order to take measure of myself. In that sense, my application for the position of area director was not vain, but courageous, and the fact that it was not accepted did not necessarily reflect negatively on me at all.

Chapter Ten

Leading the Parade

"The seeker must come to know the extremes of life via the most challenging path. Knowledge is not what he can be taught, shown, or told; it is only what he can discover for himself by long and arduous search."

—Andreas Leo, *The Face of the Eternal, Book Two,* 122

One day, I happened to contact Dee Hughes, and asked if she could help me edit some articles that I had written. Dee, who was a would-be writer herself, agreed. Since she had no car of her own, I agreed to pick her up at her house on a Saturday afternoon. I arrived at the appointed time, but it had been a long time since I had visited her place. After turning onto the street, I couldn't remember exactly which house was hers—the last one on the left or the second-to-the last one. The two houses, separated by a sloping swath of lawn, looked virtually identical, except that the latter had dark shutters and a dark door. The former had no shutters at all, and there was a white screen on the front door that looked completely unfamiliar.

I turned into the empty driveway of the penultimate house, honked my horn, got out, and knocked on the front door. There was no answer. I peered inside. It looked like the interior of Dee's house all right. I directed my attention across the lawn, toward the house next door. There were two vehicles in the driveway, but neither of them appeared familiar. I left a note on the house with the empty driveway, and drove home.

When I got back to my apartment, I called. Sure enough, Dee answered.

"Where have you been?" she asked. "I've been waiting for you."

"Is your house the one on the end?"

"Yes."

"Then I knocked on the door of the wrong house," I told her. It was inexplicable. I could easily have checked out the other house, and was at a loss to explain why I had not. She invited me to try again, so I drove back to her neighborhood. I finally picked her up about an hour and fifteen minutes later than we had planned.

Dee was a bulky woman. As she slowly eased herself into the passenger seat of my tiny Tercel, I noticed a black cat with yellow eyes sitting on the grass in front of her house. It blinked at us, without making another move.

"Is that your cat?" I asked.

"No," Dee replied.

"Is it the neighbor's cat?"

"No."

"Well, whose cat is it?"

"I don't want to talk about it," Dee said emphatically.

Now my curiosity was aroused. "What do you mean, you don't want to talk about it?"

"If you want to know, it's not a cat," Dee answered. "It's an entity."

"What do you mean—an entity?"

"An evil entity," she insisted.

Now, this wasn't a completely out-of-character pronouncement for Dee to make. She was a psychic, intuitive type, who often made remarks of this sort. Whenever she did so, I tended to change the subject or make some kind of bland remark that could be interpreted as accepting what she said, without directly committing myself one way or another. In this fashion, we always managed to get along. She was an entertaining individual, and we generally found lots of things to talk about. I was aware, however, that she expected her utterances to be taken at face value, their truth unquestioned.

I was stumped as to what to say. As an animal lover, my instinct was to make friends with whatever creature I encountered. I looked again at the cat sunning itself on the grass as we pulled out of the driveway. It looked perfectly harmless. I didn't accept Dee's pronouncement, nor did I necessarily disbelieve her, either. After all, Dee had all sorts of perceptions that I did not. It was an eerie feeling, looking at the cat, and considering the possibility that Dee might be right. At the same time, I had the perverse urge to play the Devil's advocate. "Even if it's an evil entity, couldn't you make friends with it?" I thought of asking her. I held my tongue, however. I had the strong feeling that a remark like that would only aggravate her.

"How long has it been hanging out in front of your house?" I finally managed to ask.

Dee looked at me as if she resented even this minuscule question. "Three months," she replied.

"Three months? Isn't that sort of a long time?" I observed.

"Yes. You don't know what I've been going through!"

"Well, do you want to talk about it?" I asked, trying to be helpful.

"No," she said, with finality.

We drove into town, and found a place to discuss the articles that I had brought with me. After an hour or so I drove her back. "Do you think the cat will still be there?" I couldn't help asking, although I sensed the question was provocative. Dee refused to reply to my question.

"A cat used to hang around my house when I lived in Huntington Park, and I ended up adopting it," I prattled on, skirting around the subject. I was trying to soothe Dee's ruffled feathers, talking in a neutral way about what was, on the surface at least, a similar incident. It wasn't doing the trick, though. I felt that Dee viewed my very inclination to talk about the cat as a sign that I was attracted to it. I could sense that, since she believed it was evil, anything I said on the subject had the effect of casting suspicion on me, in her eyes.

When we pulled into the driveway, there was the cat, waiting for Dee. I let her out of the car and watched as she made her way to the front door. The cat hopped up on the window ledge, and arched its back in anticipation, as she opened the door. When it was open just a crack, the creature made a move to get inside, but Dee elbowed it out of the way at the last minute and disappeared into the house.

The next day, I received an unexpected e-mail from Dee:

> The incident with the cat and the fact that you went to the wrong house, unable to differentiate which house was mine, show that YOU DO NOT GET ME! I told you that the cat was an evil entity. Your interest in getting closer to the cat and perhaps even getting to know her shows me one of two things. Either you want to form a relationship with the very evil the cat represents, or you feel it was simply MY perception that the cat was an evil entity, and that this was not truly what it was.
>
> I think you are stuck on the fact that you have been pursuing a spiritual path for a longer period than I have. You feel that you have greater spiritual knowledge of things than I do. Why else would you pursue the cat? You will discover that the number of years spent on a spiritual path in no way defines a person's level of spiritual attainment. It would shock you to know what my true level of spiritual attainment is.
>
> We have nothing to talk about. I cannot explain myself to you because you do not get me. I don't wish to talk to you on the phone or by e-mail. There is no reason for us to continue to talk or see each other. It's too painful to me that you don't even see me!

It was quite a stunning communication. I tried to think about it in a way that gave Dee all the benefit of the doubt. I could easily assume, for instance, that her level of "spiritual attainment" was far higher than mine was. What did I know about my measure of spiritual advancement, after all? Personally, I didn't feel that I had any idea of my place in the vast spiritual hierarchy that encompassed all of humanity. Clearly, Dee had an idea of her place in this hierarchy, however—too clear an idea, I felt, to be genuine.

I thought about what I would consider the marks of true spirituality. Certainly true spirituality would not need to call attention to itself, assert itself, or defend itself. It would be able to get along with people regardless of their inability to recognize it for what it was. Dee's note conveyed the impression that she desperately wished to be seen by others as she saw herself. This was a normal human desire, but one that most people did not expect could be fulfilled. Our human vanity wished to be recognized. If it was not, however, we made the best of it. We lived in the company of others despite the lack of recognition that we received. Spirituality implied that we placed a higher value on the intangibles of life, which could only be apprehended through love, feeling, and intuition. To seek recognition for one's spiritual attainment put a person in the position of making claims for which there was no visible demonstration.

Spirituality, to me, involved the use of common sense. What I found remarkable about Dee's relationship to the cat was that she had allowed it to plague her for over three months. If I had an unwanted animal hanging around my house, I would simply have chased it away, or caught it and taken it to the Humane Society. Even if it were an evil entity in the body of a cat, I would still be rid of it. Why, if Dee felt the cat was evil, would she simply allow it to hang around her house? Whatever this cat was, or represented to Dee, couldn't she have invited this visitation, be tolerating it, or have brought it upon herself?

To Dee, my failure to recognize her house was evidence that I couldn't see her for what she was. Perhaps she was right. If Dee was all she claimed she was, maybe I was the one who was spiritually blind. My common sense, however, told me that she was the one with the black cat sitting on her doorstep. If my instinct was correct, the advice I contemplated giving her might have been sound—to make friends with the cat. We all had a negative side to our nature with which we ultimately had to come to terms. The black cat, with its eerie yellow eyes, was a symbol of the dark side within us that we had to befriend.

Shortly after this incident, I heard that Dee had sent a letter to the local League center in which she made grandiose claims concerning her spiritual status, and formally cut her ties with the local League community. The word was that she claimed she was a spiritual Master, although she had never been a formal League member, or received any of the outer initiations. Finally, she vented at the members of the League community who had failed to perceive or acknowledge her spiritual stature. I dropped in at the Center, found the letter in an envelope on the desk, and read the following:

> Because of the same thread that has run through my entire experience at the League Center, I will not be attending any meetings there, ever again. Years ago, the Inner Master told me to stop going to the Center. He said it did not deserve my presence. I enjoyed the fellowship of the people there, so I went anyway. There has never really been a reason for me to be present, however, since I am not a member of the League. A true spiritual Master does not have to be a member of the League. I am such a Master.
>
> I have been putting up with the pettiness at the League Center ever since I first stepped through its doors almost ten years ago. I have been advised by the true Masters to inform the Center of the following: You do not know what the Holy Spirit is.
>
> I never wanted to divulge my status. I told it only to a few people. I came here because there were certain experiences I had to go through before I could begin my mission. They were hard experiences. My status as a Master did not make them easier. I suppose the judgments that you formed of me because of my circumstances in life were the same that you would have made of the bum lying in the street. Take care. Judge not, lest you receive judgment according to the same measure.

> I don't think any of you will want to talk to me after receiving this letter. I know that many of you will say that I am crazy and having delusions of grandeur. I do not expect that this letter will make any of you move past your petty feelings and consult the Holy Spirit about what I have said, because, as I said, you don't know the Holy Spirit. I do not wish to talk to any of you. Please honor my wishes. My foray into your world is over. It didn't work because none of you wanted me here even as a member of your community, let alone as the spiritual Master that I am.

Eventually, news of the letter made the rounds of the local League community, and there was some discussion about it. The consensus was that Dee's claim to Mastership was obviously unfounded, for if she were a true spiritual Master, she would have no need to boast of the fact, or even make such a claim public. I remembered asking Lee Nakamura how one could differentiate between someone who talked to God, as opposed to someone who just thought they talked to God.

"People who just think they talk to God are projecting their desires," Lee replied. "Everything you see, every dream you have, you can interpret to fit your want or need. It has nothing to do with reality, though. You have to be objective to see the answers."

"So a lot of what we see is what we want to see, instead of what is?" I asked.

"Yes," he told me, "if you don't know the difference."

I thoroughly agreed with this reasoning, yet felt that it too easily dismissed what was a complex issue. What would cause a person to have such a conviction? What were the mechanics that underlay it? What experiences did Dee have that convinced her that she was in communication with the invisible hierarchy of the League, and was a Master herself? I felt this was a great mystery, and was frustrated that most of the other local League members were so disinterested in this subject. I saw this as further evidence of their lack of spiritual curiosity. Dee's evaluation of atmosphere at the local Center, moreover, largely coincided with mine. I, too, felt something oppressive whenever I went there, which I attributed to more than simply Ray Hardcastle's presence.

Not long afterwards came the news that Dee passed away from a sudden heart attack. I attended her memorial service, feeling the whole time that she was possibly looking down on us. It suddenly occurred to me that I was no longer thinking of her as a personality, but as a spiritual being. From this perspective, Dee's ideas concerning her spiritual status were not necessarily as spurious as I originally felt them to be. I considered that we were all spiritual beings, and the only thing standing in the way of achieving spiritual freedom was our lack of conscious awareness that we had already done so. The process of spiritual attainment began with the exercise of the imagination. Dee had the imagination to see herself as a Master. How, therefore, could this be a complete untruth?

I longed to discuss these issues with League members, but found few who were interested. Most frustrating of all were my attempts to broach the subject of her death with Leonard Carlisle, one of her closest friends. She had passed away at Leonard's house, and it was rumored that she had confided to him many of her inner experiences. I was curious to know what she had said to him about her visitations from the Masters, and whether he felt they had been genuine. Each time I had tried to bring up the subject with Leonard, however, he had given me the brush-off. "If we're friends," I finally complained to him, "why can't we talk about this?"

"If you need some kind of understanding about Dee's purpose in your life, the Inner Master can give this to you," Leonard replied. "You just have to ask."

I was resentful at Leonard's attitude, and took his refusal to talk to me as a way of hiding, of concealing his own set opinions. Initiates within the League often invoked the Law of Silence, which ostensibly prohibited them from talking about their inner affairs in relation to the Path, when they deemed such discussion unnecessary, provocative, or hurtful. For me, on the other hand, spiritual understanding involved discussion, argumentation, and questioning. I would have liked nothing better than for the League community to function as a kind of extended family, its members freely sharing their thoughts and feelings with one another. For Leonard, however, spirituality was purely a matter of one's own personal connection with Spirit. The more I encountered this type of attitude among the initiates, the more I felt that the League community was infested with an undercurrent of unspoken thoughts and assumptions that stifled true communication.

Dee had essentially made two claims—that she was a Master, and that she had received no outer initiations in the League. This brought into question the very nature of the League initiations. The initiations were the great incentive in the League. They were the seal, the proof—or at least the evidence—of spiritual advancement. Through the initiation, the individual was connected, via the Living Master, to a greater flow of the Force, the Audible Life Stream. Each initiation, therefore, represented a stepping up of the individual's own vibration. If Dee was not a member of the League, and had received none of the outer initiations, could she have gotten them in another way?

She had made a third claim—that she was in contact with the Masters of the invisible hierarchy that was behind the League. It stood to reason that these Masters worked through channels other than the League organization known to most initiates. Did they work through other organizations, as well? Were they present in the world in other guises? Were they known by different names in other languages? Could one establish a connection with them without ever being aware of the existence of an organization called the League? What about those people who lived in cultures that had no access to the League? Were they prevented from making contact with the Living Master, or did they simply do so through different channels or via different methodologies?

I happened to pay a visit to George Blackstone around this time. George was my closest confidant within the League, the one person with whom I could always be completely candid. His life was as ramshackle as mine was, and the trajectories of our experience in the League had followed a similar arc. I lounged on a beat-up sofa in his dilapidated living room, which looked like an antechamber to the underworld, and asked him, "Do you think that a person can receive the initiations without being a member of the League?"

"Yes, I believe so," he replied. "The initiations occur on the Inner, anyway. I wouldn't be surprised if there were people who have already had all the initiations before they ever come into the outer organization."

"Well, we know that the League initiations are progressive," I continued. "They connect the individual with the Sound Current at an increasingly higher level of vibration. We have no idea, however, as to where those initiations stand in relation to the initiations of other groups. We don't know what the experience that we refer to as self-realization might mean to a Tibetan Buddhist, a Sufi, or a practitioner of Zen. How do we know that the initiations offered by the League are any more significant spiritually that those of another group?"

George shrugged. "Maybe it doesn't matter," he replied. "Maybe it's just a matter of choosing the best path for us and sticking to it."

Toward the end of our conversation, George mentioned that he had visited Buddy Webster at a psychiatric hospital in nearby Eastland. I knew Buddy casually from occasional League meetings we had both attended. He was a stonemason by profession, and was interested in Native American spiritual traditions. He had friends in the Indian community, and had participated in their ceremonies. The last time I had seen him, he was about to embark on a spirit quest in South Dakota, and had expressed some concern to the other League members about the wisdom of mixing two different spiritual paths. I had been among the most vociferous in support of his spiritual adventure. Then I heard through the grapevine that he had gotten in trouble with the law. There were rumors of spousal abuse and divorce. His whole life had come unraveled, and he had gone to prison. I wondered whether his involvement in Native American religion had backfired, and if I had possibly been wrong to encourage him in pursuing this type of experience.

George told me that Buddy had recently suffered a psychotic episode, and had claimed to be Jesus. He was doing better now, however, and was interested in having visitors. I lost no time in getting directions to the hospital, and paying him a visit. I signed in at the front desk, took the elevator to the fourth floor, and entered the ward. There were so many people milling around, it was difficult to distinguish the staff members from the patients. I checked in at the nurse's station. The man at the desk had the build of a football linebacker. When I gave him Buddy's name, he called out "Webster!" and immediately pointed behind me. I turned around to find myself staring into Buddy's familiar face.

"Wow, it's really great to see you!" he said, obviously surprised.

I grasped his hand in reply. His handshake was firm and his eyes were rock solid. Whatever he had gone through, I could see immediately that he was very sane, and had lost none of his spiritual spark. He suggested we go outside to talk, and led me first down to the basement where we purchased something to drink, and then out to an area next to the parking lot. The area was dotted with wooden benches and picnic tables, interspersed with sparse, colorless grass. I asked him right off to tell me how he had gotten into this situation.

"It all started with my daughter," he said. "She had a tumor that had wrapped itself around her optic nerve and was gradually blinding her in one eye. We took her to the Eastern University Hospital, but the doctors wanted to put off an operation until the tumor was at a more advanced stage of growth. I'd gone to a medicine man previously with some health problems. He had done a ceremony and prayed over me. I felt I had received some beneficial effects from it, so I went to a peyote service up north. The priest who officiated at the service wasn't even a North American. He was an Inca priest from Peru, recognized by the Native American Church.

"The Native American way that I learned among the Lakota Sioux wasn't the peyote way," Buddy explained. "If you wanted a vision, you went up on a hill and you didn't eat for four days or drink for two days. You went up on a butte with a blanket and prayer ties and prayed. When I went to South Dakota, my healer gave me a prescription of what I needed to do. I was to walk with my *chanupa*, my pipe. I brought the pipe to my healer, and he blessed it. Then, I was to do a *humblachia*, which is a vision quest, and attend the sun dance."

"Why, however, would you go from a pure kind of experience like that to something like the Native American Church's peyote ceremony?" I asked him.

"It was an exploratory experience. I wanted to see how it might be of benefit."

"OK," I replied. "I can understand how the peyote could enhance your inner experience, but how could your inner experience have a bearing on your daughter's health?"

"The peyote ritual is considered to be like the experience of a sun dancer. The sun dancer has to endure great physical pain. He has to go without food or water for four days. He has to dance under the hot sun from morning to night. That's a sacrifice. Well, some of the people who take a lot of the peyote consider themselves to be undergoing a similar trial or test of strength. I was encouraged to take as much of the peyote as possible. I was told that the more I used the stronger my prayers on my daughter's behalf would be.

"Every time the little container would come by with a small spoon, I took a heaping spoonful. It went around numerous times. The ceremony was an all-night thing, from dusk till dawn. By morning, I was still strongly under the influence. We went into a sweat lodge. I put my pipe by the altar, between the sweat lodge and the fire, and went in with the group and sweated. The ground began moving, seething up and down. I felt that I was riding on the back of a serpent. I freaked out. I failed the test of endurance. Two days later, I began to become extremely mentally disturbed."

"Well, hold on," I interrupted. "Perhaps it was a mistake to follow two spiritual paths at the same time, and taking the peyote clearly was not a wise decision. Instead of looking at the experience as a failure, however, I'd encourage you to interpret it positively. If you truly believe in the heroism of the peyote experience, you can look at your present situation as part of that experience. If the ceremony was as powerful as you suggest, then the sacrifice may have been for you to go through this whole thing so your daughter's operation would be successful. That would include not only the ceremony itself, but also the trouble with your wife, your arrest, and your incarceration in this hospital."

"Well, last fall my daughter went to the Eastern University Hospital," Buddy responded. "She had the operation, and it was a success. If I had to do the entire experience all over again just in order to facilitate my daughter's healing, I'd do it."

I asked Buddy how long he had been in a psychotic state, and he replied that it had lasted about six weeks. "It started about two or three weeks after the peyote ceremony," he said. "During that period, I couldn't sleep. My thoughts were racing. Then I started to hear voices. I kept the voices at bay for a long time, but after a while I stopped fighting them."

"What kind of voices were they?" I asked.

"They were mostly inaudible," he explained. "I'd watch TV, and there would be messages there for me. I'd see billboards on the way to work with messages for me, as well. Messages like: 'You know that you're Jesus, and that you've come back again.' One day, I came across three ministers who appeared to be stranded by the side of the road. They had their Bibles out. They looked at me as I drove by in my truck, and I thought they were venerating me as Jesus. I also heard voices telling me that I was Jesus Christ, and that I needed to fulfill my destiny for mankind. They told me that I wasn't doing my job. Even on the radio, I'd hear things like, 'You're failing now. You're not working your spiritual program. You should be saving people, not making tombstones.' One voice told me, 'Let the dead take care of the dead.' That's a quotation from scripture.

"There was another incident," Buddy added. "A parade came down Washington Avenue, past my shop in Wyanoke. It was a Christian parade on a Saturday afternoon. I thought that I was getting a specific invitation to lead the parade. I just stood there in front of my display area, inside the gates, and waved to everybody."

"What made you feel you were supposed to lead the parade? Did a voice tell you that?"

"No. It was just a feeling. My wife tried to tell me that I wasn't Jesus Christ, but I said, 'What if I am? We need to set up a website so that we can start sharing the good word with the world. The churches will fight it, to begin with, but they'll fall into place eventually. We just need money.' So she asked, 'How are you going to earn that kind of money?' I just told her, 'Don't worry. Money won't be a problem. We're going to do spiritual work. That'll take care of everything.' Occasionally, I'd hear the voices through radio and television, as well. I would hear the voice of the announcer, but the words would change to fit my delusion. In a psychotic state, everything warps, just like on an acid trip, except without as many fancy colors."

"When you thought of yourself as Jesus," I inquired, "did you think of yourself as the actual historical person, or more as someone graced with a certain state of consciousness?"

"I thought of it as a state of consciousness," Buddy replied. "The body that belonged to Jesus two thousand years ago was a different body from mine, but I felt the mentality was the same."

As Buddy explained all this, I was thinking of the similarity between his experience and Dee's. Dee may truly have had experiences with the Masters of the League's invisible hierarchy, but somewhere along the line, the message evidently got garbled. Similarly, Buddy's voices could have been malicious entities that invaded his personal space. The peyote could have opened a hole in his aura and let them in. The point was that one couldn't rely on inner voices or visitations for spiritual guidance, any more than one could rely on other people's advice or on religious doctrine. The only true guide was one's own inner guidance, that tiny voice inside us that was worthy of so much greater attention than we gave it.

"People develop delusional systems to compensate for feelings of insecurity or lack of self-worth," I commented to Buddy. "They suffer from delusions of either grandeur or goodness. There's a certain degree of grandiosity in the attitude you're describing. Your feelings are not that different from those of most other people—the desire to be constructive, to make the most of your life, to be a channel or conduit for Spirit. The problem is just how to do this. You don't have to lead the parade. Your talent is probably not in preaching the Gospel, but rather in your stone carving.

"Wanting to spread the word of God, and considering yourself a failure for just sticking to your work as a stonemason, are within the range of normal feelings, too. People our age commonly go through a mid-life crisis. They look back at their lives and feel that they have wasted their time, or haven't achieved their potential. This can be particularly true of people who have a spiritual orientation, and feel that they need to contribute something to humanity.

"This is a world of duality, in which positive and negative forces coexist. The human state of consciousness is actually a delusional state. Each step that we take to a higher state of consciousness is a kind of rebirth. In that process of being reborn, we're apt to look on the world with innocent new eyes. Yet, paradoxically, the transition to a greater state of awareness is often accompanied by a greater illusion. The heroism represented by the peyote ceremony may involve working your way through that illusion. If you see that you can be Christ, and still stick with being a stonemason, then I think you've got it."

"Well, I don't think I'm Jesus Christ any more," Buddy replied. "I just believe that we all have the spark of God inside us. And I can live with that."

Chapter Eleven

A World of Abundance

"Everything in life contains some degree of truth. Even pure fantasy is woven from the fabric of God, so how can it not also be truth?"

—Andreas Leo, *The Lion's Paw*, vii

One day, I was browsing in a bookstore and picked up a book entitled *Spellbound Love* by Marjorie Williams, which was about the spirituality of intimate relationships. The author was a nationally known author on spirituality, and the head of a prominent new age church. I purchased the book out of curiosity, and began to skim it, but soon had to put it down because I was so repulsed by its tone and apparent message. The book was meant to sell readers on the idea of "true romance" as something that could fulfill their spiritual and emotional cravings. Its author claimed to see romance as not only fulfilling the need for adventure, but also as supplying the individual with a sense of identity. She characterized the notion that romance is not for everyone as a big lie, a social conspiracy, and a perverse doctrine designed to convince us that our lack of courage was some form of psychological health. Although many people were looking for love, she said, they were actually committed to not finding it.

Here was the full-blown premise of pop psychology that we could be anything we wanted to be if we could only stop ourselves from sabotaging our own efforts. It was the classic brainwashing technique described by Lama Sangsu—convince people that they were in need of something, and then that they were the ones responsible for not possessing it. This one-two punch kept people in perpetual servitude to all forms of hucksterism, whether political, commercial, or spiritual.

The fallacy of this argument lay in the notion that we were not complete until we had found romantic love, and until then, we were deficient, flawed, and not whole. In essence, the author was trying to sell us on her own experience. She was setting herself up as a paradigm of love, a swashbuckler on the field of intimacy. It was hardly surprising that such a person had founded a new age church, and now commanded a following of people dazzled by her amalgam of spirituality and romanticism.

The laudatory quote on the cover of the book stated that it gave new meaning to the search for heaven on earth. That, indeed, was the apparent purpose of the book—to market the proposition that people could find paradise in the physical world. I was reminded of Donald Trump's numerous books, such as *The Art of the Deal* or *The Art of the Comeback*. Neither author claimed that their books would enable readers to duplicate their experiences. The disclaimer, however, was part of the sell. I was more convinced than ever that intimacy was a commodity, like money. Some people had it and others didn't. Those who didn't have it would always pay to read about those who did.

I also felt that we lived in an age in which spirituality was sold to us as some kind of commodity. Our whole society was built on achieving tangible results, productivity, success, material comfort, and reward through consumerism. The new age movement had infused our culture with a renewed spiritual impulse, but like many impulses, it had faded over the years. Older, more settled doctrines had reasserted themselves. Spirituality was increasingly equated with self-reliance, and allied with success. If one's brand of spirituality "worked," one should be able to achieve whatever one wanted in life. If one failed at this, one must somehow lack the requisite belief, faith, or positive mental attitude. This was a marriage of the old Calvinist doctrine that virtue was materially rewarded with the Freudian idea that neurosis had its origin in repressed impulses. It had little to do with true spirituality. Rather, it was more closely related to the myths of political and economic conservatism—that all people were created equal, and all they needed was the right attitude, determination, and work ethic, to make it in life. It was a philosophy of the rich, for the rich.

My view was that people were no more created equal in their capacity for intimacy than in their inheritance of wealth, physical beauty, dexterity, intelligence, or drive. The laws of karma and reincarnation dictated that we experienced the effect of our prior actions, including those taken during previous lifetimes of which most of us were unaware. Achievement, fulfillment, and even happiness were not for everyone in this world. Like material wealth, they were for the few, not the many. The true realization of heaven on earth was to be found in the NOW, in being content with what we had this moment. It was not a matter of striving after romantic love, recognition, or material things in an attempt to emulate other people's experiences, nor of blaming ourselves for our lack of success. Lack of intimacy in one's life was not a sign of cowardice. We could be spiritual adventurers regardless of whether we experienced romantic love or not. In fact, to live without such intimacy required a special brand of courage.

I knew so many people who had a deep capacity for love—who were sensitive, giving, kind, responsive to others, and yet had never experienced the type of intimacy that the author of this book described, and probably never would. They might have set up certain conditions for themselves before they ever entered this world. Perhaps they had a particular mission or purpose in life that required that they remain independent, even alone. They may not have had the attractive power or social skills needed to initiate relationships. Their capacity for love may have gone unrecognized because of other people's superficial standards of appearance or financial stability. Maybe they simply didn't need such an experience in this lifetime.

From a cosmic point of view, life was impeccably fair. From the human state of consciousness, it was not. The mistake that people often made was in feeling that life had to be fair in what it doled out to them, that they were all owed their portion of riches, companionship, security, and conjugal love. For those blessed with the capacity for romantic love, it was wonderful, but it in no way set them apart from others, nor elevated them in spiritual status. Quite the contrary, the deepest spirituality was most often found in those who had experienced poverty, exile, loneliness, or even physical, emotional, and mental instability.

We were being sold a "bill of goods." We were relying on other people who set themselves up as spiritual authorities to tell us what kind of lives we should want to lead. People who were already rich in wealth, beauty, fame, or intimacy were cashing in big time by setting themselves up as models for others. If they were attractive, affluent, or socially adventurous, they wrote books extolling the virtues of their experiences. Their narratives were then sold to us as emblematic of some type of modern virtue. This was the romantic illusion that we lived in a world of infinite possibility, and that it required a special kind of courage to catch the nectar in our cup. There might be some validity to this, but an equally valid viewpoint was that we were all right the way we were. Everything was here and now—not at some point in the future when we, too, would have good looks, money, and a glamorous sex life. True abundance was in living in the world with joy and happiness regardless of our station and circumstances in life.

A short time afterwards, I went out for coffee with a young female League member named Kylie Gardiner. When I mentioned the book to her, she immediately got excited. "Isn't it great?" she enthused. I tried to exhibit a poker face, but failed at it, and she recognized that my reaction to the book had been highly negative. I got the typical response from her, mouthed at me so many times by well-meaning people who had succumbed to the sell: "Well, with that kind of attitude, it's no wonder that you don't have a relationship. It's no wonder that you're not successful. It's no wonder that you're not happy!"

It was an amazing demonstration to me that this pop spiritual philosophy had no boundaries. It could infect adherents of diverse spiritual paths like a virus, driving a wedge between their members. There was no use in explaining my viewpoint to Kylie. She was a single mother living alone in a small apartment, and underneath the surface, she was probably as deeply distrustful of the prospect of an intimate relationship as I was. Like me, she had chosen the League as her spiritual path, and she was most likely aware in the distant recesses of her consciousness that her commitment to that path constituted a renunciation of life and its illusory consolations. Still, she needed to believe in the myth of those consolations to keep her going. I was also fighting against those myths, and the very fact that I reacted to them so violently was perhaps an indicator that I had more in common with Kylie than I cared to admit.

The next day, I received an e-mail communication from a member of the League, reporting some remarks made by the current Living Master on the subject of prosperity. The Master had evidently commented on the mentality of people who envied the rich and tried to equalize the distribution of wealth through taxation. He said that people in Congress were multi-millionaires who created tax reform out of impure motives. This, he said, was a spiritual fallacy.

"Soaking the rich belies the spiritual power of Soul," he was quoted as stating. "Soul is a spark of greatness. The power of Divine creativity has no limits. This is a world of abundance! To say that someone has too much in a world of boundless opportunity is wrong. If you visit the higher worlds of God, you will find places that make the largest mansions on earth seem like beggar's homes. Anything that we can create here is like a shack compared to these heavenly buildings. God's love is so great, that he created every kind of abundance for all people."

This statement—whether part of a larger whole, or taken out of context—upset me more than anything I had ever heard or seen attributed to the Living Master. I was shocked by how politically loaded it was, how much part and parcel of a ubiquitous form of American political rhetoric. "How could the Living Master say such a thing?" I fumed. "As a spiritual leader, why would he go out of his way to make such a blatantly political point?"

I had no doubt that the higher worlds of God were places of great majesty and that the wealth found there would dwarf anything our imagination could conceive. Nor could I quarrel with the observation that it was pointless to envy other people's wealth. I didn't dispute that people had the right to their rewards in life, to amass riches, and even build palatial homes for themselves if they so desired. Nor (although it was difficult for me to understand why members of Congress, who were undoubtedly rich, would envy multi-millionaires) would I ever have claimed that our legislators always acted out of the purest motives.

What bothered me were not these individual points, but the partisanship of the statement as a whole, and the implication that this form of political philosophy was divinely favored. In his biography *In My Heart I Am Free*, Brett Singer quoted Andreas Leo as saying:

> The essence of the Science of the Soul is total freedom and complete independence. This depends on cultivating an attitude of detachment. When we hang on to particular ideas and limited viewpoints, we cut ourselves off from God and exile ourselves from the freedom and independence that we seek. (147)

The Living Master's statement that soaking the rich belied the spiritual power of Soul reflected the idea that, in an ideal society, the freedom of Soul would find the highest degree of expression. The less government interference, the more society was seen as running in accordance with natural, hence spiritual, laws. The trouble, to my mind, was that we weren't living in heaven. Certainly, it was a worthy goal to make our society one in which spiritual ideals were reflected. To what extent, however, could society be made to fit such an ideal before the reciprocal force of human nature undermined its balance?

Sooner or later, as I saw it, one came up against the fact that all truth was relative truth. Just as this was a world of abundance, it was equally a world of limitation. This world would always be a testing ground for Soul, and no matter how much we tinkered with our man-made laws, we would always have to take into account the human state of consciousness. The world certainly contained much beauty, light, and that which was good, but it was not part of the higher worlds of God. We couldn't create a heaven on earth, and if we did, it would defeat the whole purpose of this world.

The problem, therefore, was the very human tendency to absorb relative truths and turn them into absolute truths. A person could take a statement such as the Living Master's, comparing freedom from taxation with spiritual freedom, and use this to develop, maintain, and justify a narrow set of political opinions. This would accomplish exactly what Andreas Leo advised against—that is, creating special points, ideas, and distinctions about certain aspects of life and our present-day culture, which actually obscured the broader view of reality.

I immediately called Brian Davidson, a League member of markedly conservative political persuasion, looking for a fight. Brian expressed the typical conservative argument—the less government interference in the lives of individuals, the better—and then justified this position in spiritual terms. "Laws," he said, "exist to reform people, to change their behavior by giving back to them in as exact measure as possible that which they inflicted on others. They constitute an imperfect reflection of the Law of Karma: 'For every action, there is an equal and opposite reaction,' or 'You reap what you sow.'"

"I don't think laws are meant to reform people," I replied, "nor are they a reflection of the Law of Karma. If you believe in karma, why do you feel we need to duplicate this with our own laws? You're assuming that the Law of Karma operates in the heavenly worlds alone, but it also operates in this world, right here and now. We only fail to see its effects. If you believe in karma, why would you feel that we need man-made laws to fulfill the same purpose?"

"Well, if laws aren't designed to change people, to make them better, or even more responsible, what is their purpose?" Brian asked.

"I'd say that their purpose is mainly to preserve, protect, and strengthen the society as a whole," I replied. "If you think of the entire society as an organism, laws can be thought of as an adaptation to ensure the survival of that society, in the same way that a species develops certain traits to adapt for its own survival."

"But if laws don't provide a deterrent or reform the individual, how do they strengthen society as a whole?" Brian wanted to know.

"Well, they mainly provide us with a model of the way we would like our society to be. The main question we have to ask ourselves in deciding what laws we want to create is what kind of society we want to live in. We can have a society in which we reward the rich and penalize the poor, or vice versa. Alternatively, we can strive for some kind of balance between the two. It's our choice. Whatever structure we choose to create, however, the Laws of Karma, which dictate an equal reaction for every action, will continue to operate, dispensing divine justice in a perfect manner. Cosmic laws are not subordinate to man-made laws. In fact, it's just the reverse.

"I think that there's a dichotomy, a split in the field of spirituality that mirrors a similar schism in politics," I added. "Eastern religion, like liberalism, stresses the interdependence of human beings and the relativism of all concepts and opinions. Western spirituality is allied with conservatism in its focus on people's responsibility for their fate and the need to live by moral guidelines and precepts. Conservatives look at this world as a place of unlimited opportunity for those who have the will, ingenuity, and self-confidence to work toward their goals.

"The liberal response to this would be that while it's true for some people, it's not true for all. It's equally true that this is a world of limited resources. There will always be poor people in the world, as well as rich. Many individuals will not experience success, no matter how hard they work, strive, and dream. Our society values some talents and abilities more than it does others. The work of a stockbroker may be rewarded to a much higher degree than those of a teacher, although the teacher may affect the lives of many more people in a positive way."

My argument made no impression on Brian. He started going on about Darwin's principle of natural selection, commonly expressed as "the survival of the fittest," touting the virtues of the entrepreneurial spirit, and invoking the brave settlers who made a new life in America, despite tremendous obstacles. I listened for a while, shaking my head sadly. Then I simply asked him, "How do you think a Native American would react to your view of history?"

This exchange prompted me to stop in a Native American shop on Fifth Street a few days later. I got into a conversation with the young man at the counter, who suggested that if I was interested in finding out more about American Indian beliefs, I could look up Kathleen Carpenter, a Native American anthropologist who taught at Eastern University. I duly called her up, made an appointment, and the next week drove down to see her at her home on the lozenge-shaped island of Grande Isle, in the Wyanoke River.

I arrived an hour late for my meeting after having had a flat on the highway, and was therefore nervous and apologetic as Kathleen ushered me into her spacious home. "That's OK," she said, when I expressed regret for my tardiness. "We Native Americans don't worry about time." She led me into a sitting room, its walls covered with a bewildering variety of masks from Central and South America, Africa, Southeast Asia and practically everywhere else, which she had collected during her periods of anthropological research around the world. She told me that she was now working on behalf of the Wyanoke Indians, who were applying for Federal recognition and needed an anthropologist or historian to write the petition.

"Are you a member of the Wyanoke tribe yourself?" I asked.

"No, but in 1729, there were twenty-nine of our families, Chickasaw and Choctaw, living out here on the islands with the Wyanoke. I'm Cherokee and Choctaw, myself. The Chickasaw and Choctaws are from Mississippi. That's where I was born." She explained that the Chickasaw and Chocktaw met with the Wyanoke in this area for centuries, that the tribes moved back and forth, met one another on hunting expeditions in the Kentucky region, and often visited or stayed with one another. This was enlightening for me. I didn't know that there was such a tremendous amount of interaction between the tribes.

"Why has it taken so long for the Wyanoke to apply for recognition?" I asked.

"Originally," she replied, "the tribes that got Federal recognition were those that were taken from their traditional homeland and moved to Oklahoma. Oklahoma was a new territory that was supposed to be Indian Territory forever. Forever lasted about twenty years. Then, it was opened up to settlers. The Wyanoke didn't feel they should have to leave their traditional lands, so they went to the islands out here in the Wyanoke River, and hid out until General Hugh Bladey's regiments of soldiers were gone. A hundred and fifty still live on the island."

I told Kathleen that I was interested in Native American religion, and wondered if there was a similarity between the belief systems of all Native Americans from North to South America.

"Absolutely," she replied. "They do the same ceremonies that we do. The smudging ceremony, performed by the Quichua and Amara in the Andes, involves the taking in of the smoke from sacred plants similar to those we use here." She got up and came back with a display case of sacred plants. "These are four various kinds of sage that come from different locations," she said, pointing to a row of plant stalks that did, indeed, look like relatives of the sage I was used to buying fresh in the supermarket. "Traditionally, if we go to a location such as the Southwest or the Andes to visit with other tribes, we bring some of our own sacred plants to share with them. When we come back, we bring some of their sacred plants to share among ourselves.

"This, for instance, is universal among us—the tobacco tie." She pointed to some small bundles wrapped in red cloth. "If you come to learn from them, the first thing you do is give them a gift of tobacco. This," she pointed to a cord of braided fibers, "is sweet grass. We braid it first and then we dry it. We use it in our ceremonies, as well."

"Is tobacco universally recognized as a ceremonial plant in the Americas?" I asked.

"Yes. The Creator gave us tobacco so that we can speak to him. Our prayers and our thoughts go up to the Creator on the smoke of the tobacco. The white man took the tobacco and abused it," she added vehemently. "As a rule, we didn't take it into our lungs. The white man used the tobacco as a commodity, and look at all the sickness it's caused!"

"It had no meaning for them?" I asked.

"That's right. They didn't care about what meaning it had. They didn't ask about or understand our attitude toward the plants. We believe that the Creator made the plants before he made us. We need the plants to survive, for food and healing, but the plants don't need us."

"Does the Native American belief system," I asked, "have a particular name by which it is identified, like other religions?"

"Sure. It's called the Medicine Wheel," Kathleen replied. She pointed to a circular wall hanging mounted close to the ceiling just opposite us. "This wheel symbolizes our belief system. There's an outer circle, with forty-four places. Those forty-four places represent gifts of wisdom and knowledge. We believe that you're born at a particular place on the Medicine Wheel, which represents your starting-point, your gift from the Creator. Your job, as a person following this tradition, is to learn all forty-four places on the Medicine Wheel.

"This belief system is very similar to that of indigenous people in other parts of the Americas. There are no dos and don'ts. There's no concept of sin or salvation, no notion of eternal damnation. The important thing is how you live your life and how you treat others while you're here. There are forty-four places on the outer circle, but there's also an inner circle, again with forty-four places, each representing a different animal. Each animal, no matter how insignificant it may appear, has a different lesson to teach us if we watch, respect, and understand it. The porcupine, for instance, raises its quills to scare away its enemies. It represents a type of survival strategy, teaching us how to discourage or repel someone without hurting that person, and thus allowing us to accomplish our own goals."

"Each creature has a spirit that has to be respected," Kathleen emphasized. "They're indigenous to this land just as we are. In the world today, however, animals are discounted. Man has set himself up in this society as being the center of all existence, when in fact we're just part of the Medicine Wheel. Our spirituality is based on the idea that everything is connected and interdependent. We're just one link in the circle of life. We have a responsibility to all the things in this world. People haven't honored other living things. The environment is finite. Once it's destroyed, we can't get it back. Six inches of topsoil, sunlight, water, and clean air sustain everything that lives. When one of those is gone, everything will die.

"I was in China for the Fourth World Conference on Women," she continued. "Fifty-five thousand women from around the world came to talk about women's issues. I waited for the women with whom I was traveling to notice that there were no birds in the trees. Nobody noticed but me. Finally, after about eight days, I pointed it out to them. To American Indians, of course, this is horrifying. Not only were there no birds in the trees, but there were no squirrels, no rabbits, nothing. There were no four-legged creatures at all, just two-legged ones, and way too many of them. The whole situation was just very sad."

What Kathleen said supported my sense that, as in eastern religions, the stress in the Native American tradition was less on the salvation of the individual than on communal responsibility, less on preparing for life in the hereafter than on living harmoniously in the here and now.

"I try hard to avoid anything that causes me disharmony," Kathleen added. "I believe that if I'm not in harmony with myself, I'll disrupt the harmony of my children, my husband, my people, and the disharmony will just spread."

"So by taking responsibility for yourself, you're contributing to the world as a whole."

"Yes," she replied. "The Medicine Wheel presents a way to live your life in a harmonious way. It's a very tolerant belief system. It doesn't say 'Thou shall not.' Instead, what it tries to do is present to you a way to live by example. Each one of these points on the Medicine Wheel represents a lesson about life. We believe that sometimes you can learn the lesson through a single experience, but some people have to experience the lesson many times before they learn. So to get around the Medicine Wheel takes a long, long time.

"Our belief system is older than Christianity," she said. "It has survived because there's validity to it. We believe that eventually the whole world will have to focus on what we believe to be true—that it's necessary to respect the Earth as you do your own mother. When you destroy and pollute that Earth, everything will suffer and die. We believe that everything is linked together spiritually, and we have to understand that link if we're to survive."

I mentioned how distressed I had become over the reported remarks by the Living Master. "Just because we feel that this is a world of opportunity," I said, "doesn't mean we can just go blindly pursuing personal ambitions for ourselves without recognizing limits to resources. If you take the idea that this is a world of abundance to an extreme, you'll become a despoiler."

"I was raised in a very poor family," Kathleen replied, nodding her head in agreement. "Most of my life I had practically nothing, materially. Nevertheless, I've been fortunate. I have this beautiful house and all these masks and art that you see here. I don't measure my wealth by these possessions, though. I've been all over the world, and I know that there isn't abundance everywhere. In other lands, or on an Indian reservation, people couldn't begin to comprehend the way I live—and I clean my own house, do my own cooking and gardening, and work very hard.

"I always say that Indians are the poorest people in America," she remarked, "but culturally and spiritually we're the richest. Most Americans simply don't know us. We don't go out and talk about our spirituality, because it's been the source of a lot of pain. Our beliefs are often viewed with disdain. People make comments like 'How come you are not Christians? How come you don't believe in the same God that we believe in?' That's why we usually don't wear our beliefs on our sleeve. We're very careful about who we share our beliefs with, because we've been the subject of a lot of ridicule, oppression, and discrimination based on our belief system."

I told her about my sense that there was a dichotomy among religions and spiritual groups—that some tended to be more rigid, hierarchical, and absolutist in their doctrine, while others held to a tolerant, open, and relativistic philosophy. I was aware of the irritation behind my words. In my mind, the League clearly belonged to the latter group, and I chafed against its hierarchical structure. I realized that the League was an organization, and that organizations had to be grounded in the physical world. They had limits. They needed internal harmony to survive. I considered myself a questioner, however—always seeking what was behind appearances—and felt I had a right to be discontented with answers cast from a single mold. I had found a like-minded person in Kathleen Carpenter.

"The whole world is too rigid and too organized, and religious organizations are the same way," Kathleen agreed with me. "Why does it have to be that way? If the Creator made all of us, and everything that lives is the same, why does everything have to be ranked and stratified?"

"It's easy for religious or spiritual groups to get wrapped up in themselves," I responded. "They believe that their God is the true God, or that their path is the highest path. They have gotten out of the habit of listening to people other than those within their own group."

"They stay within their own comfort zone," Kathleen said. "To go out of it is to challenge their own beliefs, their own dogma, and themselves. Most people don't want to do that."

"I agree that Americans, in general, don't get out of their comfort zone a whole lot, because it's so big," I said. "The whole country is a big comfort zone. It requires courage to go outside your own religious group, or even outside your own state or city."

"Or to just go outside of your own head," she added, "and try to view the world through someone else's eyes."

I thought back to my conversation with Brian Davidson, and reflected that Andreas Leo's challenge to maintain a non-attached attitude—without creating special points, ideas, and distinctions—

applied to both of us. I had to deal with my feeling of opposition to the viewpoint expressed by the Living Master. My challenge was to cease struggling against an uncomfortable idea, to remain receptive to the truth it represented, and respect those who needed to hear that truth. Brian, on the other hand, was comfortable with that same viewpoint—perhaps too comfortable. His challenge was to resist the temptation to build, reinforce, or maintain an ideology based on that viewpoint, even if it came from as revered and respected a spiritual authority as the Master himself.

Our conversation wound down. Kathleen showed me around the house, and I snapped some pictures of the masks and the artwork. Before heading back home, I took a little tour of Grand Isle, stopping at a bridge overlooking a peaceful canal, its borders hung with willows, a cluster of recreational boats moored in its estuary. As I gazed down on the water, I had the sense of what it might have been like to have lived among the Wyanoke Indians, hiding on this island from General Hugh Bladey's regiments those many years ago. For an instant, I felt connected with the continent's past, and with its indigenous culture. That culture was still present, breathing spiritual vitality into the land, even as the forces of modernity trampled over it. I was an outsider, who knew nothing really about Native American culture. Yet, just by gazing in the water and inclining my ear toward the wind in the trees, I felt welcomed like an old friend into its secret fraternity.

Chapter 12

The Fourth Synagogue

"The spiritual experience is not the same as the religious experience. There's an important relationship between the two, but it's not as direct as most people think."
—Andreas Leo, *The Face of the Eternal, Book Two,* 33

My feeling of irritation with the League was exacerbated by a relatively minor incident that occurred shortly after my conversation with Kathleen Carpenter. I had been invited to a memorial service for another fellow League member who had recently passed away. The service took place at a funeral home in downtown Belle Harbor, to which I drove with a League member named Helen. I counted almost a hundred people there—mostly relatives and co-workers of the deceased. Only a few League members were present. The service was divided into two parts. A Christian minister conducted the first part, while a member of the League clergy presided over the latter half. I found the Christian portion of the service particularly lively and stirring, punctuated by gospel singing and the minister's vigorous oration. The League cleric acquitted himself well on the whole, although some of his comments seemed designed more to introduce the League to the largely Christian audience than to honor and commemorate the deceased.

After the service was over, the League cleric came up to me. "Wasn't it wonderful!" he exclaimed. "What a contrast there was between our part of the service and the Christian part, though. That Christian minister was so loud, and the music, too!"

"I thought it was great," I deadpanned. "I felt the presence of the Force in both parts of the service."

"You did?" the cleric responded in a startled manner. He was apparently used to League members confirming one another in their sense of superiority to other religions and spiritual paths. Without commenting further, I left him to ponder the implication of my remark, and rejoined Helen outside in the parking lot.

"I can't believe what I just heard," I muttered, after relating to her what the League cleric had said to me. "How can he hold himself above the Christian minister? As a member of the clergy, he should have respect for other faiths above everything else."

This small incident highlighted my continuing discomfort with the League community as a whole. Was this what we had become—a group of religious adherents, smug in our separateness, believing that we were somehow better than other groups? Even as I voiced these objections to myself, I was aware of a contradiction in my own feelings. Although I objected to the League cleric holding the League above other groups, my disillusionment with the way the League presented itself to the public was fundamentally an elitist one. Was I really upset about the cleric's arrogance, or was I more discomfited by the fact that the League no longer clearly set itself apart from other groups? What was really at issue here—the cleric's elitism, or my own?

I recognized, first and foremost, that I had to be responsible for my own state of consciousness, instead of worrying about that of others. Nevertheless, I felt the problem went deeper than simply the attitudes of certain members of the League. It was connected with the whole way in which the organization currently defined itself and presented itself to the public. The very stated purpose of the League had been watered down, presumably to appeal to people who had grown up within a sectarian religious tradition. A recent memo sent to League members from the current Living Master stated that:

> The League is a new religion that is growing in size and importance. Its teachings define the nature of Soul more scrupulously than do those of other religions. Each person is a spark of God sent down to earth to gain spiritual experience. Purified by his practice of the spiritual exercises, the individual comes in touch with the Force, or the Holy Spirit. His goal is spiritual liberation in this lifetime.

I eyed the statement critically. Of what importance was it that our teaching defined the nature of Soul more scrupulously than other religions? Didn't all religions claim to bring the individual in touch with the Holy Spirit? Wasn't spiritual liberation the goal of many religions? If so, what set the League apart from the rest? If not, why did the Living Master insist on calling it a religion at all? Was it simply a public relations strategy, a move to make the League seem more a part of the mainstream?

In a subsequent message, the Master aimed his remarks directly at people like me:

> Some entered the League with the mistaken idea that it was no religion. Yet, it claims a God, a Living Master, a set of Holy Scriptures, a temple, and an invisible hierarchy of Masters that sponsors its activities. There's an old saying: 'If it looks like a duck, walks like a duck, and quacks like a duck, it's a duck.' This holds equally true for the League. It has all the characteristics of a religion, yet that is only the outer form it has taken at this time. Those who criticize the outer organization forget that the essence of the League lies in its spiritual core.

Here I felt that the Living Master was both defending his strategy of presenting the League as a religion, and at the same time reminding League members that it was more than that. If it was truly more than a religion, however, why present it as other than what it was? I could not dispute the truth that the League had the outer characteristics of a religion, but I questioned the emphasis placed on those characteristics.

If the Living Master intended to cloak the League in the guise of a religion, I was out of sympathy with this goal.

The truth was that I had never been interested in joining a religion. I had been raised without a religious upbringing, and had inherited a negative view of religion from childhood. I associated religions with inherited dogma, empty ritual, and reliance on received information rather than one's own experience. These feelings set me apart from most other League members who had grown up within the Christian tradition. Many of them had drifted away from their inherited religion because they were looking for something more, something that satisfied a deeper spiritual need. Yet, they were nevertheless used to the authoritarianism of religion, to leaders who told them what to think. They had come into the League by questioning, but once they found a new and higher authority, they had ceased to question.

Andreas Leo had clearly stated that the religious and spiritual experience were not the same, yet he had not explained the difference between the two. When I asked League members what differentiated a religion from a spiritual path, none of them could give me a satisfactory answer. From my perspective, their unquestioning acceptance of the League as a religion marked them as uncurious, timid, and self-satisfied. Where, I wondered, was the spiritual curiosity, the questioning, and the debate that had once invigorated us, and set us apart from other groups?

One day, as I was pondering this question, I happened to bump into Lionel Small. I had met him a number of times in Belle Harbor, and knew that he belonged to a prominent Sufi order. He invited me to attend a *dhikr*, a type of prayer session consisting of the repetition of words in praise of God. I would also have a chance to meet Shaykh Ala ad-Din Talabani, the head of the order in the United States.

A few days later, I drove to a small town about forty miles north of Belle Harbor, and turned in at a gateway on a rural stretch of road. It led past a pasture where a couple of handsome horses grazed, and up to a long, brown-painted building shaped somewhat like a barn. I went around to the back, where a large green banner with the words

"Al-Kabbani Center World Islamic Conference" was hung near the entrance. Listed on the banner were the names of countries from all over the Islamic world, including many republics in the former Soviet Union and the present Russian Federation. I encountered a number of people walking around the grounds, and guessed at their origin or nationality—Saudi, Pakistani, Lebanese, Central Asian, and possibly American. I felt as if I had been transported to a remote outpost of an Islamic-centered world. Eventually, Shaykh Talabani emerged from his cottage, wearing a peaked turban and carrying a thick walking staff. A number of men came out to greet him, having just finished attending to their evening prayers. A group of women and children appeared as well.

Our assembly entered the barn-like building. We moved down a long hall until we reached the midpoint of the structure. Abandoning our shoes, we ascended a narrow stairway in our stocking feet. This led to an immense loft, decorated like a mosque with a wall-to-wall green carpet, and numerous small oriental rugs. The walls were festooned with plaques and banners displaying Koranic verses, and to the side was a makeshift prayer niche. Shaykh Talabani strode to the far end of the room and sat down on a high-backed chair. Children roamed around while the women gathered in a corner of the loft, separated from the main group by some cabinets.

The *dhikr* was quite contrary to my expectations. I had imagined a restful, peaceful repetition of the word HUW (pronounced "who"), which in Arabic simply meant "He" or "It," and was therefore a coded reference to the Almighty. Instead, the chanting was a forceful, vigorous, singsong of Koranic verses that reminded me alternately of the cadences of campfire songs, sailor shanties, and field hollers.

Since I was familiar with the Arabic language, I was able to follow the procession of words to some extent. Eventually, the repetition of verses gave way to the chanting of the word HUW, sounded with a good deal of force, in short, sharp syllables. The chanting shifted to HAQQ, meaning "truth," and then to HAYY, which meant "to live." The name ALLAH was chanted in turn, even more forcefully. I noticed a crescendo, during which the Shaykh literally shouted the word into the microphone at his side.

After the *dhikr*, the Shaykh asked the adults to escort all the children out of the room. Perhaps twenty men remained seated on the carpet in front of him—some in skullcaps, others in peaked turbans, with short beards and long, and all in a variety of attire that reflected the diversity of their ethnic backgrounds. Shaykh Talabani gave a brief opening speech in a sonorous voice:

"Many people today are interested in spirituality, or what we know as the Science of the Soul. Spirituality is the source of energy that cleanses and enlightens the heart. Think of light that goes through a prism, and now think of that prism as your heart. To the eyes, the light is the same. To the heart, however, it is differentiated. Each color has a different taste. Just so, the light that goes through a person produces different colors.

"Now think of your body. It consists of over a trillion cells. Each cell is under the direction of an angel. The angels carry the light for every particle in existence. The smallest particle in the world has an angel assigned to it. If the angel were to disappear, the particle would disappear. Since angels never die, however, energy can never be destroyed, only transferred. The heavenly light is like a rope from heaven coming down toward you. Hold on tightly to that rope..."

I guessed that when the Shaykh talked of the different colors produced by light going through an individual, he was referring to the aura—the magnetic field surrounding a person that could be seen by some people as rays of color. When he spoke of the heavenly light that was like a rope, I suspected he was alluding to the experience of seeing the Light in one's inner vision. After the discourse, the Shaykh rose, and we all followed in unison. The devotees formed a circle, and each one approached him to pay their respects. Then the Shaykh walked to the back of the room and sat in a more casual posture, choosing the very seat that I had vacated. The rest of us sat cross-legged on the floor in a rough semicircle around him. After some brief conversation, I asked if I might be permitted a question. "You spoke of spirituality and also religion," I began. "What is the relationship between the two?"

Shaykh Talabani nodded his head, acknowledging the question as a sound one. "Religion is the car, and spirituality is the gas," he replied. "If the car runs out of gas, it will sit and rust in the sun, a mere heap of scrap metal. If you prefer, you may make a comparison to a nut. In this case, spirituality is the kernel, and religion the shell. The shell protects the kernel. This is a world of matter and energy. An atom consists of both. It is not energy alone. It has a nucleus, around which the electrons spin. Every person is happy with spirituality, because it is freedom. Spirituality needs a structure, however, just as structure needs spirituality. Everyone needs discipline, and this is what religion provides. The discipline of religion is the complement to the freedom of spirituality. Both are necessary for an individual to achieve balance.

"We have a *shaykh*, a Living Master," he added, "who is connected with the Prophet Muhammad via direct lineage—a continuous, unbreakable connection spanning over 1,400 years. In the field of spirituality, there is a new discovery every day. For this reason, you cannot depend solely on the teachings of departed Masters. If you don't have a living *shaykh*, you can't get that direct connection from the heavenly source that will keep you in tune with the new realities that are appearing daily."

Shaykh Talabani's reference to the importance of relying on a Living Master to stay in tune with a changeable reality could have been expressed in virtually the same words by a member of the League. This was why the concept of a Living Master was distinct from that of a world savior such as Jesus, Muhammad, or Buddha. These world saviors appeared at a particular moment in history and then disappeared, leaving disciples, perhaps, but no Master of comparable stature to continue their work. A Living Master, by contrast, served in an appointed position that was continually passed on to someone else. Thus, a fundamental precept of the League was that the world was never without a Living Master, charged with the unique mission of leading souls back to God.

A Living Master, of necessity, had to embody the Living Word—that is, to be a vehicle for Divine will and expression. As such, his message had to be given in a form that was as accessible and understandable to others as possible. A religion based on the teachings of an ascended, or departed, Master always had to cope with the elements of historical, cultural, and linguistic change. The factionalism that infected virtually every major world religion, most of it based on questions of textual interpretation, was ample evidence of the problems created in the wake of an ascended Master. Lionel had told me that Shaykh Talabani's order was distinct from other Sufi sects in that it was less specialized, and thus able to appeal to people in a more universal way. This comment also reminded me of the way that the League was often described, as an ancient teaching rendered more accessible for the modern spiritual seeker.

There were thus many commonalties between Sufism and the League. The biggest difference, it seemed to me, was in Sufism's relation to the religious structure of Islam. According to Shaykh Talabani, religion was meant to protect and safeguard spirituality by providing the stability necessary for it to exist in this world. To prevent the inflexibility of the structure from inhibiting the spiritual core that it was meant to protect, Islam had developed a two-tier system, consisting of an outer religious structure, and an inner spiritual one. Even Muslims who were not Sufis recognized Sufism as constituting the spiritual core of the Faith.

The League, by contrast, was still in the process of becoming established as a religion. Initiates were not used to differentiating the function of a religion from that of a spiritual path. It was easy, therefore, to confuse the religious and spiritual aspects of the League—to assume that one's level of responsibility in the outer organization was a measure of one's spiritual status, or to interpret the guidelines issued by the League's head office as sacred rules or dictates.

What I found strange was that I could accept the reconciling of religion and spirituality on the part of Shaykh Talabani, but not on the part of members of the League. As an outsider, I could appreciate the harmony and tranquility of the Sufis, but within my own Order, the same attempt to maintain unanimity produced a powerful negative reaction in me. Troubled by this contradiction, I was determined to take advantage of any encounters I might have with members of other faiths that would help me get to the bottom of my attitude.

Another such opportunity presented itself almost immediately after my visit to the *dhikr*, when I paid a visit to Sidney Bluestein, a retired teacher who lived in my mother's apartment building. I had told him something about the League, and he, in turn, invited me over to chat about Judaism.

"I have a book here," I said to him when I arrived, fingering a paperback volume in my hands, "written by a comedian who is a Scottish Jew. It contains some humorous stories."

He arched his bushy eyebrows so that they peeked over the rims of his oversize glasses. "That's an unusual ethnic combination," he replied.

"Yes," I agreed. "You don't hear too much about Scottish Jews. The man's name is Arnold Brown, and the book is entitled *Are You Looking at Me, Jimmy*. One of the stories is about a couple, Abraham and Judy, who decide to leave Lithuania and sail for Scotland with their son, Herschel. One week before the family is due to depart, Abraham decides it is time to have a serious talk with his son:

> 'Herschel, I have to tell you one important fact. We Jews are the Chosen People.'
>
> 'Chosen for what, Father?'
>
> 'Chosen to ask questions, my dear Herschel.'
>
> 'Is it good to ask questions, Father?'
>
> 'Yes, Herschel, the Almighty has put us on this earth to do this.'
>
> 'Father, are there answers to all these questions?'
>
> 'Ah,' said Abraham. 'That's exactly the point. The Jewish contribution to civilization is to try to find answers to all these questions. Questions like...Why are we here? Where are we going? Who is going with us? Are we coming back? And above all: Will we be taking sandwiches?'

> Herschel thought for a few seconds. 'What kind of sandwiches, Father?' he asked.
>
> 'What an important question, Herschel,' his father replied. 'You're learning already.'

"I like that story," Mr. Bluestein replied. "It really hits at the philosophy of Judaism—always questioning. If you read the Bible the way I do, you see it not as a history of people doing the right thing, but of *wondering* whether it's the right thing. Have you ever seen "Fiddler on the Roof?" Zero Mostel plays a poor man who sells milk. All kinds of things happen that lead him to question God. He's a pious Jew, but he can't help asking: 'Why is this happening to me?' That's the way Judaism is. Jews DO ask questions. We have a tradition of challenging the status quo.

"There's a story about Hillel, a rabbi who lived around the time of Jesus," Mr. Bluestein continued. "A Gentile approached him, saying that he would convert to Judaism if Rabbi Hillel could explain the Torah in the time that the Gentile was able to stand on one leg. Hillel told the Gentile, 'The Torah says not to do anything to anyone else that you would not want done to you. That is the whole law. Everything else is commentary. You can go study it by yourself.' Many people believe that Jesus was a student of Hillel, because he said the same thing only slightly differently: 'Do unto others as you would have them do unto you.' That's also thought to be one of the reasons that Jews are noted for studying a lot. Hillel's instruction was for them to study and get the details for themselves.

"I'll give you another example," Mr. Bluestein added. "When I was in the Boy Scouts, back in the thirties, the handbook told us to avoid masturbation, because the Bible said so. The origin of this idea is in an ancient law handed down by Moses, which stated that if a man died his brother had to marry the widow. The reason for specifying this was so that she would be financially provided for, because in those days, all the property was in the man's name. Instead of having sex with her, however, he masturbated, spilling his 'seed' on the floor. As punishment, lightning struck and killed him. The Christians interpret this to be an absolute prohibition against masturbation. According to Jewish interpretation, however, the man was simply not living up to his conjugal responsibility. He was repudiating the marriage itself."

"So you're saying that, from the Jewish point of view, the Christian interpretation is a complete misunderstanding of the story. There was a practical purpose to the prohibition against a man spilling his seed. The Christians are ignorant of this, and interpret the prohibition in a moralistic way. Is that right?"

"Yes," Mr. Bluestein replied. "The essence of Judaism is simple and practical. It has to do with doing good, helping others, and helping yourself."

"But what does doing good have to do with questioning?"

"How do you do good, rather than evil?" Mr. Bluestein replied. "How do you arrive at an idea of justice, without questioning? Justice is one of the main ideas in the Bible. For example, Moses supposedly said, 'An eye for an eye, and a tooth for a tooth.' That's not true, however. He actually said 'No MORE than an eye for an eye, and a tooth for a tooth.' In primitive times, if you hit me in one eye, I could come back and hit you in two eyes. If a member of your tribe killed one of my people, I could come back and kill three of yours.

"All this became a matter of interpretation. As the more liberal elements in Judaism see it, you do not enact justice that involves MORE than an eye for an eye, or a tooth for a tooth. That doesn't mean that you are either for or against capital punishment, however. Some later Jewish writings tended to view any Jewish court that condemned even a single man to death as a bloody court. The tradition is that it's not a good idea to kill in retribution, but it doesn't say you CAN'T. It says, before you do, you have to make sure that the man is guilty, and that the punishment fits the crime. You get an idea from this why there are so many Jewish lawyers."

"Well, there are a lot of Jewish lawyers, but there are also a lot of Jewish comedians."

"We laugh at ourselves," Mr. Bluestein agreed. "Isn't it better than suffering? For example, there's a joke that goes back to Hitler's time. A

German Jew was walking down the street, and a bunch of Hitler's storm troopers grabbed him. 'Hey, dirty Jew,' they said to him. 'Who started this war?' Of course, the man was supposed to reply 'The Jews,' but instead he said 'The Jews and the bicycle riders.' This puzzled the storm troopers, and they asked, 'Well, we can understand the Jews, but why the bicycle riders?' And the Jewish man replied, 'Why the Jews?'"

"Why the Jews indeed," I replied. "Humor derives from suffering. The certainty of the Nazis' racist ideology left them without any perspective on what they were doing. That's why I tend to react negatively to certainty. I recognize that belief is of undeniable benefit. If one is convinced of something, one acts with a greater degree of decisiveness. I'm skeptical, however, of anything that cries out that it is the truth. Holding to rigid interpretations of the truth breeds authoritarianism."

"That reminds me of another story," Mr. Bluestein interjected. "A good man, known for his learning, righteousness, sense of justice, and studiousness, was dying in the hospital. The rabbis, priests, ministers, and Islamic clerics all came to his bedside. The man died, and the clerics were all huddled around the bedside, saying, 'He is surely in Heaven. He's there with God.'

"After commiserating for fifteen or twenty minutes, a young medical student came in and said, 'We've just been studying new methods of revival.' He got on the man's chest, banged on it, and the man came back to life.

"The clerics were all excited. 'You were dead for almost a half hour,' they said. 'Were you in Heaven?'

"'Yes,' the man responded.

"'Tell us, then. What is God like?' they asked.

"'Well,' the man replied. 'In the first place, she's black…'"

I smiled. "That's an old story, and a good one," I replied.

"I'll leave you with one of my favorite jokes," Mr. Bluestein said. "It's an old one, about a Jewish man who was shipwrecked on a desert island for twenty years, all by himself. Finally, a ship came and rescued him. They got him on board, and the captain said to him, 'I can see four buildings that you've built on this island. What are they for?'

"The man replied, 'They're synagogues. The first one is in case I feel like being an orthodox Jew, the second one is in case I want to be a conservative Jew, and the third one is if I want to be a reform Jew.'

"The captain asked, 'Well, what about that fourth building, way on the other side of the island?'

"And the Jewish man replied, 'Oh, that's one synagogue I'd never be caught dead in!'"

"That's a great joke," I said, "but what's your interpretation of it?"

"To me, it means that there's such a diversity of viewpoints," he replied. "And we ourselves can change. The man could be an orthodox one day, a conservative another, a reform the next, and just in case, he's even built a place that he wouldn't be caught dead in!"

"That's a good interpretation," I commented. "Mine was probably a little bit off."

"There are many interpretations. What was yours?" he asked.

"Well, to me, it had to do with the difference between religion and spirituality," I replied, unable to shake my preoccupation with this subject. "Religion is a way for people to bring God down to their level of understanding, a way for them to feel comfortable about themselves and go about the daily business of living. Temples, churches, mosques, and synagogues help make spirituality comprehensible for us. True spirituality, however, takes us beyond the limits of our understanding.

"In the story, the man built three synagogues, and each one was a kind of refuge. The fourth synagogue, however, represents something that has no name and yet is truly universal. Most people don't want to face it. I think the fact that the man in the story built that fourth synagogue represents something very brave, though paradoxical, in Judaism. It shows that Jews are willing to recognize the existence of something beyond their own religion, even while they express the urge to contain it, to render it comprehensible."

"Well, maybe we need both," Mr. Bluestein suggested. "Maybe we need to be challenged and at the same time be able to go about the daily business of living."

"Yes," I replied. "I've learned that the two don't actually represent such a contradiction."

"There's the saying that water can either be a danger or a help to you," Mr. Bluestein added. "You can drown in water, or you can relieve your thirst."

I mentioned to him Shaykh Talabani's dictum that religion is a protection for spirituality.

"You just have to make sure it's not too solid," Mr. Bluestein commented. "If it's too rigid, it can be torn down. The more supple the tree, the greater its ability to weather a storm."

"The true protection," I agreed, "is not a completely impermeable shell, but rather something that can bend, or can breathe, or can let in the light. If it is too protective, whatever is inside will just dry up and die. Questioning renders that membrane permeable, allowing light and air to get in. That's why, whatever group we belong to, we need to get out of our shell once in a while, look around us, and appreciate that truth is everywhere around us. Religion can be a protection for spirituality, but it can stifle it, as well."

My meetings with Shaykh Talabani and Mr. Bluestein caused me to grudgingly accept the notion that spirituality could live within the framework of a religion, but I still could not embrace the idea wholeheartedly. The current Living Master had recently written:

> There is a difference between the League and other spiritual paths. The Living Master is the Living Word. This power is not granted to leaders with imperfect understanding. If its foundation is strong, the destiny of the League is to become a world religion.

The Living Master's mission was clearly to bolster the framework of the League to make it more enduringly serviceable to mankind. He intended to mold the League into a world religion, and was relying on its hierarchical structure to accommodate a line of Masters that would presumably endure for centuries, as the Sufi and Tantric lineages had done. The success of such a project depended on one thing—the consciousness of the Living Master. The League rose or fell upon his understanding of his own mission. I had already seen one such Master fail. What guarantee was there that others would not fail, as well?

The structure itself was no guarantee. The Force couldn't be tied down by creating an organizational edifice. The title of Living Master might continue to be passed down from one individual to another, but that was just a title. The spiritual authority of the true Living Master—that individual uniquely empowered by God to lead Soul to its true home in the spiritual worlds—could pass to any individual, working within any culture or group. What, then, was the point of founding a world religion if the eternal function of the Living Master was something entirely separate, which would endure irrespective of what name or title was applied to it?

One day—perhaps sooner rather than later—the League would have a titular Master at its head who would not be the true Living Master. That spiritual authority would have passed elsewhere. The League would go the way of all religions—torn by schisms, its hierarchy ossified, the title of Living Master rendered meaningless. The game would have begun anew, and it would be up to those individuals who had kept their spiritual perception intact to distinguish the true Master from those less empowered.

There was nothing wrong with supporting the Living Master in his mission to build an enduring foundation for the League, as long as it did not cause us to lose sight of the true goal. The moment we substituted the mandates, guidelines, and culture of the League for our own personal experience, we were retreating from our primary spiritual responsibility. We were allowing the League to become merely a place of refuge and solace, reducing it to our level of comprehension, and failing to hold on to the essence of its teachings in our very attempt to grasp it. The true spiritual test was not to remain loyal to the League at all costs, but to find the courage to see beyond it, to continually rediscover in it the fourth synagogue—the gateway to spiritual challenge and eternal mystery.

PART FOUR

The Knowledge of the Divine Self

"The greatest tenet of life is 'I AM.' Whoever concentrates intently upon this principle will discover the knowledge of the divine Self—that there is no center of the Force other than himself. Thus, he is liberated before the death of the physical body, while still in human form."

—Andreas Leo, *The Face of the Eternal, Book One*, 22

Chapter Thirteen

The Way of Water

"The Force embraces all the universes of God. It rules and supports all living things. It will show man how to live, if he will only permit it to do so."
—Andreas Leo, *The Face of the Eternal, Book Two*, 89

One day, I bumped into a former student of mine who knew something of my spiritual interests. She handed me a poster announcing the visit of a South American shaman, named Don Antonio, to the area. A member of a Quichua tribe in Ecuador, he was currently staying with a family in the small town of Livingston, about twenty miles southwest of Belle Harbor. This appeared to be worth investigating, so I called the number as soon as I got home and spoke to Robin Steiner, the shaman's host, who invited me for dinner that evening.

It was already quite dark as I made a left turn that brought me just opposite the dirt road that led to the Steiner house. As I straightened out my wheels, I nearly had a head-on collision with an enormous buck. I brought my car to a dead stop about four inches from the creature's nose and found myself face to face with it. It stood frozen like a statue for several seconds, gazing directly into the windshield, before it bounded off.

When I arrived at the Steiner residence, I stepped onto the front porch. Through the window, I could see the shaman stretched out on a bed, as he relaxed in a private room just to the right of the main entrance, his long, dark hair spilling over a faded yellow shirt. I knocked on the door, was greeted by Robin's husband, and introduced to about a half-dozen other dinner guests. Eventually, Don Antonio emerged from the room where he had been resting. He was an unassuming man with deep brown skin, a barely wrinkled face, cheerful eyes, and a gentle manner. I grasped his hand, and immediately noticed the firm grip.

Over dinner, I learned that Don Antonio and other Ecuadorian shamans were coming to the United States to fulfill an ancient prophecy that told of the uniting of the materialistic and intellectual North—the Land of the Eagle—with the spiritualistic, holistic, and heart-centered South—the Land of the Condor. Don Antonio had already come to the United States many times, speaking, conducting workshops, and offering spiritual "cleansings." He had also set up a shaman apprenticeship program for Westerners at a center in Ecuador.

After dinner, the Steiners passed around some photos taken of Western apprentices in Ecuador, as well as of Don Antonio, his wife, and an exotic orchid-like plant. "This is the *tatzo*," Robin explained. "The flower blooms year-round, and has medicinal qualities. Don Antonio's personality is like that of the flower—delicate and healing."

I inquired about the cleansing sessions. Robin told me that appointments were still available for the next day. I decided that this would be a worthwhile experience, so I signed up. I was instructed to bring some cut wildflowers with me, and to think about a spiritual request that I would like to make inwardly.

About eighteen hours later, I returned to Livingston. It was shortly past midday. The sky was cloudless. I had with me two long stalks of purple irises that I had harvested earlier that morning from a suburban street in Belle Harbor, where they had been on the verge of wilting. As I drove, I felt uneasy, and made a mental list of all the things that were bothering me. I was frustrated with my present job, meager salary, lack of employment prospects, and concerned about my mother's health. On top of that, I had mislaid the steno pad on which I minutely recorded all my appointments, plans, and priorities. I felt lost without that steno pad.

I arrived at the Steiner house with all these worries on my mind, sat down in the foyer with my two large stalks of flowers, and waited my turn to see Don Antonio. Eventually, a pair of double doors opened, and he ushered me into the room designated for the ceremony. I handed him the flowers, and he wordlessly motioned me to stand facing him. Immediately, my eyes closed involuntarily, and I felt myself go into a deep contemplation.

I could hear Don Antonio chanting in his native tongue as he made several passes around me, stopping each time at the four points of the compass. With each cycle, I was exposed to a different sensation. First, I felt strong bursts of air aimed at me from each of the four directions. Then I was alternately sprayed with water, touched with the feather of a bird, and whipped with something soft, like chamois. On this last pass, I opened my eyes just a bit and saw that Don Antonio was holding the purple irises I had brought with me. Throughout the entire ceremony, I was aware of the pungent smell of incense. At the end, I could feel the shaman anointing me with an aromatic balm, which he smeared on my nostrils, the bridge of the nose between my eyes, and the top of my head, as well as my arms and hands.

As the ceremony progressed, I felt myself moving through various states of contemplation. Periodically, my body stiffened, I felt my eyes roll back in their sockets, and noticed that I was nodding my head backwards and forwards. Under my breath, I began to chant a word that I regularly used in contemplation. It blended with Don Antonio's utterances, and did not appear to interfere with his conduct of the ceremony. Just as suddenly as I had started my chanting, I stopped, became silent, and felt more peaceful and at ease. Without any signal from Don Antonio, I found my eyes opening. He was standing before me, just as at the beginning of the ceremony, bowing slightly in my direction. I bowed in return, and we embraced briefly. The "cleansing" was over as quickly as it had begun.

Before leaving, I wanted to thank Don Alberto. I remembered that I had a copy of Andreas Leo's *The Lion's Paw*, translated into Spanish, in my car. I ran outside, retrieved the book, and presented it to him, out of breath. "I want you to have this," I told him through Robin. "It has meant a great deal to me over the years. I think you will enjoy it." Don Antonio thanked me, and promised he would read it. I didn't know if this gesture of exchange from one spiritual path to another would amount to anything, but felt a certain satisfaction that I had made the attempt.

As I walked back to my car, I noticed that my thoughts were indeed clearer. I expected the worries that had preoccupied me earlier to immediately come back, but that was not the case. They had receded from my mind as if I had previously experienced a muscle ache, taken an aspirin, and now was suddenly relieved of pain. In place of the previous discomfort, there was ease. My memory lingered on my encounter with the buck on the way to the Steiner's house, particularly the way it had so calmly regarded me through the windshield of my car. The shaman and the buck were dual symbols that represented a connection with the natural world. In both encounters, I felt that nature itself was extending an invitation to me.

I had a chance to follow up on my encounter with Don Antonio a few weeks later. The occasion was an apprenticeship program sponsored by the shaman, which took place in the vicinity of River Bend, just across the state line near the shore of Lake Millikin. The decision to attend the program was not one that I made lightly. Apprenticeship implied following a different spiritual path. I was worried that attending the program would further undermine my delicate relationship to the League, so I decided to call Lynne Silva and ask her opinion before deciding to go.

"Spirit is in everything," she replied in response to my query. "It's in our path, and it's in all these other spiritual and religious groups. If you choose to explore this shaman's teachings, you just have to remember where your foundation is. If you view your experience as just an extension of your own path, then that's what it will be for you.

Consider that the Inner Master has sent you to Don Antonio, and then you will be able to transmute whatever you learn from him to the highest spiritual value. Remember that the most important thing is to be yourself, and unashamedly yourself. Follow your interest, your passion, and look for the hidden guidance of Spirit in all the facets and events of your life."

Thus reassured, I drove down early on a Saturday morning. It was about a three-hour drive to the state line, and then a few bewildering miles down a maze of county roads. Finally, I arrived at Christine Kandinsky's house, the site of the apprenticeship program. The weather was unseasonably cold and wet. About twenty-five participants were seated in a wide ring in a large, comfortable basement, mostly in chairs, but with a few people lounging directly on the carpeted floor. Don Antonio entered the room, dressed with utter casualness in a cardigan-like jacket of native origin, and bare feet.

"Every moment of our life can be a party, a *fiesta*, a celebration," he began. "Every moment can be enjoyable. Our meals, our chores—everything can be a party, a celebration. Even our difficulties can be part of the celebration. Our mind wants to take us out of the party, out of the celebration. We have now reached that point in our spiritual path, however, when we have the option of remaining in it at all times. Whenever our problem is too big, we can ask for help from the elements of nature—the earth, the air, the fire, or the water. No ideal place exists for you other than where you are right now. It's all here and now, not at a different time or a different place. The elements of nature are not only outside, but also within us. The element of earth is represented by the minerals in our body, water by its fluids, fire by its temperature, and air by the oxygen we take into it."

After a lengthy discussion on the principles Don Antonio had outlined, we paused for lunch. It was immediately evident that food was a big part of the program. Participants had the option of paying for a full meal plan, bringing their own food, or fasting. I had decided to eat very sparingly, but we had a wonderful cook named Erin King, who had a knack for preparing Ecuadorian-style food. Steaming pots of quinoa, *fava* beans, and large, white-kernel corn were among the memorable dishes she served. Don Antonio stressed the importance of eating with a reverential attitude. Some of the participants seemed to take this to an extreme, eating in silence and utter seriousness at the marble dining room table. Others sat at a smaller table near the kitchen entrance, engaged in more animated conversation.

During the lunch period, Don Antonio approached me and said that he had read *The Lion's Paw*. "I enjoyed it greatly," he stated. "It made me laugh, because it was so true."

I was surprised that he had looked at the book at all, and delighted by his response. "Most people who read the book say that it reads like pure fantasy," I commented.

"That's exactly why I liked it," Don Antonio replied. "There is nothing truer than our imagination."

In the afternoon, Don Antonio gave us a ritual exercise to carry out, which he called a sand painting. This was only the first part of a larger ritual that was to conclude the next day, and which didn't actually involve sand at all. We were to go into the woods and find a place where we could mark off a circle. Then we were to embellish the space within the circle in any way that we wanted. We could draw in the earth with a stick, place objects within the circle, or do anything else with it that we desired. Afterwards, we were to find an object to place to the left of the circle, as we faced it, and another to put on the right. The object on the left was to represent something that we wanted to get rid of, and the one on the right something that we wanted to obtain or keep.

I went out and found a perfect spot in the woods where some earth had been previously dug up and was already heaped in a kind of mound, which made it quite easy to mark off from its surroundings. I drew a circle with a stick. Then, unsatisfied with the bare look of the earth, I took leaves from the surrounding foliage, and covered the earth in the circle until I had a perfectly round green shape in front of me. Following this, I took little twigs and pushed them into the leaves like skewers to hold them in place. I put a ring of pebbles around the perimeter of the circle. Finally, I placed a large spray of white flowers to the right of the circle, symbolizing what I wanted to keep, which was my relationship to the League. I placed a smaller sprig of white flowers to the left, representing all the doubts and frustrations that I wanted to release.

I drove back to Belle Harbor for the night, and returned too late the next day to catch the morning program. I asked some people what Don Antonio had talked about. "Mainly he stressed the fact that he was not a holy person, not a guru," one of the participants told me. "He can't see into the future, and he can't read people's minds. He doesn't really know what people necessarily want from him unless they come out and tell him. He's just a person walking on a path, and if people want to accompany him for part of the journey, that's their choice. He's come here to talk to us, rather than teach us, because really he's just on the same path as we are."

The weather was still bad, so in the early afternoon we met again in the basement of Christine's home. Don Antonio talked about some of his experiences during his own apprenticeship training. "Often I made the mistake," he said, "of putting a person at a particular point on the path just because I wanted to show him what I had experienced. Sometimes, it was not that person's time to experience that, and the result was actually that they took a step backwards on the path. One of the tasks I was given during my training was to live with a dog for three months in a cornfield. At the end of the three months, I let the dog go. It was so glad to be set free that it ran amok and made a mess of the cornfield. This lesson was meant to show me that I had to be careful about taking people where they didn't belong."

The image of the dog being penned up and then suddenly set free reminded me of the way I sometimes felt about the Law of Silence. My desire to constantly question and debate could, I supposed, be likened to the undisciplined behavior of the dog, although I didn't like to think of it that way. "In my spiritual group, we have a principle called the Law of Silence," I volunteered. "The rule of thumb associated with it is that if you are in doubt about the wisdom of speaking, you should ask yourself three questions: 'Is it true, is it necessary, and is it kind?' Sometimes, however, I feel that this principle is taken to the point of absurdity." I was hoping that Don Antonio would say something that would support me in my viewpoint.

"This is a very good principle," Don Antonio replied, denying me the satisfaction I was seeking. "I agree with it entirely. As we walk on this path, little by little, we will talk less and less. I have practiced being in silence, and it is a wonderful thing. Similarly, just as it is necessary to husband our words," Don Antonio added, "it's necessary to guard the sacred fire, known in the *yogic* tradition as the Kundalini."

He explained that there was no word for sex in the Quichua language, nor did people in his culture feel that the act of sex required an accompaniment of words. He also noted that sexual activity in a rural society tended to be less than in an urban one. "In the city," he stated, "people tend to lead a sedentary life, and their sexual activity increases proportionally to the lack of other forms of physical stimulation. In the countryside, people work quite hard. They're tired at the end of the day, so there are fewer sexual urges."

As I listened to Don Antonio's explanation, I reflected that one could not really separate the sexual from the non-sexual aspects of life. Simple vitality, hard work, and vigorous activity were like sex, in a way, because they brought one closely in touch with life itself. From this perspective, it was easy to understand why the Quichua language might lack a word that specifically referred to sex. It also made sense that Don Antonio would speak of sex in the context of the Law of Silence. Words were a form of communication, just as sexual activity was. Thus, the Law of Silence was akin to chastity. One had to respect the power of words, just as one did the "sacred fire."

In the afternoon, Don Antonio asked us to go back in the woods, find our sand painting, and remove the object that we had placed on the left. We were told to cover up the area that we had previously decorated and return. Once inside, we assembled in the basement. We were each given a large sheet of paper, together with some tobacco. Then we were shown how to make a circle on the paper with the tobacco, starting clockwise from the bottom. We were to divide the circle into four parts with two more lines of tobacco—vertical and horizontal. This basic figure represented the four directions, as well as the four elements—earth, water, air, and fire.

At this point, we were offered some freshly picked herbs, including mugwort and angelica, and shown how to make a sprig of one, three, or five leaves, called a *kintu*. We stood up with the *kintu* in our hands, and faced each one of the four directions in blessing, blowing on it with each salutation. Then we were told to place the *kintu* in the middle of our tobacco symbol. After this, we received flower petals to place on the paper for decoration. A number of other things could be added: animal fat and bones, herbal essences, corn, brown sugar, and chocolate—all deemed pleasing offerings. Finally, we placed the object that we had retrieved from our sand painting on the paper, wrapped it up in a package, secured it with string, and placed any additional adornments on it that we wanted.

When we had finished, Don Antonio announced the ritual of the fire ceremony. We stood in a large circle around the fire, playing drums or flutes, as each person in turn came up to the fire, and with whatever gestures, words, or ritual observances they chose, placed their ceremonial packages in the fire. I approached, inwardly repeating the secret word that I used in contemplation. I felt the presence of the Force. Something was lifted from me, and the emotional weight I had been carrying around was replaced by a sense of equilibrium. Now I understood why it was important to place objects on both sides of the sand painting. To simply get rid of something would be to create a vacuum. Something else had to move into that space.

Instead of driving back to Belle Harbor that evening, I decided to camp by the lake. I followed a small road down to a camping lodge, and made my way past the lodge down to the shore. Aside from the remnants of a large campfire, the shoreline was unremarkable, littered with rocks, driftwood, and other debris. I decided, on an impulse, to look for a camping spot in the neighboring woods, and found a grove of cedars. As soon as I entered it, I noticed the way the trees shut out the wind that blew in from the lake, offering a feeling of intimate protection. I felt the Force cloaking me around the shoulders, in a manner similar to that of the trees. I found a place to unpack my bedroll, and spent a peaceful night in that enclosure.

The next morning, I encountered Don Antonio at breakfast, and mentioned the feeling of protection I had received from the cedars. "When I entered that grove of trees, it felt almost as if I was in a place of worship," I remarked. I had expected to be cold during the night, but I wasn't. The place was remarkably warm.

Don Antonio nodded. "That's the nature of cedar. It has a feminine, protective power."

The weather had lightened up, so after breakfast we convened on the deck of Christine's house. Don Antonio gave us an exercise that involved touching one's feet, looking at them while massaging the soles quite vigorously with the nails in a stroking motion, and then closing our eyes while continuing the exercise, breathing deeply all the while.

"This," he said, "is a way of activating the mind without thinking. We think of the body as divided into three different *pachas*. The word *pacha* means 'realm,' in a loose sense, but there is no exact translation. In Quichua, we do not differentiate between the words for space and time. There is only the word *pacha*, which signifies a unified realm of time and space.

"These *pachas* correspond to the three major areas of the body—the body from the genital organs down represents the earth, the head represents the sky, and the torso from the genitals to the neck represents the physical world that we inhabit—at the meeting point of earth and sky. By stimulating the feet, we stimulate the torso, and ultimately the head. We begin to light part of the sacred fire. You can feel this in your heart. This, in turn, will activate the brain. It is a way to stimulate the mind to think in a natural, rather than a mechanical way, by activating the brain through the heart. All these exercises I have shown you today are meant to balance the physical, the emotional, and the mental processes in the individual."

In the morning, the weather had cleared, and we assembled on an outdoor deck. Before him on a small table were two tumblers that he had brought from the kitchen—one filled with water, the other empty. "I'm going to give you the sound of water," he began. "I want you to listen to your heart, and let it feel whatever it wants to feel. Let yourself see whatever your heart wants to see." He began pouring the water from one glass into the other, and back again. I closed my eyes, and experienced a strong surge of emotion. Don Antonio was right. The mere sound of the water could bring me in touch with my deepest feelings.

He continued his discourse. "In our lives, there will always be difficulties. We want immediate solutions, but we have to wait for an adequate time and place. Water can remind us of this. It's interesting when difficulties appear in our lives. The great force of life has much love for us. It has so much to teach us. A problem that is large and difficult has the appearance of destroying everything. One can feel that one's life is finished. One can arrive at a point of desperation. Water, however, never arrives at such places. The water doesn't turn back. It is always moving forward.

"Problems present us with an opportunity to find an adequate time and place to put into practice the things that we know, and to remember the things that will help us in life. As individuals, we all have different personal resources. We all have different talents, and different ways of contributing. Let us remember to experiment and discover. Life is immense and infinite. Our problems represent opportunities. God does not punish us. A difficult circumstance or problem is small in comparison to the immensity of the universe.

"The quality of one's life is determined by more than merely whether it is long or short. We existed long before we took on this body, and we will exist after it. Water is a symbol of just how immense life is. The lessons of water are beautiful and great. Let the water be your teacher. Learn to flow the way the water flows. Allow your life to be like a permanently flowing river. Allow yourself to be what you truly want to be."

His voice became more urgent, more eloquent. "Many people in the world today want only information. You can amass a great amount of information, but if you only have a little experience, you will not know truth. If, however, you have only a small amount of information, but many experiences in life, then you will know the truth. The only useful knowledge is that which you gain from your own experience, your own experimentation.

"What I am telling you is not new. You have read these things in many books. You have more than enough books. You have all the information you need. You have the knowledge. Now you simply have to live what you know. You are ready to fly. The only problem is that the knowledge is all in your minds. It has to be transferred to your hearts. The heart wants something, but the mind doesn't know how to achieve it. The mind says you are not prepared, but the truth is, you *are* prepared."

Don Antonio then gave us an exercise that consisted simply of walking, but with all the weight of the body mentally transferred to the head. He had the participants walking around the grounds for over half an hour in this fashion, practicing on the deck, the grass, the pavement, and the stones. "Try to do this first with your eyes open, then judge the distance in front of you, and try it with your eyes closed," Don Antonio recommended. The resulting spectacle was comically reminiscent of a Fellini film, with people walking very earnestly at all angles across the lawn and driveway, passing one another wordlessly as they did so.

When we reassembled, Don Antonio commented on the walking exercise. "Watching other people walk can help us with our own walking," he said. "This exercise has to do with comparing ourselves to others. It can be a positive exercise if we do it not to place ourselves higher or lower in relation to other people, but only in position to learn from them. Criticism can be harmful to the person doing the criticizing. It's best to observe others and be aware of our own mistakes. When a person thinks that someone is either behind them or in front of them, it is a way of being judgmental. When we judge in this way, we will feel superior to some and inferior to others. Neither of these will help us on our path."

Don Antonio asked us to do a variation of the massage exercise that we had done with our feet, except this time with our hands. Again, he instructed us to first look at our hands as we did this, and then to close our eyes while continuing the exercise. He then asked us to relate some of the things we had experienced that day. After a number of people had taken their turn, I spoke up.

"The most profound experience for me," I said, "came from the simplest technique, which was the palm exercise that we just did. The minute I made the transition from looking at my hands to closing my eyes, I felt a deep love pouring into my heart. I'm used to feeling this in my contemplation, with my attention placed on the Inner Master. I was surprised, however, to feel this in response to something as simple as looking at my hands and then closing my eyes. I can't exactly explain why the simple act of closing my eyes while stroking my hand would have this effect on me, but it did. It seemed to have something to do with the action of shifting my attention from the outer to the inner world."

"It's true that you can have such a feeling in response to focusing on something specific, such as a Master or teacher," Don Antonio replied. "But when we open ourselves to just feeling, then we can go even farther than when we have a particular goal."

This was the first experience I had during the apprenticeship program that challenged one of my assumptions as a League initiate. Generally, the contemplation techniques of the League involved putting one's attention on the Living Master, or on one of the departed Masters still serving on the inner planes of existence. They rarely involved focusing on something as mundane as one's hand or foot. One of the things that I felt lacking in the League teachings was that they focused exclusively on out-of-the body experiences, and very little on integrating oneself with the physical world, or one's physical body.

My natural tendency was to live in my head, in my imagination, and to neglect my physical needs. Instinct told me that my reliance on the League teachings had merely exacerbated these tendencies. I couldn't pinpoint the relationship between Don Antonio's method of contemplation and the spiritual exercises of our Order. All I knew was that Don Antonio's exercise had a remarkable effect on me. It highlighted for me the contrast between the League's ethereal teachings and his down-to-earth practices. It was paradoxical that they could both achieve the same effect. When we reconvened, I asked, "How can a simple action cause us to change our attitude or awareness? If it has this power, how can it be just a ritual?"

"Anything we do can be viewed as a ritual," Don Antonio replied. "Even just sitting together as we're doing now is a ritual. It influences us by making use of the elements of nature. Everything in nature is giving and receiving. For that simple reason, everything we do is sacred and can have repercussions in our life. If we can understand this, our life will be transformed, and we will be in a permanent state of ritual. In Quichua, the word 'ritual' also does not exist. Instead, we have a word, *raymi*, which means a *fiesta*, or party. The researchers translate it as 'sacred ritual,' but that's an elaboration. It just means party, *fiesta*.

"Everything needs to be transformed into a permanent ritual. A ritual has four parts. We greet that which we are encountering, we express our feelings at that moment, we ask for whatever we would like to occur, and we say our words of parting. This may transpire without another person even noticing. For instance, a little while ago, Christine's cat was standing in the doorway. I opened the door to go inside, and the cat came out. Most people would not notice anything in my behavior to indicate that anything else occurred, but as I passed the cat in the doorway, I went through this entire ritual. It's difficult to put into words, but it's actually a simple technique to master. We just have to make everything we do part of the great ritual of life.

"Every moment is sacred. Every place is sacred. This house is sacred, and so are your homes and the places you inhabit. You can transform your home into a sacred place, and your life into a succession of sacred moments."

Tears came to his eyes as he spoke. Out of respect, I looked away from him as he delivered his parting words. "It is not in my hands to take you deeper into this temple. I only offer that we walk together. My body belongs to Mother Earth, and it is only natural that it will return there. Let us not be concerned about the ultimate fate of the body, but simply celebrate our existence at this moment. It brings great joy to my heart to be with you. Thousands have given their lives, reputations, and fortunes in order that we could come together for this very meeting centuries after their deaths. Let us not forget to be grateful to them. The best way to show our gratitude is just to live. When you wish, and when we can, we will walk together again. And when we go to sleep, we can continue to meet and to talk with one another in our dreams."

Before driving back to Belle Harbor, I decided to make a last pilgrimage to the grove of cedars where I had camped the night before. I found the spot. It had begun to rain gently, but inside the grove of trees, it was dry. Inwardly, I thanked the spirit of the cedars for their protection. Then I walked to the shore. At a point where it curved sharply, I stood on a large rock at the farthermost tip, surrounded by water on three sides, and gazed out on the horizon.

"What do I do next?" I asked inwardly. "Where do I go? How do I make my way?"

In answer, I heard an intuitive voice inside myself:

"You need only do something that gives you great joy, and you will hear my words conveyed to you on the wings of silent sound!"

Chapter Fourteen

Something Pretty Special

"The truth about God is shocking. He is not interested in humanity, but only in the continuity of life. His desire is to open up the human consciousness so that the Force can flow out into the world of matter."

—Andreas Leo, *The Words and Wisdom of Andreas Leo*, 29

After my return from Don Antonio's workshop, I started mentally comparing what I had seen during his apprenticeship program and similar events sponsored by the League. What had impressed me about Don Antonio's program was the relaxed manner in which the shaman ran it. There was no formal schedule, no list of activities. If something of Don Antonio's method could be incorporated into our own activities, I felt it could have a positive effect on the League community as a whole. I had a sudden impulse to reconcile with Dan Koster, and find out what was going on with planning for our upcoming annual retreat in Cavanaugh City.

"That's interesting," he said, when I got ahold of him and explained the reason for my call. "I was just on the phone discussing this with the area director. The date for the retreat is only two months away, and we have no one willing to take charge of it. I was just considering whether I should volunteer to do it myself. Would you like to work on it together with me?"

I agreed, and received quick approval from the area director to help Dan with the retreat. I was struck by the uncanny timing involved in my taking on this responsibility. During the fire ceremony the previous weekend, I had asked to be reconciled with the League, and had felt a weight lift from me. The effect, apparently, had been immediate. It affirmed my sense that I had been given the opportunity to attend Don Antonio's retreat as part of my spiritual training, and that its purpose had been to restore and deepen my relationship with the League, rather than cut me off from it.

There were virtually no League members in our area that had participated in anything like Don Antonio's apprenticeship program. Either they were not curious about other spiritual paths, or they didn't want to risk the potential spiritual conflict of dabbling in them. That gave me, in a modest sense, a degree of expertise that other local initiates didn't have. I felt that the League community possibly needed this infusion of fresh perspective from an outside source. If so, I was in a position to contribute to the retreat in a way that few others within the community could.

Dan and I worked intensively on the program, trying to make it more relaxed and informal than it had been in previous years. I was able to come up with several innovations suggested by my experience with Don Antonio's apprenticeship program. Perhaps my greatest contribution was to find a guest speaker from outside the League. Jack Hathaway was a medicine man, highly respected by Native Americans in the state. Kathleen Carpenter had given me his name, and I had gotten approval from the League hierarchy for this unorthodox addition to the program, which I felt would give the League members a perspective that was quite different from the one they were used to. The program began on Friday evening, continued through Saturday, and wound up around noon on Sunday.

After the opening formalities, the main feature of the Friday evening program was a contemplation exercise that began like a party game. Pictures representing several of the Masters of the Order of the League had been cut up in puzzle fashion. These were broken, turned over, and the pieces jumbled together. Each person came up and picked one at random. The piece I picked turned out to belong to the Master Rumi. According to the League teachings, Rumi was the guardian of the third volume of the sacred text of *The Face of the Eternal*, located at the Temple of Moha, in the spiritual city of Akash, high in the mountains of Tibet. The city was said to exist at a higher rate of vibration, rendering it invisible to our senses. The only method of travel there was via the exercise of the creative imagination.

The members of each group assembled in separate rooms. Once we gathered, our group leader gave us a little bit of background on the Master Rumi, and the spiritual location at which he was said to reside. The Temple of Moha was described as resembling an ancient cathedral. The picture of Rumi showed a solid-looking individual wearing a cassock. He had a salt-and-pepper beard, piercing eyes, and his general appearance reminded me of Sean Connery in his role as a medieval monk in *The Name of the Rose*.

I began the exercise by imagining myself seated in a chair, and feeling the presence of the Master directly behind me. I turned around to face him, but was not conscious of clearly seeing his face. Nevertheless, I had the distinct sense of being escorted by him to our destination. Next, I was aware of being inside the dark and gloomy interior of the cathedral-like temple. We walked down the central nave, and toward a cluster of initiates seated in wooden pews. A yellowish-green aura emanated from them, cloaking them like a canopy.

At this point, I became preoccupied with taking away some proof that this experience was "real." In response to my request for such proof, the Master replied that he would give me three gifts, which I would be able to "take back" with me. Immediately, he held out the first "gift." The curious object was a type of amulet made of heavy, shiny metal. It was shaped like a spade, but with elongated tips and a handle as slender as the stem of a flower. The strangest thing about it was its size, which was closer to that of a garden tool than an item of jewelry.

Unlike a trowel or ladle, the object was convex on both sides, making it unsuitable for any utilitarian purpose. The metal was unlike anything I had seen, with a very shiny surface, almost like quicksilver. I took the oversize amulet in my hand. It felt as heavy as lead. It was too massive to wear around my neck, and in any case came with no string or chain. Luckily, I found I was wearing a loose-fitting brown robe, and discovered a large pocket sewn in the interior of the garment, which allowed me to carry the object clumsily around with me.

Master Rumi then led me outside the temple and into a garden, where a unique species of long-stemmed flower with the form of a daffodil and the color of an iris, grew in profusion. Its trumpet-shaped bell was milky white, with purple edges like the fringes of a tattered skirt. Extending from the interior of the bell and just visible beyond its frayed purple margin was a bright orange stamen. The Master picked one and presented it to me as the second "gift."

Finally, he led me to the edge of a small river or stream that ran through the garden. The environment suddenly became tropical. The water was muddy, and as we approached the banks, I saw the backs of some crocodiles as they slithered into the water. The Master bent down at the riverbank. I looked to where he pointed, and noticed some crocodile teeth lying on the ground, partially bleached from the sun. He picked one up from where it lay in the earth, and handed it to me. This was the third "gift." In an instant, I was back with the other members of the group, who were also just emerging from their contemplation. We took turns narrating our experiences. When I related mine, the group leader asked what significance I saw in the three objects.

"I think they represented three successive stages in one's relationship to the physical world," I replied, almost without thinking. "The process is one of progressively greater detachment. The metal amulet had no outwardly utilitarian purpose, but possessed a reserve of energy, much like a lead battery. It was so heavy, however, that there was no means to carry it without feeling burdened. I think it represented youth. We have energy in our youth, but lack the direction to apply it constructively. Consequently, we're actually burdened by our energy, and go through life in a clumsy fashion. The flower represented middle age. It possessed lightness and flexibility, but was also fragile and dependent on the elements. The moment it was plucked represented the beginning of one's awareness of mortality. Finally, the crocodile tooth was a mere relic. The spirit that had animated it had left the physical world entirely, symbolizing the ultimate form of detachment."

On Saturday morning, I took part in another powerful group activity in the main hall. Participants were divided into two equal groups, with those of one group seated in a circle, and those of the other group standing in a second circle enclosing them. Each member of the outer circle placed their hands on the shoulders of the person directly before them. The seated individuals closed their eyes, and each person behind them whispered some type of praise, compliment, or encouragement in their left ear.

The people in the outer circle proceeded to move in clockwise fashion, and repeated the process with a new person. In doing so, they were told not to take their hand off the previous person until their other hand had been placed on the next one. When the members of the outer group had come full circle, the two groups switched positions. It was then the turn of those who had been on the receiving end to give, and of those who had been the givers to receive.

I felt this was an impressive exercise because it forced people to say the best and think the best of others. The exercise was also instructive because it gave an intimate glimpse into the dynamic of giving and receiving. As the receiver, I felt emotionally filled with the Force, but as the giver, I felt strangely empty. It took an effort for me to think of the right thing to say. The gratification of finding the right words didn't come directly via the heart, but through observation. As I watched some of the members of the inner circle dabbing at their eyes with handkerchiefs, I knew that the Force had touched them, and that I had helped to facilitate this.

After lunch, it was time for Mr. Hathaway to speak. He walked very slowly, with the aid of a cane, to the front of the room, and sat down in a chair next to the podium. His hair, black as the feathers of a crow, hung from a receding hairline down to his shoulders. He had a long, drooping handlebar moustache, also ink black. A hush fell over the audience.

"Spirituality is very simple," he began. "You know when you have a connection, or make a connection, with God. You don't need anybody to tell you when you're connected. Only we know when we're connected, and just how we're doing. We know that all the time. We know when we're doing right and when we're doing wrong. We're given the choice. We're free to choose whether to do right or do wrong in everything.

"As Native Americans, we raise our children that way. We teach them that their choices have consequences. If you make good choices, only good is going to happen. If you make bad choices, you suffer negative consequences. You're going to be responsible for what you do and say. When you're going to be held accountable, however, I don't know."

He pointed to a tumbler of water on the podium. "You can look at a glass of water as a person," he said. "The amount of water in the glass is spirituality. Some people have a full glass. Perhaps it has to do with how much they have drunk over their lifetime, or with knowing how to replenish what they have. What have they done? How have they lived? How have they treated their fellow beings? We Native Americans don't take other people's word as law. We listen to what they have to say, and if what they are saying reflects nature, then it is probably true.

"We believe that the Creator gave us original instructions. He gave us four sacred medicines—tobacco, sweet grass, sage, and cedar. Tobacco was the first. That's why it begins our day, our prayers, and our ceremonies. He told us to build the sacred fire, and to make our offerings of the sacred medicines. He told us that the smoke would carry our prayers to his ears. We still do that, as native people. Many cultures, however, do not. They figure they don't have to, as long as they build their great shrines to glorify God. Their great mosques and cathedrals don't glorify God. They glorify man.

"No, spirituality isn't meant to be difficult. We don't go in for a lot of outer ritual. I know the Muslims, for instance, are bound to kneel down five times a day, and kiss the earth before they pray. I'm not saying anything against their religion, but in general, the more outer ritual that I observe people practicing, the more I see evidence of man's control in the process, and therefore the less spirituality. People can stand in these mosques or in these great churches—crowds of people all lined up in rows, doing the same thing at the same time. Yet, most of them are just paying lip service to God. Spirituality is getting up in the morning and privately praying to God. That's not for everybody to see. It doesn't depend on appearance.

"I'm told with my medicine to harm *no one* and *no thing*. We feel that all forms of life are sacred, even the crawling ones, the biting ones, the insignificant ones to man. They still have life, and that is sacred. We treat them as brothers. We're to live in balance and harmony with all of creation, not just with each other. You can see that man doesn't want to do that. You can see it on the news every day—all the fighting that's going on, the hatred in the streets, the racism. Man isn't ready for anything. He's come no further today, spiritually, than he was ten thousand years ago. God is going to have to intervene one of these days.

"That's why I say we're given the responsibility for our spiritual wellness. I can't take any of the blame for what other people do, nor can I absolve them of anything they've done. Man cannot do that. Man may elevate himself to positions such as cardinal or bishop, but he can't say, 'I forgive you, son. Go say this so many times, pay the church so many dollars, and you're forgiven.' No. If you need forgiveness, you have to get on your knees and talk to God. The responsibility for your spiritual wellness lies in your connection with God.

"God has given every man a physical side and a spiritual side. The physical man is the one that needs conveniences and shortcuts. It wants power, money, and sexual gratification. They say that the physical man lives in our brain and that the spiritual man lives in the heart.

That spiritual part of ourselves is a spark of the Great Spirit, which gives us life at the time of conception. That can't be anything but good. You hear people talking about others, saying, 'He's got a mean spirit, or an evil spirit.' Well, there's no such thing in a man. That spirit can only be good, because it comes from God. When this body dies, there's only the spirit left. The spiritual side never dies. What is of God goes back to God.

"We don't worship. We celebrate. We don't ask forgiveness for the things we do. We're given a choice, the ability to choose right from wrong. When we pray, we ask that the Creator pity us, because we make mistakes. Yet, we also learn from those mistakes. If we were punished for every little thing, every wrong thought, we would be so busy making restitution and paying penance that we couldn't live our lives. For this reason, we ask the Creator for pity. I think that, if we're going to be punished, it's for something that we've knowingly done. Humans are designed to make mistakes. What's important is what you do with those mistakes.

"The native peoples were given seven virtues—truth, bravery, honor, respect, wisdom, humility, and love. The gift of judgment wasn't given to us. That's reserved for the Creator. The first thing that man wants to do, however, is to judge. The first time he meets a person, he forms an opinion about him, without even knowing him. Only the Great Spirit can judge, yet man wants that power so badly. He wants the power that is reserved for the Creator.

"If you look for the truth in everything, you will see only truth. Honesty is a tough one for a lot of people. One time I went to the store and found a wallet on the ground, just in front of the store. I picked it up. I could see from the license in it that it belonged to a young man from Philadelphia. It contained about eighty dollars. Well, eighty dollars was a lot of money to me, at the time. I had no job. I was on unemployment. Rather than put it in my pocket, though, I took it in the store, and said, 'Hey, this was laying on the sidewalk out there.'

"The store owner put it behind the counter. I bought what I needed and went home. The next time I was in that store, the owner told me the man had come in for his wallet. He and his wife were just on the way home and stopped by to get something for the baby. He said he sure was thankful. That was all the money they had to get home on. I could have taken that money, and gotten what I wanted or needed, satisfying the physical side of life, and ignoring the spiritual.

"We look at those things as tests. Our faith is tested on a daily basis. What we do with those tests determines where we will be, and how we will be. I truly believe that we were put on this earth for a purpose. Most of us don't know what that is. If we don't accomplish our purpose, however, we'll get another chance. We'll come around again. Each time we come around, I believe we're given more tools to accomplish what we have to do.

"We think we know. We say, 'This is my job. This is why I'm here,' but in fact you need to work hard at finding out why you're truly here. You have to go back to those basic principles we were given to live by, and live by them. Eventually, you'll know. If you want answers, fast and pray. Your answers will come in visions or dreams. Our people are told, 'When you're showed something in a dream, you do that!'"

At the end of Mr. Hathaway's talk, I looked around at the audience. People were wiping tears from their eyes. During the intermission, even the area director came up to me and asked how I'd managed to find such an impressive speaker.

In the afternoon, I had the opportunity to sit down and talk with one of the League's elder statesmen, Dr. Stewart Eckland. He had come all the way from his home in Syracuse, New York, where he had recently retired from his dental practice. Dr. Eckland was one of the earliest followers of Andreas Leo, and even resembled him to some extent. He was dressed in Andreas Leo fashion—a rumpled gray suit, white shirt open at the neck, no tie, and casual shoes. There was also a resemblance in his features—the sparse hair carefully combed to one side, the fine lines etched in the face. Finally, there was a familiarity in his bearing—the way he sat leaning back in his chair, supporting himself under one arm, with his legs crossed and head cocked to one side. I asked him about his past experience in the League. "Is there a particular incident that sticks out in your memory?" I wanted to know.

"I met an individual who had written Andreas Leo for a healing in the early days, when Leo was doing this by mail," Dr Eckland responded. "He got a reply about two weeks later, telling him that his health would improve shortly, and it did. He went back to his doctors, and they couldn't believe what had happened to him. I saw him later at subsequent conferences, and he was still alive and doing well. I thought that was impressive. I also met Leo at a couple of seminars. After his lectures, he would come down and talk with the members of the audience. On one occasion, his wife was with him, and he introduced her to me directly, without even looking at my nametag. He was an incredible man."

"For people who are unfamiliar with the League," I commented, "it's hard to explain how a person like me, who never met Andreas Leo in the flesh, could feel so close to him and be so influenced by his personality. From the first time I picked up his books, his presence seemed to jump right off the pages and creep into my skin. I feel it just in talking to you. It's like you've been sprinkled with pixie powder. Does that make any sense?"

"Yes, it does," Dr. Eckland answered. "I've had some people tell me before that they sensed Leo's presence when I was with them. All I can say, however, is that he was a very brilliant and enthusiastic man.

"My greatest thrill on the Path occurred shortly after I joined the League. I was the only member of the League in my area for a while, so I didn't have too much feedback or reinforcement from other people. I used to contemplate in my office sometimes at night, but nothing happened. You were supposed to listen for various sounds in contemplation, but I didn't hear anything, so I began to think that this was nothing for me. Finally, one evening, I made up my mind that if I didn't achieve any results that night, I'd quit.

"I went to the office around nine o'clock. The walls were very light-colored, but it was totally dark in the hallway. Right there, before me, was a solid, massive blue light. It was about three feet in diameter. A cluster of rays went out from the center to the periphery and back again. The light was vibrant and strong. At first I just stared at this thing, thinking 'What is going on here?' It was utterly amazing. Then I started slowly walking down the corridor. The light moved ahead of me, gradually shrinking until it was about six or eight inches in diameter. It stood there at the end of the hall, right in front of me. I didn't dare touch it. I had no idea what in the world it was. Finally it went up the wall, made three passes over my head, and disappeared.

"Well, I thought that was something pretty special," Dr. Eckland added. "Divine Spirit—or whatever it was—had to know that I was going to be there that night, because it was waiting for me. It had to know that I was thinking of quitting if I didn't get any results with my contemplation that night. Naturally, I continued with the spiritual exercises after this happened. Eventually I did pick up on the sounds as they were described in the League literature. What I learned was that you can do some amazing things. At least, it does happen for certain people."

The retreat ended for me on this note. I drove back to Belle Harbor in a reflective mood, satisfied with my contribution to the event, and wondering what the future would hold. That night, I dreamed about Andreas Leo. He was sitting with me and listening amiably while I told him all about my continuing dissatisfactions with teaching and my problems in finding an additional job that would give me enough money to live on.

"The main thing," he replied, after I had gone through my litany of woes, "is to change your attitude to one of gratitude. Changing your attitude toward your situation is more important than trying to change the situation itself. You made a choice a long time ago to take a spiritual path in life, rather than a material path. Stick with your choice. If you waver now, you may wind up with nothing. The more you think of worldly things, the more you'll need them. Put your heart into your teaching, although you're not being rewarded for it in a material way. If you're a good teacher, you'll know that it's your job to help your students realize their spiritual potential. It's your job to expect more of them, and have the patience to deal with them."

When I woke up, I thought about the exercise we had done at the retreat on giving and receiving. In particular, I remembered that we had always kept one hand on the shoulder of the person before us, never removing one until the other had made contact with someone new. I felt I understood now what this action was meant to represent. We were part of an endless chain of giving and receiving. I had received a fresh spiritual perspective at Don Antonio's apprenticeship program, which I was able to pass on to others at the League retreat. In the aftermath, I had dreamt of Leo. That gift, in turn, was waiting to be passed on in some form to my students.

Following this, I agreed to give a talk to the senior citizens at Oakhurst Manor, my mother's apartment complex. My mother and I used to have frequent talks about spirituality. She belonged to an informal discussion group that met in the Oakhurst reading room after dinner, and frequently reported to the participants about what I said. On one occasion, I lent her a little book called *The Uncommon Book of Prayer,* by Elsa Bailey, which I thought was an excellent brief introduction to spirituality. The book sparked a good deal of discussion on the meaning of spirituality and led to the group's decision to invite me to speak to them. I made up a poster for the talk and hoped that my mother's word-of-mouth campaign would ensure a large turnout. In fact, over three dozen senior citizens showed up for my presentation—a good-sized audience. I stepped up to the podium, introduced myself, and explained the sequence of events that had brought me to speak before them. Then I launched into my address:

"What is spirituality? I've been interested in this question for most of my adult life, but I grew up without any religious background. My parents were non-religious people, who didn't believe in God or life after death. My own spiritual questioning grew directly out of my parents' skepticism. I remember, when I was an adolescent, my parents told me that when I died, I would simply cease to exist. After this, I went through a period in which I would lie on my back at night, staring at the ceiling, unable to sleep, trying to imagine what it was like not to exist. I never succeeded in imagining this. In fact, I found that I was able to imagine just about anything except my own non-existence.

"As a young man, I got interested in meditation and out-of-body experiences. Finally, I joined a group called the League, which taught the Ancient Science of the Soul. This involves the movement of consciousness from the physical world to the inner realms by the act of shifting of one's attention. The purpose of this type of experience is to enable an individual to prove for himself his own survival beyond the death of the physical body. This is one of the most basic spiritual principles. Soul is eternal. It cannot be destroyed. It has no beginning or ending.

"Of course, no one can convince another person that there is life after death, or that Soul exists eternally. We can only prove this to ourselves, and sometimes we do it in ways that would seem completely illogical to another person, but are nevertheless real to us. Once you've accepted the principle that Soul is eternal, many other principles follow logically. For instance, if we're eternal beings, then this life is only a temporary way station. What then, is its purpose, if not to train us for some higher form of existence? Life is thus like a school, and when we die, we simply graduate to another level. If this is true, someone or something must have set up this school for the benefit of our education as Soul.

"If life is a school, what is it that we are being taught? We're being taught to be more aware. Awareness is a matter of movement and flexibility. The human eye, for instance, is constantly moving. The eye itself does not see. It merely absorbs light. The mind converts these images to something meaningful. It does this by means of perspective, comparing images to other images. If the eye were static, it would not actually see. It would merely register the impression made by light. Consciousness comes from comparison, and comparison comes from movement. This is the principle behind the Science of the Soul—the movement of consciousness, the shifting of awareness—and it can be equally applied to daily life. Movement and comparison give us flexibility and perspective, allowing us to live in greater harmony with the ebb and flow of life.

"For those who think in terms of God or a Higher Power, greater awareness means living in greater harmony with that Force. To paraphrase Elsa Bailey, once we recognize that there is something deep within us that is much, much bigger and more powerful than our brains and our bones, we realize that we are always connected. It is always listening and always answering. When we worry, complain, carry a grudge, feel miserable or sorry for ourselves, hold other people responsible for our plight, or think that life is out to get us, we're not listening to this voice inside us. We're closing off our natural channel of communication with this Higher Power. We're allowing our little self to dictate to God, and in this state, we put ourselves at odds with God's will.

"Some people may object that this sounds very passive. 'What about free will?' they ask. Well, yes, we have free will, but our free will consists mainly of our power to choose. At any moment, in any given situation, we have a choice of whether we will react positively or negatively in that situation. When we react positively, constructively, helpfully, hopefully, then we are moving closer to God and acting in accord with its will. When we react negatively, spitefully, angrily, vengefully, then we are moving away from God and opposing its will. So how can we train ourselves to think and act more in accord with God's will? One way is through a contemplation, or spiritual exercise. Many spiritual traditions teach that certain words have a particular spiritual charge, signature, or vibration that can help lift us in a state of consciousness so that we are more in accord with God's will. We can make use of such words by singing them silently to ourselves.

"How can silently singing a particular word bring us closer to God? We can think of God as a tremendous power or force, whose energy is transmitted as vibration. Vibration is perceived as light or sound. Sight and hearing are our most exalted senses. Everything we see and hear is this light and sound, which emanates from God. We can perceive light and sound both objectively and subjectively. If we close our eyes, we can see and hear with our inner senses.

"Think of the vibration that emanates from God, or what we call the Sound Current, as a tremendous symphony. Singing a word specially tuned to this vibration is like hearing a song on the radio and singing along with it. The more we can sing in tune with it, the more harmonious the sound. This same principle is behind music itself. Some music is harmonious. Other music is discordant. You can judge just by the way it makes you feel which is more 'spiritual.'"

I then played a tape in which a variation of the word HUW, in this case pronounced "HYOO," was sung by a large group of people. The gentle hum reverberated softly in the room. I showed them how to close their eyes, place their attention on the screen of their mind, and gently sing the word in harmony with the tape. As I closed my own eyes, I felt a force that seemed to gently lift me until I was standing on my toes. After a minute or so, I opened my eyes, and saw some of the seniors dabbing at their eyes with handkerchiefs. Something had profoundly affected them. Many of them came up to me afterwards, their eyes shining, and thanked me for my presentation. As I received their thanks, I understood that this was what it was like to be a conduit for the Force.

Chapter Fifteen

The Three of Spades

"Men have endured great hardship for a momentary glance at heaven. Then, pursuing a religious objective, they have usurped their own vision in an attempt to systematize, proselytize, and preserve it. Only when they realize that they have stifled their own freedom, will they reach the goal that they seek."

—Andreas Leo, *The Face of the Eternal, Book Two,* 163

The previous year, when I had been at my lowest ebb, I had received a letter in the mail from a local psychic. "Everything is about to 'click' for you," she wrote.

> If you're worried about turning a year older, don't be. Everything in your life will soon fit together. Beginning today, an incredible period of good fortune is going to wash over you. Write down how you're feeling about life at this moment. Be honest. Now put this note away and don't look at it for six months. After that time, I bet you won't recognize your old life.

The psychic went on to claim that she had been glancing at an address list, and that my name had "jumped out" at her. "I feel you have no one you can really trust," she continued.

> I feel your loneliness. I sense a yearning for the comfort and warmth that comes only from a nurturing relationship. At the same time, I detect great strength of character. I feel you wish to be, and rightly so, respected and recognized for all the things you do and know. Your life, up until today, hasn't exactly been 'a bed of roses' for you, has it? Certainly there have been good times, but not enough to offset all the bad times and suffering you've had to endure, especially lately. With no one around to share with, you've had to shoulder all this anxiety by yourself. I see you have sought help before...unsuccessfully. No one is to blame, however.

"At the time, you weren't in the position you are in now," she concluded. "In fact, nothing was falling into place. It wasn't time yet." She then offered a personal reading that would help me take advantage of this period of luck that she claimed I was entering.

Normally, I wasn't someone who would be susceptible to this sort of mail solicitation, but everything the psychic was saying about me was true. "What harm could there be in sending in twenty dollars to get some kind of prediction for the coming month?" I thought. "Maybe it would help me make some crucial decisions." I called the psychic's office, gave the secretary some information about my date, time, and place of birth, and ordered a forecast for the coming month. Instead of the expected mailing, however, I got a new letter from the psychic, telling me that I needed special help, that there was some stubborn negative energy around me, and consequently it was necessary to analyze the various aspects of my current difficulties. She promised to help free the positive energy lying dormant in my subconscious, and urged me to act now and authorize her to perform an occult intervention on my behalf.

This letter was disturbing to me. Resorting to the intervention of a psychic seemed like an acknowledgment that the League could no longer help me. Andreas Leo's writing repeatedly warned against getting involved in the psychic sciences. I picked up *The Lion's Paw* by Andreas

Leo, and opened it randomly to a page—a technique that League members sometimes used to get answers to their personal questions. Sure enough, I found myself reading the following passage:

> If a person is insufficiently experienced in the spiritual path, an individual with psychic powers may contact him, and awaken in him the lower faculties. Psychic awareness can often be mistaken for spiritual awareness, and this has the unfortunate effect of putting a halt to our spiritual growth. (ix)

"Great!" I thought ruefully to myself. Little techniques like this rarely failed to give me seemingly appropriate answers to my questions. I would get these little nudges and hints, just enough to let me know that a spiritual presence was still subtly at work in my life, but I couldn't get an overall direction, and without this, I remained at a crossroads in my life.

As usual, I gave Lynne Silva a call, and told her about the letters I had received from the psychic, as well as the passage I had read. I could sense Lynne smiling through the phone as I recounted this. "Using these techniques for guidance is fine," she replied, "but I don't think you're giving yourself enough credit. You seem to be viewing yourself as spiritually inexperienced. You've been an initiate of the League for a long time now. You know the difference between right and wrong. If a psychic were to suggest that you do anything that you know is contrary to the ethics that you have developed in the League, you're strong enough not to allow anyone to have that kind of influence over you, don't you think?

"I think you're neglecting the possibility that you're being guided at this very moment," she continued. "The Force, or Spirit, is in everything. It's behind every experience. How do you know that you aren't being guided to this psychic, or the psychic was guided to you, to help you correct this very imbalance in yourself? The psychic could be an agent of the Living Master. You can test this for yourself by simply asking inwardly whether or not this is true."

"That occurred to me, as well," I said. "I was thinking that maybe I could view this psychic the same way that one views going to a doctor."

"That's true," Lynne agreed, "although you may ultimately find that you'll have to choose between relying on psychics and other doctors, and addressing the more fundamental problem, which is your relationship to the League, the Living Master, and the Force Itself."

"But how do I do that?" I asked.

"I think you're very close to finding out," Lynne replied.

Now, a year later, I was going through my files, and came across the letter from the psychic again. I was just as perplexed about what to do with my life as ever, so I decided what the hell! I would take a chance and see her. Mary Hibbard advertised herself as a spiritual counselor and lived in Livingston, where I had first met Don Antonio. Instead of a large house deep in the woods, however, she inhabited a deluxe converted mobile home in a sterile trailer park, where all the units looked like tract houses. She greeted me from her porch as I pulled into the driveway—a large, blonde, energetic woman, quite contrary to the dour stereotype of a psychic. The interior of her place was filled with religious and spiritual bric-a-brac—portraits of Jesus, angel pictures, and enormous candles. We sat down in a small study, on opposite sides of a card table crowded with stacks of tarot cards and metaphysical reference books.

She spread a stack of her business cards face up on the table, and asked me to choose one and show her what was on the reverse side. I did as she told me to. On the back of the business card were the words "Badger Medicine—Aggression."

"Normally, this is done with a deck of Medicine Cards," she explained. "The Badger card has to do with aggressiveness. You're not aggressive enough. You'll stand up for someone else more than you will for yourself. Badger is willing to persist. Badger people don't give up. Their certainty is a source of strength. The card says that you've been too meek in trying to reach your goal. The Badger card asks how long you're willing to wait for the world to deliver you what you desire. The key is to become aggressive enough to do something about your state of affairs. Badger is teaching you to get angry in a creative way and say 'I won't take it any more.'

"You have to keep your eye on the goal. Use your anger to pull yourself out of the doldrums and your apathy will be a thing of the past. The Badger card may be signaling that the time is at hand when you can use your healing abilities to push yourself ahead in life. Cut away the dead wood and use Badger's aggression to seek new levels of expression.

"You're clearly going through a transformation," she added. "Now let's see who you are and what you have to do next. When is your birthday?" she asked.

I told her, as she took out a reference book illustrated with pictures of playing cards by an author named Robert Camp. "Have you ever heard of the science of the cards?" she asked. "It's based on the combined influences of astrology and numerology. It's a system of self-understanding and prediction, with the same function as astrology, but much easier to learn.

"Your card is the Three of Spades," she announced, peering at a table in the book. "Spades is the highest suit. It represents action and idealism. Three is the number of creativity. The Threes tend to be romantics and spendthrifts. They can't be tied down. They have diverse interests. They need constant stimulation. Most Threes lack commitment. They start things without finishing them. The Three of Spades is different, however. In the case of these people, all their creative and romantic drive is channeled into their work. This overshadows everything else in their life. Still, as a Three, your life can get scattered in many directions. Above all, you need to find a creative channel for your energy.

"Another reason for your lack of success up to this point in your life may lie in your Planetary Ruling Card, which in your case is the Nine of Hearts. The Nine of Hearts is compassionate. People under the influence of this card tend to think about other people in their decision making. They have a soft heart for other people's suffering. They want other people to feel good. They have a tendency toward co-dependency, because they try to keep everybody happy. They won't choose to do something that they feel will hurt others, although it might be the best thing for them. In your case, if striking out on your own was something that might have caused consternation to your family, you may not have chosen to do that because of the discomfort that *you* would feel with *their* discomfort.

"You made a choice to take care of them and do what you thought they wanted you to do. Maybe that wasn't the best thing for you. It didn't really help you get a sense of your own strength or power. It's not too late for you to try something new, however. Maybe you need to divorce your family for five years, go somewhere where they don't even know where you are, and get your artistic career off the ground. That would be good therapy for you.

"In the first stage of your life, you had to serve. That's when your parents really did a number on you. They imprinted you with the need to serve their interests. In the second stage of your life, you were a leader, a pioneer. You joined a group in the forefront of the spiritual field. Now you're just coming to the third stage. In this stage, you want your freedom, and the key to your freedom is self-expression.

"You're a creative individual. You put all your value in your work, your ideas. You're willing to sacrifice everything for that. You have little interest in material things, where you live, or having a home, friends, and relationships. You're even willing to sacrifice your health for your work. You have to watch that. It's also important that you be honest in what you write. That's the nature of your transformation. You're stripping away all the layers of your self and getting right down to the bone. Be careful to give yourself some time to relax, however. You can put so much energy into your work that you burn out. You need to spend time outdoors. You'd be good at gardening, or any kind of work involving plants or animals.

"You also have protection on the other side," she added. "You get all kinds of information in your sleep. Do you want to remember more of your dreams, or go beyond dreams to travel outside the physical body? Do you want to have an inner connection with the Force? Have you heard of the League?" She reached down, pulled out a book by the Living Master, and started to show it to me.

I smiled dryly. "I'm an initiate of the League," I said softly.

"You are? Oh, isn't it beautiful?" she exclaimed. "Ray Hardcastle is one of my good friends. You remind me of him in certain ways. You have the same temperament."

I smiled at the irony of this pronouncement. I had to admit that I was impressed by what Mary had to say, and fascinated by the science of the cards. "From what you've conveyed to me about this system," I commented, "I can't help but be struck by how limited we are. We live in a day and age in which we're told that we can be anything we want to be, and I don't exactly hold with that. I think that we're dealt a hand of cards in this lifetime. We have a certain degree of freedom to operate within that framework, to make positive choices, and make the most of what we're given. That's hard to explain to people in our present-day culture, however."

"I agree," Mary replied. "The Hindu astrologers believe that everything is destined. Nothing happens to an individual that can't be foretold using their astrology. They also tell you, however, that you have to act. Although your actions are predestined, you still have to follow your *dharma*. Olney Richmond, who wrote the first book about the science of the cards, also said that life was completely destined, and that everything that happened to an individual followed strict mathematical law. Still, the individual has to act on his or her own behalf."

The consultation gradually turned into a free-for-all discussion about metaphysics and spirituality. I found out that Mary had been a student of Krishnamurti before becoming a psychic. As it happened, I had recently stumbled upon a website devoted to this spiritual leader's teachings. It had mentioned a speech that he had given in 1929, when he dissolved the Order of the Star in the East before three thousand members in the Netherlands. In this address, he maintained that truth is a pathless land, and could not be approached by any path whatsoever. Since it was limitless and unconditioned, he claimed that it could not be organized without becoming dead, or crystallized. He had become disillusioned in his attempt to communicate spiritual truth to those who were intent on reducing it to dogma.

"There's a book I want to recommend to you," Mary told me. "It's called *Thaïs*, and was written by the nineteenth century French novelist Anatole France. I think that you'll find this book bears some relation to your own journey."

I wrote down the name of the book, and promised her that I would immediately look into it. The next day, I went to the public library and checked out a copy. The short novel focused on the character of a monk named Paphnutius, who lived in North Africa during the early era of the Christian Church. This was at a time when the Church had to contend with the existence of many competing heresies, as well as the continuing presence of Hellenistic pagans and practitioners of eastern religions. One day, Paphnutius had a vision of Thaïs, the most famous and beautiful courtesan in Alexandria, which was the main cultural center of the world at that time. He concluded that his mission was to journey to Alexandria, win Thaïs over to Christianity, and induce her to enter a convent for the rest of her life.

The whole story is about Paphnutius's spiritual downfall. He never understands the meaning of his vision of Thaïs. Instead, he clings to his Christian dogma. His mission to convert the courtesan is based on pride and vanity. On his way, he meets many people, Christian and pagan, who each have found truth—or a portion of truth—in their own way, and whose greater strength of character is reflected in their tolerance of other people's views. Paphnutius succeeds in converting Thaïs, and she finds salvation in her conversion. Of all the characters in the book, however, Paphnutius is the only one who is truly beyond all hope of salvation, because of his deep attachment to his ideas, opinions, and attitudes.

Halfway through his journey, Paphnutius meets a hermit named Timocles, who has studied the Hindu teachings, and does not believe in Christ. Paphnutius cannot understand how Timocles can live a life of poverty if he doesn't believe in Christian doctrine. "Why are you virtuous if you do not believe in Jesus Christ?" he asks. "Why deprive yourself of the good things of this world if you do not hope to gain eternal riches in heaven?" For Paphnutius, the illusion of guaranteed salvation in the next life is just a version of the illusion of success in THIS life. His faith is based solely on the principle of deferred gratification. Timocles replies:

> Stranger, I deprive myself of nothing which is good, and I flatter myself that I have found a life which is satisfactory enough, though—to speak more precisely—there is no such thing as a good or evil life. Nothing is itself either virtuous or shameful, just or unjust, pleasant or painful, good or bad. It is our opinion that gives those qualities to things. Men suffer because they are deprived of that which they believe to be good; or because, possessing it they fear to lose it; or because they endure that which they believe to be an evil. Put an end to all beliefs of this kind, and the evils would disappear.

In reading this, I suddenly remembered my dream about the Lost Slipper of Soul, in which, like Paphnutius, I had lived as a hermit in the wilderness. It was now clear to me that the dark land of Röo-kel, which I had glimpsed in that dream, had not been evil at all, for what we consider evil is merely a projection of our fear of the unknown. The little girl, whom I was intent on following into that land, paradoxically represented the oldest and wisest part of me. It was not my task to rescue her, but her mission to coax me out of my hermit-like existence. Then it occurred to me that I had succeeded in entering that portal, after all—not via a mystical experience, dream, or fantasy, but simply by investigating the world around me and seeing it with new eyes.

Even more significant, in light of this new interpretation of my dream, was that Pahphnutius had clung to his limited ideas concerning the superiority of his religion, values, and way of life. His vision of Thaïs had posed a challenge to those values, but he had rejected that vision, subordinating it to his own belief system. Likewise, my dream had posed for me the challenge of broadening my spiritual horizons beyond the sphere of the League, and seeking out new experiences instead of remaining within the safe perimeters of my habitual life. This didn't necessarily mean abandoning the League entirely. Anatole France's fictional landscape was peopled not only with pagans, but also with Christians whose view of life was far broader than that of Paphnutius. It did, however, entail seeing the League as part of a greater reality.

At issue in both my case and that of Paphnutius was the necessity of becoming detached from one's beliefs, attitudes, and opinions. Like all people, we were free to choose the spiritual path that was best for us. The moment, however, that we felt ourselves to be better than someone else because of our belief, membership in a particular group, doctrine, practices, morality, or lifestyle, we were lost, stranded in the desert, reduced to the solitary life of a hermit with inflated pride and spiritual ambition. I reflected that if I had not begun to explore the perspective of other religions and other paths, Paphnutius's downfall might have been my own.

In the wake of my consultation with Mary Hibbard, I became interested in the science of the cards that she had used in her reading. I visited the new age bookstore in Belle Harbor, bought a copy of the book that she had used during the session, and began to study it. I began asking people for their day of birth, looking them up in the book, and found that in a few minutes I could ascertain underlying qualities in their personalities that I might not otherwise have discovered if I had known them for years.

The League sponsored monthly presentations at this same bookstore, and not long after my session with the psychic, I agreed to fill in for the regular speaker, although I was warned that there had been no publicity for the event. On the evening of the talk, I showed up at the bookstore. The multipurpose room rented for the occasion was completely empty. I hung around for a while, and finally a single League member, Cindy Matthews, appeared. I had known Cindy for years. She lived on the West side of town with her family of cats, worked as a computer programmer, and occasionally expressed some dissatisfaction with her job. I still thought of her as a young woman, but there were now deep lines etched in her face.

We sat together in the multipurpose room, and did a brief contemplation together. Afterwards, we chatted awhile, and I began telling her a little about the science of the cards. "It's fascinating," I said. "It's like finding a little key to the mechanism of the universe, being able to open it up, look inside, and study it." I then told her a little about the significance of the suits and the numbers. "I'm the Three of Spades," I explained. "Threes are indecisive. They can suffer from stress, especially if they don't find an outlet for their creativity."

She looked at me fixedly. "If you think that way about yourself, then you'll never change," she asserted. "You'll just reinforce that limitation." I immediately regretted having brought up the subject with her. She was reacting with the typical prejudice of a League member toward anything that smacked of the psychic sciences. Now that I had started the discussion, however, I wasn't going to back down.

"How can you think of life as unlimited?" I replied. "That's an illusion. We come into this life and take on a physical body. We're given layer upon layer of limitations. We labor under astrological, karmic, past life, genetic, social, cultural, and family influences, all piled up on top of one another. The most that we can do within these limitations is to be the best that we can be, and make the best choices we can. The very notion that there are no limitations can limit you. You can live your whole life under the illusion that you're free, and still be a prisoner!"

"But that means that you're always going to have the same basic personality," she said.

"Don't you have the same basic personality that you've always had?" I replied. "Pythagoras' maxim was to 'Know thyself.' If a metaphysical system can add to your self-knowledge, in what way is that limiting? If you have no interest in such information, how does that make you any more free or enlightened? You think the abstractions of the League are better than those of metaphysics, because they seem to you more lofty, holy, or spiritual, but that can also make them less practical, less relevant."

"I don't think many League members would agree with you," she commented. I saw her pull back as soon as she said this, as if she was aware that it sounded condescending.

I felt a sudden wave of aggression come over me. "How have you changed over the years?" I asked her. "What are you doing with your life that's so different? You're the same as you've always been. You talk about your faith in the League as something that won't limit you, but I suspect you limit yourself all the time.

"Don't you see?" I beseeched her. "We're just puppets on strings, meat bags on hooks, acting out a predetermined course of action. To recognize that is the first step toward freedom! The League is a tool, but it's also an impediment. It offers a door to spiritual freedom, but on the way, it also tests our spiritual vanity. What really sets the League apart from any other group? We have a Living Master, but even the Master can fall from grace. We have the initiations, but they're only an opportunity, not a guarantee. When we go to a League conference and listen to the Living Master speak, we come away uplifted, but the Christians experience the same thing in their churches, as do the Muslims in their mosques.

"You don't mind using this bookstore to sponsor a League event, but you look down your nose at the books that it contains. To you, the paths they represent are only stepping-stones to the League. You believe the League is superior to all other paths, and therefore your devotion to it is nothing but a form of vanity."

Cindy looked at me as if I was something alien and disgusting. We left the bookstore together, our minds far apart.

I was now plunged into renewed depression about my relationship to the League. I felt unable to relate to the League members, cut off from the statewide organization, distrustful of the overall goals as laid down by the Living Master, and unmotivated to practice my contemplation. In an attempt to make sense out of my situation, I visited a counselor I knew named Mitchell Andrews. I told him all about the League, my feelings of alienation from it, my conflict with the members of the hierarchy, and my discomfort with those who used its lofty abstractions to govern their lives.

"I don't know why," I said, "but I find these abstractions debilitating."

"Of course, they're debilitating for you," Mitchell said. "For years, you've tried to measure yourself against them, and you're frustrated as hell. You're not perfect. No one is. You see yourself as a spiritual failure, but you're not. Why are you putting yourself through all of this? Why would you make your validation dependent on other people, particularly those you know don't have a high opinion of you? Moreover, if you suspect that some of the people in the League hierarchy are not acting out of the purest motives, how can you reasonably consent to submit to their judgment? If the League hierarchy is fallible, if people at the very apex of that hierarchy can block the flow of the Force, then there is no neat solution to life, no conclusive answer to be found in loyalty to it, no matter now lofty its purpose or high-minded its goals."

"That's true," I replied. "On the other hand, the whole idea of the spiritual path is that it will turn you inside out. It will ask you to let go of everything you hold dear in order to test your loyalty. Part of the paradigm is that you're supposed to go through hell. You're supposed to get twisted every which way. You're supposed to give up every shred of ego. To leave the path is spiritual failure. That's the paradigm. It's continually enunciated in the League teachings."

"That's only one paradigm," Mitchell said, "and it's got you trapped. You're trying to fit yourself into a mold that you've outgrown. Like toothpaste that's been squeezed out of the tube, you can't squeeze yourself back in. I know how attached you are to the League, but you're attached in two ways—as someone who wants to belong and as someone who yearns to break away. You're like an adolescent whose urge is to rebel against his father, but is still attached to him. The adolescent needs the father as an object against which he can square himself. As long as he's rebellious, he's not free. He's only free when he can come and go of his own will.

"Have you noticed how you're always in conflict with members of the League, and yet are able to relate so easily to members of other faiths and other paths? That's due to spiritual competition. The members of your group are like your siblings. In a group where people have the same goals, you can expect to find competitiveness. By contrast, your encounters with individuals outside the League are liberating, yet ultimately they do nothing to solve your problem. You're looking for validation, for someone to tell you that you have the right to live the way you choose. You'll never get that validation from the League, but at the same time, you can't accept it from any other source. You don't get along with many of the League members. You're not in sympathy with their convictions. Yet, they're the only ones who can give you ultimate approval.

"I'm not saying that you must abandon the League, but just don't take it so seriously—or so personally. You can't find a mirror image of yourself in the League any more, so don't look for one. You can't expect everyone to be on the same wavelength. Why, then, do you seek the approval of these people? Didn't Hesse write that the Journey to the East was an individual path, that each person on the path had his or her own purpose, which could hardly be understood by anyone else? Do you really need the validation of the League to confirm you in your sense that you are going in the right direction spiritually?

"Why are you so at war with the League's hierarchical structure? You told me yourself that it has always taken the form of a hierarchy. Didn't Hesse describe it as a perfectly ordered, all-knowing bureaucracy? Isn't life itself built on hierarchy? Of what significance are you in the vast spiritual chain of life? Of what significance are you in the League organization? Aren't you just as obsessed with your spiritual status as those who are successful League politicians? You want to contribute to the world? The world is out there, waiting for you. The League is only one tiny portion of it. You said yourself that the Journey to the East is everywhere, and in everything. So go out there, and participate in it.

"If God is everywhere, why do you need a church? There are elementary schools, middle schools, and high schools. There's a purpose for all of them. You thought you enrolled in a high course in spirituality, but now it's turned into a kiddie course. You're not free in that system any more. You're forced to make a Faustian deal. It's become a religion, defined by its external features. That shouldn't bother you, however, because you don't need to depend on those externals. You should be able to distinguish the essence from the form.

"You no longer need the League as a surrogate family. You're ready to strike out on your own. There's no longer a role for you as a leader in this group. You served in that capacity in the past, and now it is up to other people. You have to step up to a higher form of leadership, and you can do this by writing about your experiences. You'll reach a wider audience. Thousands of people have pledged their loyalty to similar groups and are in a similar kind of bind. Others need to hear about the existence of such groups for the first time. All can learn that these paths are bound to a common purpose, that despite the fallibility of their members they can give people an important connection to the Force.

"You can do this and still be loyal to the League. You simply have to be honest about how painful and messy it is. You don't have to act on your feelings of rebelliousness, but you have to acknowledge that you have them. In some sense, you want to overthrow the League, to tell people it's full of shit. That's all right. Every spiritual path has some holes in it, just as no spiritual path is one hundred per cent flawed. The real unknown for you is to step into the messiness, the confusion, and the frustration of it, to try to express that and write about it. Eventually, you'll resolve this conflict and move on to a new level of awareness."

Chapter Sixteen

The Unheroic Man

"Those who know nothing of the spiritual path are repulsed by the renunciation of worldly life. Yet, those who possess this knowledge are not necessarily submissive people who find detachment easy. Rather, they are individuals who have a clear view of reality, who are confident in their own judgment, and whose wills must merely be disciplined in order to bend to the Force."

—Andreas Leo, *The Face of the Eternal, Book Two,* 110

One day, Solomon Dufu, a graduate student whom I had gotten to know at Eastern University, invited me to attend a play in which he had a featured role. Written in 1975 by the internationally acclaimed South African playwright Athol Fugard, "The Island" reenacted a well known interpretation of Sophocles' "Antigone" that had been staged by the prisoners of Robben Island, off the South African coast, in the late 1960s.

In the two-man production, presented at the Eastern University Museum of Art, Solomon and fellow graduate student Darius Croft played internees in the South African prison camp who have been cellmates for almost three years. John, the character played by Solomon, is a passionate, fiery, and overbearing intellectual, consumed with preparations for the prisoners' presentation of "Antigone," who bullies his cellmate, Winston, into playing the title role.

When John finds out that his sentence has been commuted and he has only three more months to serve, the roles reverse. At first, he generously offers not to talk with Winston about his impending freedom. Nevertheless, he can't help counting the days. Bitterly, Winston reminds him that he'll be left behind, and that John will quickly forget him. John tortures himself with guilt as Winston tells him what his freedom will be like. "Your freedom stinks, John," Winston tells him. "You will laugh, you will eat, you will fuck, and you will forget. Fuck slogans. Fuck politics. I am jealous of your freedom, John."

The climax of the play comes with the prisoners' performance of "Antigone." John plays Creon, the head of state. He has sentenced Antigone to death for the crime of burying her brother, the traitor Polyneices, next to that of her other brother, Eteocles, who defended the state. On a political level, the trial and punishment of Antigone is a story of the ancient struggle against injustice, and this was what made it so passionately representative of the South Africans' struggle against political oppression.

I met Solomon at a coffee shop in downtown Belle Harbor after I had seen the production. Solomon was a tall, distinguished-looking young African man, very dark complexioned, and overflowing with talent, intelligence, and charisma. He was obviously destined to go far in the academic world. From the beginning of our conversation, it was clear that his perspective on the play was primarily political, while mine was spiritual. He was interested in seeing the plot as a reflection of a particularly extreme instance of injustice, deprivation, and self-sacrifice. I saw it as representative of a universal condition. We agreed, however, that Winston was the central character in the play.

"Winston, who is doomed to remain in prison, is, for me, ultimately the more interesting character," Solomon stated. "The image we have of him is of a man who puts his head on the block for his fellow men, and then says 'Fuck them.' Winston feels crushed. He is sort of a heroic figure, because he has sacrificed everything. He realizes that prisoners like John will come and go, but he will be in this place for the rest of his life, with no prospect of being released. He tries to feel happy for John, to tell himself that there are higher ideals for which it is worth sacrificing one's life, but then he says, 'Maybe there aren't.'"

"To me, the play clearly shows how the system of injustice imposed by the white regime in South Africa didn't stop at enforcing inequality between white and black. It enforced inequality among the black prisoners, as well," I replied. "On a deeper level, however, it brings up the question of the inherent unfairness or arbitrariness of life in general. We're all stuck here, right? We're all serving some kind of penal servitude. But different people are serving different types of sentences, and some sentences are harder than others."

"Yes," Solomon replied, "but this is a particularly extreme example. I guess that I'm coming up with a very pessimistic reading of what the play is about. I think that, rather than just looking at these gestures of incredible bravery and self-sacrifice, that one might pose the following questions: Is it ever justified to put anybody in that situation, to ask anybody to put his head on the block for others? What does it really mean to say that there are higher ideals for which we can sacrifice everything—our families, our children, and our freedom?"

I was beginning to see what the play meant to Solomon. As an African, he came from an underdeveloped part of the world, yet he was immensely privileged. This caused him feelings of guilt. The issue of self-sacrifice troubled him, because he couldn't see himself as someone who would be willing to make the kinds of sacrifices that he knew many Africans had made and were still making.

"When you refer to Winston's self-sacrifice," I replied, "I assume you mean those actions that landed him in prison in the first place. In the course of the play itself, he doesn't sacrifice himself, however. His life has already been taken away from him."

"Yes. That is why he's so compelling. He's not a heroic character. He's a beaten down man who's given up on life."

"I see that Winston is beaten down," I objected, "but I think this fact gives him greater clarity. You have to be beaten down before you can realize what life is all about. His insight is greater than John's is. When he says, 'I'll forget you, John,' he's really dismissing him. He realizes that the reality of his future life in prison will have nothing to do with the fate of others, but will hinge purely on how he is able to adapt to his own personal circumstances.

"To me, the play doesn't necessarily have to do with extreme desperation and deprivation," I added. "I see the same issues in the most ordinary situations in daily life. I see people measuring themselves against others, people who are not content with their lives, who wonder what they have done with their lives. Society has tricked or coerced these people to think less of their own achievements than those of others.

"In 'Antigone,'" I added, "the main character honors both her brothers, despite the fact that one receives approbation, the other vilification, by the state. The lesson here is that there is dignity in the most ordinary and even wretched human circumstances. It's only when we allow ourselves to be convinced that, because of our circumstances, we have lost our dignity, that we are undone. This principle can be applied to every facet of life, not just to political inequality and injustice. It refers to any situation in which we're made to feel unequal or unworthy, whether because of our appearance, our background, or our achievement. The play isn't necessarily only about people who make great sacrifices for a higher cause, but about the way ordinary people choose to live their lives on a daily basis."

"Well, I'm not looking for a great big cosmic answer," Solomon commented. "I'm not about to make dramatic gestures of self-sacrifice like either Winston or John. Personally, I don't think that I have the capacity."

"I don't think I have that capacity, either," I replied. "Most people don't. Self-sacrifice is a double-edged sword, however. It can be the gesture of a hero or a fool. The hard thing to do is to accept your life, your destiny, and who you are.

"Of course, the extremity of the circumstances in the play dramatize the existential situation," I conceded. "If you have a person facing life in prison, that's about as dramatic an existential situation as one can find. Nevertheless, it's an existential situation that we all share. Just the other day, I saw a show on TV in which they interviewed prisoners who were serving life sentences. Although these prisoners had their whole lives ahead of them, the most fulfilling activity they could look forward to was picking up trash on the prison grounds. One of them told how he helped a wounded bird to heal, and later set it free. For him, that was the most meaningful thing he had been able to do in years. That's an extreme example, yet it applies to all of us. We're all wrestling with the same problem of how to make a contribution to life with whatever limited resources and opportunities we possess."

Our conversation ended with Solomon unconvinced that the play had the type of universal significance that I saw in it. From his point of view, there was a danger in drawing universal parallels to the story, because that would put the greatest human injustices on par with the most trivial ones. For him, that would have represented an anti-political viewpoint. Erase the differences of the human condition, and you erase the arguments of all political causes. From my perspective, however, no human experience was trivial. It was only through the universal experiences addressed in the play that all members of the audience could relate to it. I thought of the example of Antigone, who buried the bodies of her two brothers—a loyalist and a traitor—side-by-side. The difference between them was an illusion.

The apparent gulf that separated the spiritual from the political was an illusion as well. Although Solomon considered himself a "political," rather than a "spiritual" person, what could be more spiritual than politics, which was profoundly concerned with other people's welfare? What was more representative of this than the work of an actor, which required a person to sacrifice his own identity by putting himself in the role of another character?

As Solomon and I exited the coffee shop, a young Eastern University co-ed came up and started flirting openly with him. I could see the look of casual acceptance on Solomon's face. The attentions of women appeared to be something that he took for granted. I wondered for a moment if he would take the high road and put her down gently. After engaging her in conversation for a few moments, however, he turned to me with a look that said, "Our business is done, isn't it?" The girl barely gave me a passing glance. Solomon spread his arms in a gesture that seemed to cloak her in his charisma, and he went back with her into the coffeehouse, leaving me standing on the street corner with nothing to do except transcribe my conversation with him.

At that moment, I saw Solomon—the powerful actor, the skeptical intellectual who did not believe in spirituality—in the role of John again, and I saw myself in the role of Winston. Solomon was the man of talent and ambition, while I was the man who felt trapped in circumstances of life beyond his control. His very talent and charisma produced an underlying feeling of guilt, which chained him to pessimism. By contrast, despite my privileged background, I had experienced difficulty, frustration, and lack of achievement in life. Like Winston, underneath the futility that I often felt, I possessed a smoldering sense of hope and purpose.

Shortly after this, I met a young Cuban woman in Belle Harbor named Anna Estefan. She ran a translation service in town, which I had engaged for help on one of my writing projects. Anna was a beautiful young woman, just recently engaged, with whom I felt an immediate connection. I cultivated a modest friendship with her, and in return, she introduced me to a civic group that was attempting to establish a sister city relationship between Belle Harbor and a provincial town in Cuba. I told her that I was interested in visiting Cuba and perhaps doing some interviews and travel writing while I was there. She was supportive of my idea, knew a number of prominent writers there, and declared herself willing to supply me with a list of contacts.

Shortly thereafter, I had a long and vivid dream about going to Cuba. I remember visiting a primary school, where the teachers showed me around, and introduced me to the children. They all seemed happy, well nourished, and enthusiastic. It was a heavenly vision of Cuba—a Cuba as it no doubt existed on some other plane of existence. The next day I booked a direct flight from Toronto to Havana. I had the strange feeling that Anna was sending me on this journey like Helen of Troy, whose face launched a thousand ships full of men eager to engage in heroic missions on her behalf.

My main reason for going to Cuba, however, had to do with my continued spiritual questioning. I was more convinced than ever that some of our most cherished ideas about spirituality were closely bound up with our own particular modern-day culture. Our society in the United States was predicated on individual freedom and responsibility. Spirituality in our culture was all about being self-sufficient. The assumption was that where there was less individual freedom, there was less responsibility, self-sufficiency, and spiritual maturity.

The only problem with this concept was that those with the greater resources had the greater advantage. In the affluent society of the United States, it was easy to ignore economic differences. The rich could build their mansions without guilt. Equality of opportunity was the reigning cultural myth, and there was little evidence to contradict it. In a society with plentiful resources, the only poor people were those who lacked gumption.

Sure, self-reliance was an admirable attribute, but was it the litmus test of spirituality? Wasn't compassion a spiritual attribute, as well? Competition endowed the individual with toughness and resilience. Survival motivated those at the bottom, and greed those at the top. How could one live in such a system without becoming corrupted by it in one way or another? I wanted to explore these questions in a country that had taken the opposite path, which was as much the opposite of my own as I could find, that ran on different principles and assumptions, as well as on different myths and illusions. What better country than Cuba, which, almost alone in the world, still held defiantly to socialist doctrine?

To study Cuba was like examining the anatomy of a small, wayward fish, which stubbornly refused to be eaten. The Cuban revolution had been a dismal failure, except that it had kept Cuba for the Cubans. Now, however, even that minor victory was threatened. Cuba had few natural resources. Sugar, tobacco, and tourism were the main sources of hard currency. To this basic economic problem was added the inherent inefficiency of the socialist system, the U. S. embargo, and the loss of its patron state, the Soviet Union. In the wake of the latter blow had come the legalization of the dollar and the full shift to a tourist economy.

The "dollarization," as the Cubans called it, was, in effect, creating a new class system in Cuba, eroding one of the few achievements of the revolution. People were now divided into those who had hard currency and those who did not. They could obtain dollars in three principal ways: they could work in some aspect of the tourist industry, work for a foreign firm operating in Cuba, or receive cash from relatives in the United States or Europe.

On my arrival in Havana, I met an old schoolmate of Anna's named Lisa Perez, who worked as a Spanish-English translator for a Chinese firm. She agreed to accompany me over the weekend. We went to the beach together and walked around the Old City, visiting restaurants and shops. Lisa told me about her current job, for which she was paid in hard currency, but the work environment did not sound attractive. The Chinese managers spoke English poorly, and she felt her command of the language had suffered. The work was tedious, and she was confined to a desk in an overly air-conditioned office throughout the day. As Lisa talked about her life, I contemplated the difference between her and Anna. How had Anna managed to leave Cuba, get U. S. residency, and build a successful business, while Lisa was left to toil in the office of a foreign company, unable to leave Cuba?

Lisa told me that she had been to the United States for an entire year, but had seen little of the country during that time. When I asked her if she would like to go back and visit the States, her chest heaved with a sigh. "I would like to, of course," she replied, "but it is not possible. The year I spent in the United States was a once-in-a-lifetime opportunity." I wished that I could do something to help her, but I didn't voice my thoughts. Instead, I just told her that I would like to come back at the end of the year, and if I did, I would see her again.

As soon as I got back to Belle Harbor, I got in touch with Anna. She came over to see me at my apartment—an unusual gesture, given her busy schedule, and one which she couldn't help acknowledging. "You don't know how privileged you are to get a visit from me," she quipped, as I greeted her at the door. "Since you visited my home country, however, I'll make an exception." I forgave the touch of queenly arrogance in her remark because, after all, she was Anna.

We sat down together, and I briefed her on my trip, going on at considerable length about my concern for Lisa. "Isn't there anything I can do for her?" I asked.

"Of course, I went to school with Lisa," Anna replied, "but there are so many people like her in Cuba. She had a chance when she was in the States. She could have made American friends. She didn't take advantage of the opportunity when she had it."

"I don't care," I said, somewhat petulantly, taken aback by Anna's cold response. "I didn't meet all those other people. She's the one I met, and I'd like to help her."

To Anna, Lisa was just one friend among the many she had left behind in Cuba, and not even the most deserving, because she didn't have the boldness to make the most of her opportunities. I sensed that her cold attitude had its roots in bitter experiences that I could barely comprehend. Indeed, she confided some details of her personal life by way of explanation, which accounted for the alacrity with which she had adapted to the fast-paced American lifestyle. It was nevertheless a little shocking to me how Americanized she was. She was young, beautiful, the owner of a successful business, and about to be married to a handsome intellectual. She was one of the lucky ones, living the American dream. The briskness in her demeanor, however, was a defense mechanism. She couldn't afford to think too much about the people she had left behind in Cuba. There were, after all, so many of them.

For a moment, Anna's attitude reminded me of that of a young businesswoman I had met years ago in New York City. The woman had taken a flirtatious interest in me until she saw me give a few coins to a bum, at which point she had recoiled in horror. "If you give money to beggars, it means you secretly identify with them," she declared, in response to my gesture. That was the kiss of death, as far as she was concerned, and after that, she dropped me like a hot potato. She didn't want to have anything to do with me because, in her estimation, I lacked the ambition and drive that would have made me worth the investment of her time and attention.

"So there's nothing I can do to help Lisa?" I asked wearily.

"Not unless you want to marry her," Anna stated. Our eyes met for an instant, and she saw that I was not treating her remark as a joke.

"There's nothing I'd rule out if it involved an opportunity to help someone," I replied in a subdued tone. "Such opportunities don't come around often, at least not for me."

As I said good night to Anna, I reflected that the exchange I had with her was similar to my conversation with Solomon. Anna and Solomon possessed a charisma, drive, and personal magnetism with which neither Lisa nor I could compete. We didn't move as fast as the Annas and Solomons of this world. We lacked their aggressiveness and drive. We were more introspective, more doubting of ourselves, more risk averse. Despite the vast differences between the United States and Cuba, both countries could be equally unforgiving to the meek and the sensitive. My heart went out to Lisa, for I felt that underneath our mutual timidity, we also shared an unrecognized and unacknowledged heroism.

Almost as soon as I returned to Belle Harbor, I faced an unpleasant situation. For several years, I had been involved in helping my mother settle estate issues that had lingered in the wake of my father's death. We had engaged a whole series of lawyers over a period of years, doling out money to them in return for incompetent work that had to be rectified by still more lawyers. Finally, we found an attorney who had both expertise and integrity, and worked with efficiency on our behalf. My mother's estate matters were gradually resolved, but one minor matter remained—a final payment of six hundred dollars that I had not yet made to a lawyer whom I had previously engaged on my own.

The sum was paltry compared to what our family had spent on legal fees, overall. Although my finances were at the zero point, I could easily have borrowed the money, paid the lawyer, and gradually earned it back. The money was not the issue.

This lawyer, Franklin Engler, had a history with our family. In fact, he had been my father's lawyer years ago. I had met him in his office at an East Side mall when I was still an adolescent—a tall, distinguished-looking man, with an air of utter confidence in himself that bordered on smugness. My father eventually broke with him in a billing dispute. According to my father, Mr. Engler had charged him exorbitantly for copying and mailing of materials. A minor sum was involved, but my father was a man of principle. He settled the bill, and wrote Mr. Engler a terse letter, which no doubt communicated his scorn.

Years passed. Our family had gone through several lawyers already and the estate situation had only gotten worse. I decided to take my mother's affairs into my own hands and set out to find a new lawyer. The only attorney I knew was the one who had represented Ray Hardcastle in court. His manner with me had been initially aggressive, but when I had explained my side of the story, he had become very reasonable. I went to his downtown office and asked him if he could help me with an estate matter.

"That's not my field," he replied, "but it happens to be the specialty of my partner next door. I recommend you go and see him."

I went next door, and found to my surprise, that the partner was none other than Mr. Engler, ensconced in a new downtown office. In my naïve way, I took this as some kind of sign from heaven that he was the man to help us. He already knew a great deal about our estate situation, which made me feel curiously in touch with my father as I sat down to meet with him. It all seemed logical, so I engaged him to draft an agreement that would form the basis for an amendment to my mother's trust. Mr. Engler took to the task like a marlin after a hook. I got my mother on board, and she contributed the bulk of his fees. He made a big show of getting input from the whole family, but there was an ambiguity the whole time as to whether he was representing the family's interests, or only mine. Gradually, I came to feel that he was manipulating me, fostering unrealistic expectations on my part, and playing me against other members of my family. The agreement he drafted proved unacceptable to the other family members, and we were left at square one, looking once more for a new lawyer.

Now, a reminder came from Mr. Engler of the six hundred dollars still due. I couldn't bring myself to pay it. I consulted our new attorney who advised me to offer him half the fee, as a compromise, but I wasn't keen on doing that, either. Instead, I sent Mr. Engler a letter in which I simply informed him that he had achieved no results for us. "I leave it to your sense of honor and fairness to guide you in your course of action," I stated.

He replied with a letter, in which he compared himself to an auto mechanic. "I put in the time and send you a bill," he wrote. "If you get the desired results, great. If not, as long as I did my best, I have the right to be paid. You still owe me six hundred dollars."

At this point, I happened to glance at the book I had purchased on the science of the cards. I turned to the section on my card, the Three of Spades, and read the following passage:

> As with all creative cards, the Three of Spades feels the temptation to take shortcuts with regard to obligations and financial transactions, but the Law of Karma won't let them get away with it. It is relentless. Whatever is owed will be paid. There is no judgment or prosecutor behind it. It is simply a divine law that governs the world we live in, and cannot be broken. The moment we try to get away with something, we will pay the consequences. For the Three of Spades, the punishment may have an extra kick to it, due to past-life karma. It may seem to the individual that they get punished way too much, but this is because of the additional past-life payments that are being made.

Chastened, but not entirely convinced, I called up Lynne Silva to get her opinion. "What we have here," I told her, "is a conflict of ethics and values. I'm sure that Mr. Engler considers himself a man of principle, as do I. We just follow different principles. His sense of ethics revolves entirely around his time clock and fee schedule. For me, ethics go deeper than that. He may be "right" in the sense that our society and its legal system support his type of ethics. That doesn't make him right in my book, though.

"By his own admission, he doesn't consider it part of his responsibility to secure any results for his clients. It's possible that the whole legal profession runs this way, but what other profession so separates itself from its own clients' interests? If the sole operative principle is that the client pays irrespective of result, there's no incentive whatsoever for the lawyer to do anything more than make a show of busying himself. Even worse, an unscrupulous lawyer could attempt to manipulate his clients into paying for services they didn't need. He could bilk his clients for as much as he could and still justify his actions in his own mind as long as he observed his own private rules of ethics—marking down the time he had spent, and billing his clients according to his set rate. Moreover, lawyers don't offer their clients any proof that they worked the number of hours they say they did. All the clients have is their word of honor.

"This man was unscrupulous in his dealings with us. On occasions, he claimed to represent the interests of the entire family, while at other times he placed himself solely in the position of my advocate. He manipulated me by playing me against my sister, fostering unrealistic expectations on my part, while by his own admission attempting to trap my sister by her inconsistent statements. He didn't further our cause in any way. He compares himself to an auto mechanic, yet surely, that's a false analogy. Even auto mechanics have to stand by their work. Most of them today guarantee the quality of their service. Nevertheless, according to the science of the cards, I'm going to have to pay him because he represents some kind of higher principle. What is he, a representative of the Negative Power—the cosmic bureaucrat who number-crunches our karmic debts for all eternity?"

I could hear Lynne laughing at the other end of the phone. "The idea that you owe this Mr. Engler six hundred dollars is his opinion, his construct," she replied. "Just because he's the lawyer, that doesn't mean he's right. Lawyers are only interested in winning, even if it's in the most despicable and devious ways. There's something very small and sad about it. Instead of allowing yourself to be run over by everyone and everything, why not go with that urge to stand up and say you're not going to take it any more? This is your chance at an epiphany. You've been emulating Kaye Tyson your whole adult life. Is your whole mission in life to be stepped on, like she was? Kaye was old and crippled. She wasn't able to be active. She had no other way to be a channel for the Force, but you have options.

"Maybe this science of the cards has validity. Maybe you get into situations like this because of past karma, or something that you have to learn. Yet, what do you know about Mr. Engler's role in this? Why do you necessarily elevate him to a representative of the Almighty? Why do you assume that you're in the wrong, and that you're going to get taken, or be punished? How do you know that he doesn't have a lesson he needs to learn, as well? Maybe you can tell him something that he has to hear. Maybe he needs you to tell him just where to stick his fee. Maybe no one has ever had the gumption to tell him off before, and you're the only one who can give him that valuable experience!"

As Lynne spoke, I caught a view of a whole different way that I could be. I suddenly remembered what the initiator had said to me during my initiation: "You've moved past working with pain. You're now working with love, joy, and freedom. There's a world out there. It's not a world of limitation, but of possibilities and opportunities." The startling thought occurred to me that I was only now stepping through the door that the initiation had opened for me.

A panorama of my experiences in the League since that day flashed before my eyes. I realized that I had created a philosophy out of the League teachings that was unduly fatalistic. I had reacted negatively to those people whom I correctly saw as clinging to only a portion of the truth, while I, in turn, clung to a different portion of it. These were nothing but two sides of life, ever reflecting back on one another.

If the spiritual life was not about personal gain or achievement, neither was it about resignation. Instead, it involved walking a thin line, a razor's edge. It meant maintaining a balance, being neither for nor against. It required that the seeker not only maintain a distance from other people's viewpoints and opinions, but also mercilessly root out those that that had become so much his own that he could no longer recognize them. To achieve that kind of perspective on oneself could not be accomplished overnight. It could not be absorbed in a single lecture, or in a single encounter with a more enlightened individual. It had to be driven home again and again until there was no alternative to seeing from that new point of view. With this realization, came a feeling of gratitude that washed over me in a wave of long-repressed emotion.

Conclusion

The Cop in the Trunk

"What is man when, having been used by the Force, it has ceased to use him? He is in possession of himself again, yet he is not what he was before. He is changed by knowing that he has been, and potentially still is, the instrument of God."

—Andreas Leo, *The Face of the Eternal, Book Two*, 24

It was the first beautiful spring day of the year. The semester was almost over, the sky was clear, and the sun warmed the still brisk air. My mother was again in Florida, and I was on my way to her apartment to tend to her cat, which she had left behind during her absence. Suddenly I had a brainstorm. I would take my mother's cat outside! The creature had never been outdoors in her life, and did little else except hide under the sofa and meow whenever anyone came near her.

A plan quickly unwrapped itself in my mind. I would get a piece of string, tie it to her collar, take her on the grass next to the apartment building, and acquaint her with nature. I found a spool of string, dug the cat out from underneath the living room couch, and tied the string securely to her little collar. Then I hoisted her up in my arms, and carried her down the hallway, through the elevator, and out into the fresh air. She was meowing dangerously the whole time in a low voice utterly different from the usual sound she produced.

When I set her down, she started slinking around, belly pressed to the ground like a snake. Then she made a beeline for the woods. The string was long enough to allow me to let it play out for a while, but it soon reached its limit. I could barely see her still. Some jerky movements in the shrubbery indicated that she was tangled in a small tree. I followed her, reeling in the line, until I was able to grab hold of it just near her collar. At this, the cat became alarmed and tried to wrench herself away from me. All at once, her head slipped free of the collar, and she went bounding off in the woods.

A small grassy strip separated the woods from a commercial parking lot, completely empty on this Saturday afternoon except for a single car. I saw the cat go under the car, and made my way there in no great hurry, sure that she would pause there. When I bent down and looked underneath, however, she was gone. I fruitlessly combed the lot and adjacent woods. Returning to the apartment building, I told a few people what happened. "If you don't find that cat before your mother gets back, you'll have to move to Canada!" one of the residents quipped.

The remark hit home. With a feeling of calm desperation, I printed up a flyer and posted it throughout the neighborhood. When I returned to my mother's apartment, I called the Humane Society. It was already late in the afternoon, so they suggested I come in the next day and file a report in person. By evening, I was out of ideas, so I called my friend George just to get things off my chest. I related to him the whole sequence of events.

"The last place you saw her was underneath the car. You didn't see her scoot off anywhere else?" he asked.

"Nope."

"They can crawl up from underneath inside the motor, you know."

As soon as George mentioned this possibility, I realized that it fit the nature of the cat. Her first instinct would be to hide. What, however, if the owner of the car came back and tried to start it? It would be like putting the cat in a blender! I asked George if he could come over quickly, and he agreed. A couple of hours later, he pulled up in his beat-up red pickup. He was burly, tanned, balding, and always looked like he had just come from working in his yard or garage. He got on his back and peered up into the bowels of the car.

"I can see her," he said.

"Let me see." I crawled under the car, but was unable to see a thing. "Where is she?" George showed me again. I got on my back and looked very carefully. Finally, I could see part of the cat's head—a patch of white and gray fur, and one green eye. George slid underneath the car once more. I could hear him fiddling around with something, and then the hood suddenly popped open. When we lifted it up, there was the cat, sitting right on top of the engine.

As I took the animal back to my mother's apartment, the whole incident started to sink in. "You know, George," I said, as he was preparing to drive back home, "I'm trying to pay attention to everything that happens to me. This situation with the cat was no accident. It was trying to tell me something about my life. I wanted to play the great liberator, take the cat outside, show her the world, and teach her not to hide under the sofa all the time. It's been ruled by its fear instinct its whole life, but am I really that different?"

The next evening, I had a vivid dream in which I was driving down a street in Belle Harbor, looked into my rearview mirror, and saw a police car. The more carefully I drove, the closer it followed me. Eventually, the cop stopped me and told me to get out of the car. Then he started to get abusive, like in some grade-B movie. He was standing in front of me, getting in my face. Finally, he pulled out two magic markers—a yellow one and a blue one—and started painting my lips with them. He painted my upper lip yellow and my lower lip blue.

All of a sudden, I got a jump on him, took his gun away, and pointed it at him. Of course, I couldn't kill him. That would have gotten me into real trouble! At the same time, I couldn't allow him to go free, because then he'd haul me off to jail, so I stuffed him in the trunk of my car. Then I got on the highway and drove without stopping for a day and a half, all the way down to Florida. Finally, I came to a forest of Southern pine. There I released the cop, ensuring that it would take him a long time to make his way back north.

As soon as I woke up, I had an intuition about the meaning of the dream. In the League teachings, the color yellow was associated with Soul, and the color blue with the Mind. The cop had painted my upper lip yellow and my lower lip blue. The dream seemed to be referring to the spiritual principle that the Mind was subordinate to Soul—or, as we said in the League, it was a good servant, but a bad master. The cop wore a blue uniform, so I reasoned that he represented the Mind, as well. The dream was warning me that I was giving the Mind too much authority.

I had attracted the cop's attention by driving so slowly and carefully, and took this as an additional warning—that by attempting to avoid risk, I was actually increasing it. The encounter with the cop represented the consequences of approaching life too carefully. The dream was modeling fear for me, just as the incident with the cat had done the year before. The cat, ruled by fear, had sought refuge in the most potentially dangerous part of the car. Similarly, I, with my slow driving, had attracted the attention of the cop. Fear attracted the very conditions it sought to avoid. I could not eliminate my fear, but I could bypass its authority by metaphorically packing it away, like the cop in the trunk, in a neutral part of my mind. I decided that the dream was telling me I needed to quit teaching for good, leave Belle Harbor, discard all my expectations, and look for something that would point me in a new direction.

The next evening, I happened to go to Brian Davidson's house to listen to the current Living Master deliver a talk via a satellite transmission. The Master was speaking on some innocuous subject, when suddenly he made a comment about people who were ready to leave the League. "When the individual asks 'Is this all there is to life?'" the Master said, "it means that Soul has gathered all the experience it needs in a particular area, and is ready to move on to another. You become the seeker all over again. When you're facing a busted bank account, that's the point when you let go. You fear that although you visualize what you wish to be, it won't really happen, yet you are daring to think of your life as being different." The Master's words were ambiguous. Was he politely saying to dissenters, "If your must go, go," or was he truly giving his blessing, affirming that the true Path had no boundaries?

Before I left Belle Harbor for good, however, I decided to attend a local meeting of League high initiates. It was actually the second in a series of monthly workshops, the first of which I had missed. Their purpose was to study a book, written by the current Living Master, which was concerned with how to become a greater channel for the Force. The meeting was scheduled for a conference room at the local district library that weekend. When I arrived, I found myself in the company of seven other high initiates, with Lynne Silva presiding over the meeting.

The meeting was desultory, or at least it seemed so to me. Participants made use of a companion workbook, with exercises meant to supplement the text. Lynne did her best to inject some life into the discussion. When asked how they could be of greater spiritual service in their daily life, most of the members expressed themselves in vague platitudes. One said that he tried to do everything in the name of the Living Master. Another hinted at a writing project he was considering, but voiced concern that it did not involve the League teachings, per se. The conflict that registered in his face brought back a flood of memories. He was still hung up, as I had been, on the idea that the way to be of service had to be connected with spreading the League teachings. The teachings, however, didn't say that. They only spoke of being a channel for the Force, which could be found universally in all of life.

I found the overly structured nature of the workshop numbing. These students not only had a book, but a workbook to follow the book. The facilitator, specially trained to lead such workshops, possessed an additional set of guidelines to assist her in leading the sessions, as well as videotapes to be used as occasional instructional aids. I wondered how it had come to this. Did we really need a workbook to teach us how to be a conduit for the Force? We were given layer upon layer of instructional tools—all in order to understand something that was so simple, that in fact was the easiest thing in the world. All we need to do to be a channel for the Force is to do whatever moved us or gave us joy. What could be simpler than that?

These initiates were all good people. They were living their lives the best they could, and trying to make sense out of life, just like me. This discussion group simply fit the pace of their spiritual education. They were like students at any level, still in need of an organized curriculum. I saw that there was a need for the League, just as for any school, to minister to students at various levels of understanding.

The sole cause of all my complaints with the League community was simply that I was seeing things from a slightly different perspective than the other members. I couldn't expect them to see things exactly as I did, however. The spiritual path was becoming longer, and lonelier. I realized that I was now a graduate of the school, still with attachments to my alma mater, but needing to turn my attention to the path of life ahead. To strike out on my own meant leaving the confines of what had once been an intimate family. It meant not being able to rely on the support of a community for my future education. It meant confronting my fears, and putting my trust completely in the Force.

After an hour and a half, the group took a break. I didn't see any reason to stay. I left the conference room and approached Lynne in the lobby of the library.

"I'm going, Lynne," I told her. "There's nothing more for me here."

Lynne instantly understood. "I'll miss you," she said. "You've contributed a lot to this area. You tried to change things, and many of the League initiates recognize that, and appreciate it. I think you realize now that the path is within you. Some of us may choose to work within the organization as a way to be of service, but that's simply a choice. Many of the initiates haven't grasped that yet, but that's a matter of their own spiritual growth. It can't be rushed, but must be allowed to come about naturally.

"You have to define yourself according to who you are. You may feel that you're on the edge of a precipice, but you need to give yourself credit. It takes a lot of imagination to think of a future that's so far outside the box you've been used to keeping yourself in. Go somewhere where you really want to be, and do what you really want to do. You can't define yourself simply according to the League. If you do, you'll remain at an arrested state of development."

As Lynne spoke, I had a sudden inspiration, and inquired whether or not there was an opening for me to give a farewell talk at an upcoming meeting before I left for good. She told me that they were looking for someone to give such a talk in Brighton that weekend, and I immediately volunteered. When I arrived for the event, my mood had changed. Many of my old friends were there, and they brought back memories of former camaraderie. I felt affection for them again, as well as for the League as a whole. Some of the old spirit was in the room as I began to speak:

"I've been thinking about the difference between religion and spirituality for a long time because I believe that many members of the League are confused on this issue. I've gotten into some heavy arguments with fellow initiates because I have maintained for a long time that the League is not a religion. I've said this in private and in public, in one-on-one conversations and at League meetings. The reaction I've gotten from most people is that I'm dead wrong, because we all know that the League calls itself a religion. Not only that, but the implication that I've drawn from their looks of displeasure, their grimaces, their coldness, is that I'm no longer loyal to the Living Master, because he's said many times that the League is a religion.

"Finally, I thought of an analogy that would help me explain my viewpoint. The League to which we belong is like a school. Think of the high school or college that you attended. Was it unique? Was it the only high school or college around? No. You could have chosen to attend many other schools. You chose the one you did for certain reasons—maybe it was the most convenient to get to, or the only one in your immediate vicinity, or it was more cost effective, or it was safer, or it had a better curriculum.

"That's the way it is with religions and spiritual groups. There are many to choose from. Each has its own name, its own curriculum, its own teaching methods, its own instructors, its own symbols, and its own rules. Some of these schools, like the League, may have a more advanced curriculum. They may recruit more elite students, and some may see a greater number of their students achieve success and go on to higher levels of responsibility in life. Yet, all of these schools have one thing in common, and that is to prepare their students for life. The day that their students graduate, they are released into a far greater school, which is the school of Life itself.

"What I have to say to you may go against the grain, because many of you are still students. Like typical students, you think that you're going to be in school forever. You think your relationship to the League will never change, but it will. In fact, it's supposed to change. You're supposed to graduate.

"There's a common assumption among League members that the League presents us with a series of tests, and that the point of these tests is to see if we will stumble and fall. The test of spiritual failure, according to this view, is whether we'll stay in the League, or drop out. Now, it's true that some people fail spiritually in this way, just like some people, in fact, drop out of school. The goal is certainly to avoid this kind of failure. The goal is not to drop out. However, the goal is ALSO to complete the curriculum successfully. The goal is NOT to stay in school forever.

"We're told in the League that we need to do our spiritual exercises, and we need to follow the guidance of the Living Master, but that is simply like being told that we should do our homework, we shouldn't cut classes, and we should obey the principal's guidelines. These things are important, because they'll help us successfully complete the curriculum and go on to graduate. Once we graduate, however, it's up to us to choose our own spiritual disciplines and impose those disciplines upon ourselves. We're free of the rules and guidelines that we were asked to obey while we were in school.

"If we graduate, does that mean we'll cease to be League members? Not at all. We can continue to have an affiliation with the League. We may go on to become members of the faculty or administrators, or we may just become alumni and visit for annual reunions or send occasional donations. In any case, we can continue to be part of the League family. The important thing, however, is that we are no longer students in the school. Once we've graduated, we are only students of Life.

"The Force doesn't want us to be perpetual students. The Master doesn't want us to be perpetual students. The Master, like the school principal, wants us to successfully complete the curriculum and go on to graduate.

"This gets to the heart of my distinction between religion and spirituality. Religion is the domain of the school. Spirituality is the domain of life itself. It's as simple as that. The reason that this is not made clear to us in the League is that while we're in school, we tend to think within the parameters of school life. If we look back on our high school years, we remember that our principal, teachers, and fellow students all reinforced us in this way of thinking. Apart from the occasional job fair in our senior year, little attention was put on the world that awaited us upon graduation.

"In fact, we have a semantic problem in the League, because there isn't just one League, there are actually two. There is the League that is a religion, and there is the League that is a spiritual path. Some will say that these are not mutually exclusive, but in an important sense, they ARE. The religion is only the temporary school from which we will graduate. The spiritual path is something that we won't truly know until we DO graduate, and have to stand on our own two feet. The sooner we realize the difference between the two, the sooner we will approach spiritual maturity.

"When do we graduate? That's hard to say. Is it possible to stay in the school your whole life and never graduate, regardless of what initiation you receive? It's possible. Is it possible to graduate while you're still in school? Yes, I think so. Generally, however, people who are in a school are in a school for a reason. They have to finish the curriculum before they're ready to graduate.

"The current Living Master has the mission of establishing the

League as a world religion. In that sense, when he speaks, he often does so as the headmaster or principal of the school called the League. If he is indeed the highest spiritual authority on earth, then he has the responsibility to lead ALL Souls back to God. The way in which he works in this capacity, however, is outside the boundaries of the school known as the League, and cannot be seen by most of those who are students in that school.

"If you want to know what lies beyond the League, and what lies in store for you after you graduate, I recommend that you study the writings of Andreas Leo. If you read them carefully, you will see that the League that Leo talks about is NOT the religion, but only the spiritual path. Leo's name for it was the Ancient Science of the Soul. It's not a religion, but a spiritual science that runs through all of life, and through all religions and philosophies. This science will guide you through life once you graduate from the school of the League. What you learn in the school are only tools, the pieces of this science. When you graduate to the school of Life, you will be asked to put those pieces together.

"There is a lecture by the famous Argentine novelist Jorge Luis Borges, in which he recounts a tale from the Arabian Nights, called the story of the Two Dreamers. A man in Cairo dreams that a voice tells him to travel to Isfahan, in Persia, where he will find a great treasure. He makes the long journey, and, exhausted, falls asleep among a group of thieves. All are arrested and brought before a magistrate, or qadi, who asks the man from Cairo why he has come to the city. When the man tells him his dream, the *qadi* scoffs at him, for he, too has dreamed of a treasure—located in a house in Cairo! Although he puts no credence in it, he minutely describes his dream to the man before him. Behind the house is a garden, in which there is a sundial, a fig tree, and a fountain. Beneath the fountain is the treasure. The man recognizes his own house in the *qadi's* description. He returns home, digs beneath the fountain, and finds the treasure.

"The story illustrates the difference between religion and spirituality. The League is twofold. The outer League is like a journey—

the Journey to the East that Hesse wrote about, or the journey of the man from Cairo, retold by Borges in his lecture. The man from Cairo represents the seeker, and the qadi represents the Master. The seeker dreams of a goal, a treasure, a Holy Grail. His search takes him far and wide. At the end of his journey, the Master tells him that all he needs to do is go back home. The Master is a dreamer, as well. He dreams of the treasure that resides in the seeker."

When I had finished, one of the League members asked a question. He mentioned a prominent high initiate who had recently left the League, and written an exposé that challenged the veracity of Andreas Leo's writings. What was my opinion on all this, he wanted to know.

"First, I think it's absurd to criticize Leo's writings on the basis of their adherence to facts," I said. "Leo's purpose was to fire people's spiritual imagination. The League is not something that can be documented. The existence of the invisible spiritual hierarchy is not something that can be proved or disproved.

"As for those who leave the League, there is the tendency for us to view them as lost sheep who have strayed from the path, but that is merely a reflection of our own feelings of self-importance. The League is not one path, but many. Moreover, we must remember that our relationship to the path does not remain the same. Many of these people who leave the fold have come to that point where they see that the path is universal and that their relationship is to the Force itself. In that realization, they forget that they reached this point via the guidance of the Living Master. Their memory of their experiences in the League fades, and they drop away. They are still on their own path, however, and since it is a universal path, they are still with us. They are still our spiritual brethren."

It was my last week of final exams. In my spare time, amid the stale task of correcting student papers, I prepared for my journey. I went down to the weekly Kiwanis sale and bought a sleeping bag and some mosquito netting, in case I decided to do some camping. I also found a light tent that was on sale at the Army surplus store. On the last day of the exam period, I turned in my grades. My car was already packed, but I had some loose ends to tie up. The stress of the long semester had made me anxious. It seemed to take forever to get out of town. It was like tearing off something that had been glued to my skin.

I knew that my greatest difficulty would be to go slowly. Once I got on the road, I tended to keep my foot on the gas until I reached my destination. In this instance, I didn't have a destination, and it would be crucial to avoid manufacturing one. I finally took off around midday, and drove steadily south. I drove for two days, until I came to the Outer Banks of North Carolina. That evening, I camped near Kitty Hawk, and the next morning went out to the public beach and swam in the tide. The sun was still red and low in the sky. In the afternoon, I visited the Wright Brothers Memorial. The monument was inscribed with the following words:

> In commemoration of the conquest of the air…conceived by genius, achieved by dauntless courage and unconquerable faith.

The inscription brought tears to my eyes. It seemed strange that I would cry at a mere inscription, and I wondered why these words had touched off such a well of feeling within me. They had something to do with the idea of greatness, of making a difference in the world. I knew in my heart that I was not a person who was destined for great achievement in this lifetime. Yet the desire, the ambition to make an imprint, a singular difference, or a contribution to my fellow man appeared to be a hidden, but important, aspect of my personality. I walked out to the beach, watched the sunset, and remembered a quotation from Andreas Leo's *The Lion's Paw*:

> We are all navigators of the spiritual seas. Our little selves, like boats, serve to carry us toward a distant shore. (2)

I returned to my car, packed up my things, and continued until I came to a little town in Florida, where there were no members of the League. I started writing articles for the local papers, and after a while began to receive an income that could sustain me. I got interested in raising medicinal plants as a hobby, and found great satisfaction in getting more in touch with the natural world. I had remained in e-mail contact with Lisa during the months after my return from Cuba. We began to discuss the possibility of getting married, and I initiated the process of petitioning to bring her to the States as my fiancée. Eventually, I found that I again had the patience to sit and do my contemplation for twenty minutes a day.

After many months, however, I felt the familiar itch to once more be of service. I went down to the local bookstore in town, and asked to put up a poster that read as follows:

> A study group is now forming for anyone interested in studying the Ancient Science of the Soul as a means of liberation. It will follow the techniques as set down by Andreas Leo, founder of the present-day Order of the League…

Finally, I began to write about my experiences. I wrote and rewrote, but after I had finished the umpteenth draft, there was still something that nagged at me. I had been determined to use the true name of the League and that of its modern founder to demonstrate my continuing loyalty to the outer organization. Eventually I came to a point where I realized I could not do so and truthfully represent the universal path that was at its core. As Hermann Hesse had done, perhaps just as regretfully, I went through my manuscript from beginning to end and expunged the present name of the League from my chronicle, so that by reading the record of my experiences, more might find it in their heart, where it truly exists.

Additional copies of this book can be ordered from
The Spiritual Traveler website

http://www.spiritualtraveler.com

SPIRITUAL  TRAVELER

PRESS